SPECIMENS

OF

BANTU FOLK-LORE

FROM NORTHERN RHODESIA

TEXTS (Collected with the help of the Phonograph)
and ENGLISH TRANSLATIONS

BY

J. TORREND, S.J.

WITH MUSICAL ILLUSTRATIONS

NEGRO UNIVERSITIES PRESS
NEW YORK

Originally published in 1921
by Kegan Paul, Trench, Trubner & Co., Ltd.

Reprinted 1969 by
Negro Universities Press
A Division of Greenwood Publishing Corp.
New York

SBN 8371-1398-9

PRINTED IN UNITED STATES OF AMERICA

CONTENTS

CONTENTS

SAMPLES OF BANTU FOLK-LORE

PRELIMINARY NOTES.

1. LANGUAGES ILLUSTRATED IN THIS WORK.—This little work is the result of an attempt to illustrate both the folk-lore and the language of the Bêne-Mukuni and the Ba-Tonga of Northern Rhodesia. The first are spread north of the Kafubwe, *alias* Kafukwe, Kafue,[1] the second south of it. Both to a certain extent have intermixed and intermarried with the Ba-Sara, the Ba-Sori, the Ba-Ila or Ba-Sukulumbwe, the Ba-Twa, the Ba-Ramba, the Bêne-Rwano, the A-Cikunda from the Lower Zambezi, etc. Their folk-lore, partly on account of this amalgamation, partly owing to the insertion of poetry, which claims the right to use any dialect known to the story-teller, is, likewise, to a certain extent, impregnated with words borrowed from the dialects of their various neighbours. That is why the compiler has thought it advisable to give to this book the somewhat comprehensive title of *Samples of Bantu Folk-lore from Northern Rhodesia*. The main geographical position of the languages purposely or accidentally illustrated in this book may be seen from the following map :—

LANGUAGE MAP OF PART OF NORTHERN RHODESIA

[1] The true native names of this glorious river are *Kahubu*, " a little paradise for hippotami " ; *Kafubwe* " let it be a true possession," from *fuba*, " possess " ; *Kafukwe*, " let it be dug " ; *Rwenje*, " skim it," *i.e.*, " catch fish there," etc.

2. THE ALPHABET.—Having to deal with a variety of languages, I have had to face the eternal difficulty of a general alphabet. Lepsius's Standard Alphabet would, it might appear, have served well enough. The fact is that it does not. Printers, especially those in a smaller line of business, find his symbols, *ń, ṅ, š, ž*, etc., inaccessible, unless it be at prices which do not suit them, particularly when capitals are wanted, or they have to apply to a foundry other than the one they usually deal with, and that is what they do not care to do.

The principal difficulty comes from the sound which I write *ñ* (*ñ* of Spanish, *gn* in French, *nh* in Portuguese), a sound which many English people find it difficult to catch. They mistake it for their own *ni* of "onion," which in Bantu must be written *ny* if we follow analogies, since we write *dya, lya,* or *tya,* "eat"; *pya,* "burn." The two sounds, *ñ* and *ny*, should be carefully distinguished in Bantu, where it only by reason of the different meanings they convey. Thus *ñama* means "meat," and *kañe* means "once," while *nya ma* is "quite shocking," and *nkanye* means "Let me go to the bush." Besides *ñ* is a single sound, while *ny* is a double one, like *dy, ly, py, ty,* etc., Ñ being a well-known symbol, adopted long ago in a great neo-Latin language, must certainly be preferred to Lepsius' *ṅ*.

Another difficulty comes from a sound similar to *ng* in the English word "song." This sound being single, the combination *ng* cannot do for it in Bantu if we adhere to the principles "one sound, one letter" and "no letter or combination of letters with two different values." Worse is for this sound the combination *ng'*, as ' represents an elision, and here no sound is elided. After many trials I have come to use the symbol *ᴎ, ɯ* (a mutilated *M* or *m*), which every typographer can form for himself with a stroke of the knife. Thus *ᴎombe, ɯombe,* "cattle,' *ᴎanda, ɯanda,* " house."

Having once found how practical was a mutilated letter for a Bantu sound not represented, or not well represented, in European languages, I have come, naturally, to the conclusion of using mutilated letters for all other sounds giving trouble, as *ꓘ, ʞ* (mutilated *K, k*) for the modern Greek χ ; *ʍ, ʋ* (mutilated *W, w*) for the Dutch *w* ; ⅄, ⅄ (mutilated X, x), for the Xosa and Zulu lateral click. This, while saving the principle, "one sound, one letter," saves also to the English printer the trouble of applying to a foreign foundry for types of difficult access.

Instead of the combinations *ch* and *sh* for single sounds I use respectively *c* and *x*, as good scholars have done before me. They are both single sounds, so let .them be expressed by single letters. Examples in Bwine-Mukuni : *caxa*, keep; *cintu*, a thing; *xintu*, things.

The evident contraction of two vowels has to be marked in certain cases. We then use the circumflex accent, as in *mêno*=*ma-ino*, teeth.

3. LINGUISTIC POSITION OF THE LANGUAGES ILLUSTRATED IN THIS WORK.—To what linguistic group or groups do the several languages belong of which samples are given here ? Our answer to this question will depend on the principle of classification which we adopt. Geographically they are all languages spoken by natives of Northern Rhodesia, each of them predominating in one or another part of the country. But a definite philological classification is not so simple, since fusions have taken place between languages geographically remote. Practically, the way of expressing " three people " in a Bantu language is one of the most convenient means of tracing its family relations. This expression is sounded :

(*a*) *ba-ntu bôtatwe* in Rhodesian Tonga, Bwine-Mukuni, Ila, Sara, Totera, Subiya. Here we have a well-defined group and the one best illustrated in this work. We may call it the *bantu bôtatwe* group, apparently the most archaic, on the whole, in the Bantu field.

(*b*) *a wa-ntu wa-tatu* (*w* like Dutch *w*) in Bemba, Ramba.

(*c*) *wa-ntu, wa-tatu* (*w* like Dutch *w*) in Sori, Rwano, etc.

(*d*) *wa-ntu wa-tatu* in Nsenga.

(*e*) *a-nthu a-tatu* in Ñungwe, spoken in the Feira sub-district ; also in Sena, Ñanja, etc.

(*f*) *ba-nthu ba-hatu* or *a-nthu a-hatu* in Mbwera.

(*g*) *ba-tu ba ba-lalu*, in Kololo.

(*h*) *a-tu a-raru* in Kelimane and Kúa in general.

In some of these languages the full sentence showing best where affinities are closest would be the following :—" Weep, eyes mine, over the death of these three people." (p. 4).

4. THE TYPICAL OLD BANTU TALE.—It consists of two distinct parts, one narrated, mostly in the form of dialogues, the other sung. It is melo-drama of a kind. Its name is in Bwine-Mukuni *ka-labi*, lit. " it opens a little one's eyes," in Tonga *kâno*, lit. " let one repent a little there," in Ramba *ci-ximi*, lit. " one tells the news," in Ñungwe, *ci-ndzano*, lit. " where I play (?)." Of the two parts the more important is the one that is sung, so much so that in many tales the narrative is to it no more than a frame is to a picture.

ENGLISH.	WEEP	EYES	MINE	THE DYING	OF	MEN	THREE	THESE.
Rhod. Tonga, Mukuni, etc ...	*A mu-lire*	*mênso*	*á-ngu*	*hu-fwa*	*hwa*	*ba-ntu*	*bó-tatwe*	*aba*
Ila or Sukulumbwe ...	*A mu-lile*	,,	,,	,,	,,	,,	,,	,,
Subiya	*Mu-lire*	,,	,,	,,	,,	,,	,,	,,
Ramba	*Rirêni*	,,	*á-nji*	*uhu-fwa*	,,	*a ua-ntu*	*ua-tatu*	*aua*
Sori	*Ka mu livêni*	,,	*á-kane*	*hu-fwa*	,,	*ua-nu*	,,	,,
Mbwera	*Nga ijivênu*	*mênlo*	*á-me*	,,	,,	*ba-nthu*	*ba-hatu*	*aba*
Nsenga	*Rira-ni*	*mênso*	*á-ngu*	,,	,,	*wa-ntu*	*wa-tatu*	*awa*
Ñungwe	*Rira-ni*	*ma-so*	*á-ngu*	*hu-fa*	,,	*a-nhu*	*a-tatu*	,,
Sena	*Rira-ni*	*ma-so*	*á-nça*	,,	,,	*a-nhu*	,,	,,
Kololo	*Lira-m*	*mêto*	*á-ka*	*hu-xwa*	,,	*ba-tu*	*ba-lalu*	*aba*
Kelimane	*Lila-ni*	*mêto*	,,	*o-kwa*	*wa*	*a-tu*	*a-raru*	*aa*
Kûa	*Unla-ni*	*mêto*	,,	,,	,,	*a-tu*	*a-raru*	*a:a*

The part which is sung is not only free to borrow words from any language known to the singer, but is supposed, moreover, to understand and interpret the language of birds, other animals, and nature in general. It is composed of a monologue, or a dialogue, and a chorus.

Nearly all the tales in Bwine-Mukuni and Tonga which the compiler has so far collected, belong to this old Bantu type. '

This happy combination of narrative and melodies containing " choruses " in which the hearers take part, though it makes this sort of composition somewhat slow, does in fact keep away dullness from our essentially musical natives to an extent which one who has not witnessed it can scarcely realise.([1])

These little melodramas are, in fact, such a power in Central Africa that, with a few of them, a competent story-teller can keep a troop of boys and girls interested for hours without the least thought of mischief. An evening with the phonograph repeating some of the very tales printed in this book has even been found to be far more interesting for throngs of natives than grand exhibitions with the magic lantern.

4. THE AIM OF OUR STORY-MAKERS.—As a rule, the Mukuni tale is tragic. The more versatile Tonga are able to compose comic stories as well. What Mukuni and Tonga story-tellers have in common, whatever be the purpose of folk-lore among other peoples, is their intention, not only to make their young hearers happy, but

---

[1] It is a strange coincidence, if the profane may be associated with the sacred, that the form common to nearly all the Mukuni and Tonga tales happens to be practically the same as that of the morning lessons in the Latin rite of the Catholic Church. In these every lesson is followed by an anthem which contains a chorus, and the movement of the anthem is exactly that of the songs of our tales. For instance, one may compare with our songs the following anthems of the lessons on the Holy Trinity.

" Great is the Lord, and above all praise. *Chorus* : And no number can measure His wisdom.—Great is the Lord, and great His virtue, and to His wisdom there is no end. *Chorus* : And no number can measure His wisdom. —Glory be to the Father, and to the Son, and to the Holy Ghost. *Chorus* : And no number can measure His wisdom."

The Israelites seem to have had for a number of their narratives a form akin to this movement of the Mukuni and Tonga tales, as may be concluded from the variety of hymns interspersed in not a few of their recitals of events. Among such hymns may be mentioned that of Moses after crossing the Red Sea (Ex. 15) ; that of Anna when she took Samuel to the house of God (I. Reg. 2) ; that of the women singing the victory of David over Goliath (I. Reg. 18) ; the lamentation of David over the death of Saul and Jonathan (II. Reg. 1) ; the hymns of Tobias, Judith, the three youths in the furnace, etc., etc. ; the *Benedictus*, the *Magnificat*, the song of the angels at the birth of Christ, etc., etc. In the Psalm 135 the chorus, " *Quoniam in aeternum misericordia ejus* " is repeated in every verse, exactly as the choruses of most of our Mukuni and Tonga songs in the tales.

also, and above all, " to instruct." Every tale, from their point of view, is a lesson, it may be of a principle of law, or of civilised manners as they understand them, or even of religious dogma, as in our tale NSEYANDI; but a lesson it is, though generally hidden under a legendary or an allegorical form which rubs off anything in the shape of personal application and irritation.([2])

A woman was heard once delivering herself of a tale evidently intended to give vent to ardent love.

5.   ORIGIN OF THESE TALES.—For all we know, some of these tales, both Tonga and Mukuni, may be as old as the hills; of others it cannot be proved that they are not as recent as the invasion of Africa by railways and flying machines. What is certain is that most of them are losing their hold on the natives with the advance of European civilisation, which concentrates their thoughts on money at the expense of the old happy-go-lucky ideals.

6.   THE TITLES.—By the natives themselves these tales are generally remembered by the first verse of their principal song. That is why such verses are here made to serve as titles.

7.   HOW THIS COLLECTION HAS BEEN MADE.—All these tales have been collected with the help of the phonograph, and most of the records are still preserved, so that every detail can easily be checked. The text in Bantu is given almost exactly as it was, or is, on the cylinders. The translation, however, does not pretend to be absolutely literal, a word being inserted here or there where clearness seems to require it in English. Neither am I sure that I have everywhere exactly seized the mentality of the narrators. But a trial had to be made before it was too late.

Every song has its own tune, but only a few tunes have been thought worth noting, just enough to give an idea of what Bantu music is like.

8.   A SPELLING LESSON.—Bwine-Mukuni is the language best exemplified in this work. The following table exhibits first the syllables proper to it, then, between brackets, syllables which are foreign to it, but are sometimes borrowed by it for specific purposes.

```
                      mi me ma mo mu
bi be ba bo bu        mbi mbe mba mbo mbu
pi pe pa po pu fu     mpi mpe mpa mpo mpu mfu
```

[2] A question which may be submitted to students of Bantu lore is whether the proportion of animal tales has not increased in some places in the same ratio as slavery. It is certainly a notable fact that among the Xosa, Zulu, Bêne-Mukuni, etc., who do not remember having ever been enslaved, the proportion of animal tales is insignificant or evidently borrowed.

```
                                ni  ne  na  no  nu
ri  re  ra  ro  ru              ndi nde nda ndo ndu
li  le  la  lo  lu
ti  te  ta  to  tu              nti nte nta nto ntu
    se  sa  so  su              nse nsa nso nsu
                            ñi  ñe  ña  ño  ñu
 i   e  ja   -  ju
yi  ye  ya  yo  yu              nji nje nja njo nju
ci  ce  ca  co  cu              nci nce nca nco ncu
xi  xe  xa  xo  xu              nxi nxe nxa nxo nxu
                            ᵐa  mo  mu
        a   o   u  gu       ngi nge nga ngo ngu
ki  ke  ka  ko  ku              nki nke nka nko nku
                        mwi mwe mwa
                        mye mya myo myu
                        mî  mê  mâ  mô  mû
bwi bwe bwa                 mbwi mbwe mbwa
bye bya byo byu             mbye mbya mbyo mbyu
bî  bê  bâ  bô  bû          mbî mbê mbâ mbô mbû
pwi pwe pwa                 mpwi mpwe mpwa
pye pya pyo pyu             mpye mpya mpyo mypu
pî  pê  pâ  pô              mpî mpê mpâ mpô
fwi fwe fwa                 mfwi mfwe mfwa
fô  fû                      mfô mfû
                        nwi nwe nwa
                        nye nya nyo nyu
                        nî  nê  nâ  nô  nû
rwi rwe rwa         }
lwi lwe lwa         }       ndwi ndwe ndwa
rye rya ryo ryu             ndye ndya ndyo ndyu
lye lya lyo lyu
rî  rê  râ  rô  rû          ndî ndê ndâ ndô ndû
lî  lê  lâ  lô  lû
twi twe twa                 ntwi ntwe ntwa
tye tya tyo tyu             ntye ntya ntyo ntyu
tî  tê  tâ  tô  tû
swi swe swa sô              nswi nswe nswa
                        ᵐwa
wi  we  wa  wo              ngwi ngwe ngwa
â   ô   û                   ngâ ngô ngû
kwi kwe kwa kô              nkwi nkwe nkwa nkô
```

(vi ve va vo vu fi fe fa fo ji je ja jo ju
zi ze za zo zu si hi he ħa ho hŭ)
(ñwi ñwe ñwa ; fye fya fyo fyu ; zye zya zyo zyu ;
sye sya syo syu). These are all foreign sounds.

In the languages of the *bantu bótatwe* group (see above, 3*a*) *m* and
n, coupled with a sonant, behave differently according as the following
syllable has a nasalised consonant or not. Thus, in Bwine-Mukuni,
when the following syllable has a nasalised consonant :—

m + b becomes *m'*. Ex., *m'ombe*, let me be docile = *m-bombe*.

n + r and *n + l* become *n'*. Ex., *n'onde*, let me run = *n-ronde*.

n + y becomes *ñ*. Ex., *ñande*, let me search = *n-yande*.

n + i becomes *ñi*. Ex., *ñimbe*, let me sing = *n-imbe*.

n + e becomes *ñe*. Ex., *ñembere*, let me herd = *n-embere*.

n + a becomes *ɯa*. Ex., *ɯambe*, let me speak = *n-ambe*.

n + o becomes *ɯo*. Ex., *ɯombe*, let me beat the drum = *n-ombe*.

n + u becomes *mu*. Ex., *mumpule*, let me bark a tree, =
n-umpule.

But, when the following syllable has no nasalised consonant :

m + b becomes *mb*. Ex., *mbone*, let me see = *m-bone*.

n + r and *n + l* become *nd*. Ex., *ndeke*, leave me = *n-reke*.

n + y becomes *nj*. Ex., *njare*, let me spread = *n-yare*.

n + i becomes *nji*. Ex., *njipuxe*, let me ask = *n-ipuxe*.

n + ĭ becomes *n*. Ex., *nse*, let me come = *n-ĭse*.

n + e becomes *nje*. Ex., *njebere*, let me contemplate = *n-ebere*.

n + a becomes *nga*. Ex., *ngane*, let me repent = *n-ane*.

n + o becomes *ngo*. Ex., *ngone*, let me sleep = *n-one*.

n + u becomes *ngu*. Ex., *ngule*, let me buy = *n-ule*.

n + w becomes *ngw*. Ex., *ngwe*, let me fall = *n-we*.

Thus it appears that the Bême-Mukuni are conscious that the
syllables *i, e, a, o, u, wi*, etc., contain a spirit of some sort, something
like '*i*, '*e*, '*a*, '*o*, '*u*, '*wi*, etc.

FIRST PART

TALES OF THE BÊNE-MUKUNI.*

I.—HOW CAN I SILENCE KATUBI?

This is what some people did.

The son said : " Mother, go and find a wife for me, as I am now grown up."

The mother said : " My child is now grown up."

Other people said : " Dear me! he is not grown up yet."

The mother got up and went to look for the wife. . . .

Time passed. The wife gave birth to a child, and later on to another. At last she said to her husband : " Let us get up and go and see my mother."

The husband said : " We will go."

They got up, both of them. It happened to be a time of famine. On the way they found wild figs. The woman then said : " Do climb up and give me some figs."

The husband went up the tree. He then began to shake the branches, and figs fell in abundance, the woman, meanwhile, and her children eating them.

Again he shook, and more figs fell, among them a particularly big one : " Wife," said the husband, " do not eat that one fig; if you do I will kill you".

" Hunger has no law," said the wife. " Besides, really! Would you kill me, your wife, for a fig ? I am eating it ; let us see whether you dare kill me."

The woman ate the fig. Seeing that, the husband came down and with an assegai pointed at her, said : " My fig, what has become of it ? "

She said : " I have eaten it."

He there and then killed his wife, his younger child just staring at him.

The man then said : " My children, let us go now, as I have killed your mother."

---

* The Bêne-Mukuni call their language *Bwine-Mukuni*. A. C. Madan's *Lenje Handbook* (Oxford, Clarendon Press, 1908), is a description of it.

They got up and the bigger child put his little brother on his back. Baby, looking behind, began to cry.   His brother then started this reproachful song :

"How can I silence Katubi?
"How can I silence Katubi?
"O my dear Katubi!
"O my dear Katubi!
"How can I silence Katubi?" (¹)

The father asked : " Now what art thou saying? "

The answer was : " It is not I that am speaking; it is baby that is crying."

The father said : " Let us go, dear!   There is food for thee where we are going to? "

On they went, on they went, on they went, till baby himself took up the song :

"Silence Katubi!
"Silence Katubi!
"My brother has become my mother!
"My brother has become my mother!
"Silence Katubi!"

The father said : " Now what sort of language is that, thou little child of a tendon? ²   I am coming to kill thee.   What!   As I have killed thy mother, art thou going to expose me at thy grandmother's abode? "

The child said : " No, I shall not speak."

On they went, on they went.   Baby looked fixedly behind.   Then came the song :

"What a lot of vultures!
"What a lot of vultures!
"Over the fig-trees at Môya's,³
"Over the fig-trees at Môya's,
"What a lot of vultures!"

And baby cried again.

The father said : " What art thou crying for? "

The bigger child said : " I am trying to stop baby's crying."

The man, having looked behind, saw a number of vultures hovering

---

¹ *Katubi*, lit., "Make-the-thing-white," *i.e.*," Expose-the-truth;" is the name of the baby.

² *Mukaxi*, pl. *mi-kaxi*, means properly, " Achilles tendon."   The expression "child of a tendon," generally used in the vocative, sounds somewhat like " exasperating child! "

³ *Môya* is the name of a chief introduced here merely to localise the story. The fig-trees of Moya's kraal are famous in both the Mukuni and the Tonga folk-lore.

over there, then heard this song :
> " What a lot of vultures! " etc. (as above).

He said : " What art thou crying for ? "

" Why! " answered the child. " I am doing what I can to silence baby. It is he that is crying, not I."

" What is he crying for ? "

" He is crying for mother," answered the child.

The father said : " Nonsense! Let us go ; thou art going to find thy grandmother ahead."

On they went and went, till baby looking back started again :
> " Silence Katubi ! " etc. (as above.)

This time there goes the father retracing his steps, then beating them both, beating and beating them.

" You are killing me, father," said the child. " Are you going to kill me too as you have killed mother ? "

" I mean to kill thee," answered the father.

On they went, on they went, the children this time going in front until baby looked back once more, and sang as before :
> " What a lot of vultures ! " etc.

.   .   .   .

At last they reached the village.

There first the greeting : " So you have put in an appearance ! "

" We have put in an appearance," replied the man.

But the grandmother at once began to put questions to her bigger grandchild, saying : " Now, where has your mother been left ? "

The child just shook his head. Then he said : " Do you expect to see mother ? She has been killed by father, and that for a wild fruit. It is a fact ; it was for a fig that he killed her."

At that moment baby started singing :
> " What a lot of vultures!
> " What a lot of vultures!
> " Over the fig-trees at Môya's,
> " What a lot of vultures! "

The grandmother said : " Stop, baby." She added : " We are just going to kill your father also."

People then set to dig inside of a hut, to dig a deep, narrow hole. Meanwhile the grandmother said : " Stir the porridge."

Soon porridge was brought into the hut, while a mat was being spread over the hole. The grandmother then said : " Go and call your father."

He was called. As he entered the hut, he said : " We may as well sit just there on the mat." And, as he said so, he tumbled into the

hole.   He died in boiling water (which was then poured over him.)
I am Mwana-Rumina.[4]

(IN BWINE-MUKUNI.)
M'UMBULUXE KATUBI?

Nce bâkacita bantu.
Ayi " Má, mukanjębere mukângu, ono ndakúla."
Bañina ayi " Mwana wangu ono wakula."
Bamwi ayi " Bâna ![5] tâna a kukula.
Bâñamuka bañina, bâya mu kwebera.
Mukaakwe waxara, waxara mwana.   Ay'axare mwana, a rimwi waxara.
Mukaakwe ayi " A tuñamuke tuna kuya kuli bamá."   Bânarumi ayi " Tulaya."
Bâñamuka, bâñamuka.   A nsara yakora.
Baxike mu nxira, bâjana nkuyu.   Bârutundu ayi " A mutante mumpewo nkuyu."   Bânarumi bâtanta.
A kutanta bânarumi, bâpukumuna, xâroka xinji, bânakaxi bate kulya a bâna bâbo.
Bâpukumuna, xâroka.   Rwaroka runene, ayi " Mukaangu, utarî rukuyu uro.   Citó ululye, ntôkujaya."
Bakaabo ayi " Cifumbwa yankora nsara.   A rimwi ne mukaako uncaye pa rukuyu!   Nte kululya, tubone mbwe uncaye-wo."
Bânakaxi bâlulya.   Bânarumi baraseruka, a pa risumo " Rukuyu rwangu rwaya kuli ? "
Ayi " Ndarulya."
Bâmuyasa mukaabo, kâna kâbo kakaranga-wo bulyo.
Ayi " No bâna bângu, a tuna kuya ono, mbo ndamujaya ñina wanu."
Bâñamuka, mwana wabo wabereka kâkwabo.   Karange kwisure kânike, kâtanguna kulira.   Mpêce mukwabo a rwine a kulusamputa :
   " M'umbuluxe [6] Katubi ?
   " M'umbuluxe Katubi ?
   " Katubi, o mukwêsu!
   " Katubi, o mukwêsu !
   " M'umbuluxe Katubi ?

---

[4] *Mwana-Rumina*, when he told this well-known story, was a boy about 15 years of age, from Kalulu's kraal in the Bu-Sori.   He was already thinking of getting a wife.   His mother told him this story, probably to try to convince him that he was too young yet.
[5] *Bâna!* lit., " Children! "   A Mukuni deprecatory interjection which may be translated variously by " Come, come! "   " Nonsense! "   " Dear me!" etc.
[6] *M'umbuluxe*, subjunctive 1st pers. sing. from *bumbuluxa.*

M'u-mbu-lu-xe Ka-tu - bi? M'u-mbu-lu-xe Ka-tu -
-bi? Ka-tu - bi o mu-kwê-su, Ka-tu-bi, o mu-kwê-
-su! M'u-mbu-lu-xe Ka-tu-bi?

Baixi ayi " Ino ute kwamba buyani ? "
Ayi " Ute kwamba mwanike, ute kulira."
Ayi " Katuya, bâna ! tulaya ukarye."
Bêenda-ko, bêenda-ko, bêenda.   Mpêce a kêne kânike a kâro ·
    " Bumbuluxa Katubi!
    " Bumbuluxa Katubi!
    " Má ngo mukwesu !
    " Má ngo mukwesu !
    " Bumbuluxa Katubi ! "
Baixi ayi " Ono ute kwamba buyani, o kâna kâ mukaxi?   Nte
kwĭsá mu kukujaya webo.   A rimwi, mbo ndajaya bañoko, uye
ukaambe kuli ba-nkambo yako ! "
Mwana ayi " Tawu, te-nkaambe."
Bêenda-ko, bêenda-ko.   Mwanike wasompa-ko, ayi :
    " Câunjira makubi ! [7]
    " Câunjira makubi !
    " Ku makuyu kwa Môya
    " Ku makuyu kwa Môya
    " Câunjira makubi ! " [8]
Kârira kâna kâbo.
Ayi " Ute kulira-nxi ?
Ayi " Nte kubumbuluxa mwanike."
Ingayi barange a bâro kwisule nko bâswa, bajane makubi câunjira,
bañumfwe ayi :
    " Câunjira makubi ! " etc. (as above).
Ayi " Ute kulira-nxi ? "
Ayi " Nte kuumuxa mwanike, bâna !   Ngo ute kulira, têxi ndime."

---

[7] It looks as if *makubi* were here meant to rhyme with *Katubi* of the preceding
song.
[8] Same tune as above.

Ayi " Ute kulira nxi ? "
Ayi " Ute kulira bañina."
Ayi " Bâna ! Ka tuya, ula kujana ba-nkambo yako ku nembo."
Bêenda-ko, bêenda, kacebe kwisule :
        " Bumbuluxa Katubi," etc. (as above).
Mbá bâbôrera baixi. Bâbauma a bâro, bâbauma, bâbauma.
Ayi " Tá, ulencaya.[9] Uncaye a nebo mbo wakajaya bama ? "
Ayi " Ntôkujaya."
Bêenda-ko, bêenda-ko, kuya a nembo. Kacebe-ko kwisule, ayi :
        " Câunjira makubi ! ", etc. (as above).

.   .   .   .

Bâxika ku muxi.
Baxike ku muxi " Mwaboneka ! " Ayi " Twaboneka."
Ba-nkambo yakwe kuxikira bo kwipuxa mwixikulu wabo ayi :
" Ino bañoko bâkacara kuli ? "
Mwanike kulipukumuna bulyo ayi " Mukabone bamá ? A rimwi
mbo bâkajaya batá. Pa musepo mpo bâkabajayira."
Kâimbira kânike :
        " Câunjira makubi !
        " Câunjira makubi !
        " Ku makuyu kwa Môya,
        " Ku makuyu kwa Môya,
        " Câunjira makubi ! "
Ba-nkambo yakwe ayi " Cireke, mwanike." Ayi " Tulamujaya
bulyo arakwe ixi wanu."
Bâkaba mu manda bâkaba mulindi. Ayi " A muponde nxima."
A kubatorera, a mpasa a kuyara-wo. Ayi " Kôya ukabaite baiso."
A kubaita.
Ingayi baxike bo mu manda, ayi " Tunôkara bo pa mpasa," bâku-
lukira mu mulindi. Bâfwa mu manxi arungula.
Ndime MWANA-RUMINA.

II.—FATHER, WAIT FOR ME.[1]

Another man, too, had taken a wife, and now she had the joy of
being with child, but the famine was acute.

One day, when hunger was particularly severe and the man,
accompanied by his wife, was dragging himself along in the direction

---

[9] Form more common : *ulancaya.*
[1] This tale somewhat resembles the preceding, but is told in a more classical
style, though by an illiterate woman.

of her mother's home in the hope of getting a little food there, he happened to find on the road a tree with abundant wild fruit on the top. "Wife," he said, "get up there that we may eat fruit."

The woman refused, saying : "I, who am with child, to climb up a tree !"

He said : "In that case, do not climb at all." [2]

The husband then climbed up himself and shook and shook the branches, the woman meanwhile picking up what fell down. He said :

"Do not pick up my fruit. What ! Just now you refused to go up !"

And she : "Dear me! I am only picking them up."

Thinking about his fruit, he hurried down from the top of the tree and said : "You have eaten some."

And she : "Why ! Of course I have not."

Coming, assegai in hand, he stabbed his wife. And there she died on the spot.

He then gathered his fruit with both hands. There he is eating them, remaining where the woman is stretched quite flat.[3]

Then all of a sudden he starts running. Run! Run! Run! Without stopping once till he reaches the rise.

There he slept, out of sight of the place where he had left the woman.

Meanwhile the child that was in the womb rushed out of it, dragging its umbilical cord. First it looked round for the direction which its father had taken, then started this song :

"Father, wait for me.
"Father, wait for me,
"The little wombless.
"Who is it that has eaten my mother ?
"The little wombless . . . !
"How swollen are those eyes! [4]
"Wait till the little wombless comes."

That gave him a shake. . . ." There," he said, "there comes a thing which is speaking." He listens, he stares in that direction. . . . "This is the child coming to follow me after all that, when I have already killed its mother. It had been left in the womb."

---

[2] This may be a *lapsus linguae* for "do not eat my fruit."

[3] "The woman is stretched quite flat." Among the Bêne-Mukuni it is a great sin thus to leave the body of a respectable person stretched in the veld to be eaten by vultures. The murderer should at least have folded over the arms and legs so as to give to the body more or less the shape of fœtus in the womb, and after that restored it to its mother the earth.

[4] Among the Bêne-Mukuni murderers are said to have red eyes.

Then rage took his wits away, so he killed the little child! . . . There he is, making a fresh start, then going on. Here, where the little bone has been left : " Little bone, gather thyself up! . . . Little bone, gather thyself up."[5] Soon it is up again, and then comes the song :

" Father, wait for me," etc. (as above).

The father has stopped. . . . " Again the child that I have killed! It has risen and is coming. Now wait for him."

So he hides and waits for the child, and that with an assegai in his hand. The child comes and makes itself visible at a distance as from here to there. As soon as it comes, quick with the assegai! Stab it! Then he looks for a hole, shovels the little body into it and heaps branches up at the entrance.

Then he with all speed! With all speed ! . . . .

At last he reaches the kraal, where lives the mother of his dead wife, the grandmother of the child.

When he comes he sits down. Then his brothers and sisters-in-law come with smiling faces. . . . " Well! Well! You have put in an appearance!"

" We have," he says, " put in an appearance."

And a hut is prepared for him and his wife, who is expected.

Then the mother-in-law is heard asking from afar [6] : " Well! And my daughter, where has she been detained ? "

Says he : " I have left her at home. I have come alone to beg for a little food. Hunger is roaring."

" Sit down inside there, father."

Food is procured for him. So he begins to eat. And, when he has finished, he even goes to sleep.

Meanwhile, the child, for its part, has squeezed itself out of the hole wherein it had been put, and again, with its umbilical cord hanging on . . . :

" Father, wait for me," etc. (as above).

The people listen in the direction of the path. . . . " That thing which comes speaking indistinctly, what is it ? . . . It seems to be a person. . . . What is it ? . . . . It looks, man, like a child killed by you on the road. . . . And now, when we look at your way of sitting, you seem to be only half-seated."

---

[5] " Little bone, gather thyself up! " These words are put in the mouth of the great avenging power.

[6] The common law in Northern Rhodesia strictly forbids a mother-in-law togo near her son-in-law.

" We do not see him distinctly. . . . It cannot be the child, mother; it remained at home."

The man has just got up to shake himself a little. And his little child, too, with all speed! It is already near, with the mouth wide open :

" Father, wait for me," etc. (as above).

Every one is staring. They say : " There comes a little red thing. It has still the umbilical cord hanging on."

Inside of the hut there, where the man is, there is complete silence!

Meanwhile the child is coming on feet and buttocks with its mouth wide open, but still at a distance from its grandmother's hut. " Straight over there! " notes every one. The grandmother looks towards the road, and notices that the little thing is perspiring, and what speed! Then the song :

" Father, wait for me," etc. (as above).

Great Lord ! It scarcely reaches its grandmother's hut when it jumps into it. And on the bed :

" Father, wait for me.
" Father, hast thou come ?
" Yes, thou hast eaten my mother.
" How swollen those eyes!
" Wait till the little wombless comes."

Then the grandmother put this question to the man : " Now what sort of song is this child singing ? Have you not killed our daughter ? "

She has scarcely added " Surround him," he is already in their hands. His very brothers-in-law tie him. And then . . . all the assegais are poised together in one direction, every one saying : " Now to-day you are the man who killed our sister. . . ."

Then they just threw the body away there to the west.[7] And the grandmother picked up her little grandchild.

I am CIBUTA.[8]

[7] " . . . to the west." The body is thrown away to the beasts of prey, just as the man had left to them the body of his wife. Why " to the west " ? Probably to avoid the smell, as the winds in these parts blow mostly from the east.

[8] Cibuta, who can tell a number of pretty tales like this, is a plain woman of Munenga's kraal, west of the Kasisi Mission Station, N. Rhodesia.

Tales of this kind, showing that every crime finds an unexpected revealer appointed by a superior power, are very common in the whole of the Zambezi region. In this particular tale the revealer is a child which was still in the womb at the time of the crime, in others it is a little dog, but in tales far more numerous it is a little bird, which no killing or other ingenious means of destruction can prevent from rising from the dead and singing away the criminal deed until punishment is met to the guilty person.

TATA, MPEMBE.

A bamwi bâkaringa a bakaabo, bakaabo ka bacite rifumo. A nsara yakora.

Uko nko yabakora bo nsara, mu nxira bâjana cisamo. Bajane xisepo kopere, ayi, " O mukaangu, tanta-ko tulye xisepo."

Mwanakaxi wakaka, " Ne ncite rifumo, ntante ku cisamo! "

Ayi " Ono utatanti-ko."

Bâtanta-ko bânarumi, ka bapukumuna, ka bapukumuna, mwanakaxi xisepo kâbwesa.

Ayi " Reka kumbwesera xisepo. Ino ndye wakaka kutanta! "

A rakwe, " Bâna! Ntôbwesa bulyo."

Xisepo xâbo, ayi bâramuke-ko (kujulu rya cisamo, ayi " Waryawo."

A rakwe, " Nxikwe kulya-wo, bâna! "

Bê baxike a risumo, bâmuyasa mukaabo. A mwine mulya wafwa. Bâyoranya xisepo xâbo. Mbarya bate kulya. Wacara mwatandabarira mwanakaxi.

Pukume! Pukume! Pukume pamwi pa mutara.

Bâona kwakacara mwanakaxi.

Mwana waringa-wo mu mara warapuká-mo a rukowa rwakwe. Kulangaula nxira yakaita bêxi. Warusansanta :

> " Tata, mpembe.[9]
> " Tata, mpembe,
> " Kabulanda!
> " Ngani warya mama ?[10]
> " Kabulanda!
> " Uximbya câ mênso.
> " Kabulanda kabwïsá."

Mpa a kumwenxa . . . " Uku kutôsa câmba cintu." Kusuwamo, kulanga-mo. . . . " Uyu mwana utôsa cikonkera, a rimwi! Bañina mbo nda-kêjaya! Wakacara mu mara."

Mpa a kufumpuka. A kujaya mwana! . . . Ngulya wakumbuluka-wo ute kuya!

Nko kâcara a kâro kafuwa, " Kafuwa, ribunjebunje! Kafuwa, ribunjebunje! " A mwine wapatamuka :

> " Tata, mpembe," etc. (as above).

---

[9] *Tata, mpembe*, Ramba words for Mukuni *Tá, ninde*, " Father, wait for me."
[10] *Mama*, " my mother," Ramba for Mukuni *má*. Such Ramba words abound in the songs of the Mukuni tales. As a rule, the Bantu are fond of introducing into their songs words from different dialects.

Watulumana . . . " A rimwi! Mwana ngo ndêjaya! Wabuka ute kwĭsá. Ono a muberamine! "
Kumuberamina a risumo. Kwĭsá mu kupora mbuli moomo. Ay' axike, a risumo a kumuyasa. A kuciyanda ciringo a kumukwirika-ko, a xisanswa a kubika-ko.
A rakwe a rubiro! A rubiro!
Kuxika ku muxi kuli bañina oko, kuli ba-nkambo yakwe.
Ay' axike, a kwĭkara. Ba-maramu bâkwe kumusekerera . . .
" Bâna! Mwaboneka? "—Ayi " Twaboneka."
A kubabambira manda.
Ayi kuñumfwa bañinaxara . . . " Ino mwanângu wacara kuli ? "
Ayi " Ndamuxiya ku muxi. Nte kwĭsa kwinxira xâ kulya. Nsara yaburuma."
" A mukare moomo, tá."
Kumuyandira xâ kulya. Kurimba kulya. Ay' amane kulya, a koona.
A rakwe mwana wapatamuka nko bâkamubika ku ciringo, a rukowa rwakwe. . . . .
    " Tata, mpembe," etc. (as above).
Bâsuwa-ko ku nxira . . . " Citôsa citepeta-ko ncinxi? . . . . Ciri anga ngu muntu . . . Ncinxi? . . . Mbwa kwinga, mwebo no bantu, mwana mwakajaya mu nxira. Ino mbwa kwinga mu kwĭkara mulisunteme bulyo."
" Ta tumubwene-wo kabotu . . . Tawu, má, wakacara ku muxi."
Bâñamuka kulyendauxa. A kâro kâna kâbo a rubiro. Kâxika karirakeme :
    " Tata, mpembe," etc. (as above).
Kusompa-ko. Ayi, " Kute kwĭsá kantu kafubera. Karicite a rukowa."
'Mo bâkaringa mu manda tontoro!
Eryo ute kwĭsá kusontomana—ulirakeme bo—. ku manda kuli ba-nkambo yakwe.
Ayi " Nkwece kulya." Kulanga-ko ku nxira. Ajane kayuwa. Rubiro rwenka :
    " Tata, mpembe," etc. (as above).
Bacu! Mpa a kuxika mu manda muli ba-nkambo yakwe, pirikixi! A pa bulo! . . .
    " Tata, mpembe.
    " Tata, wêsá ?
    " E, warya mama.
    " Waximbya câ mênso.
    " Kabulanda kabwĭsá."

Eryo mpa a kubaipuxa ayi, " Ino mwana ute kwimba buyani?
Mwanêsu te wakamujaya? "
Mpa a kwamba ayi " Moondomoke," uli-wo mu mânsa.   A bêne
ba-maramu âkwe a kumwanga.   Eryo ndye pa kubwarayika pamwi
masumo. . . . " Ino sunu mukwabêsu ndiwe wakamujaya! "
Mpa a kumusowa kumbo kulya.
Mpa a kubwesa kêxikulu kâkwe ako.
Ndime Cibuta.

III.—AS I AM BE-THANKFUL, I GO BACK.

Other people then picked up the song.
They said : " Let us go to the forest."
There they succeeded in killing wild pigs.   Then one of them said :
" Look here, friends, since we are hunting game, we may as well go
as far as the Bu-Twa,[1] in order to see the dogs they have there, and
bring one across." [2]
There they are on the way.
In the Bu-Twa they bought a dog. . . .   " Friends," said the
original owner, " the dog you have got, when he takes food, does
not eat from the ground, but from a little basket.   And to put his
sauce in a potsherd will not do; it must be a good earthen vessel." [3]
Now the troop has brought the dog across the river.   On the road
as they go he first kills wild pigs, then kills an elephant.   " Well
done ! " they say.   " Now let us go two by two to carry each tusk."
Finally they reach their kraal . . . " Look here, wife," says the
owner, " this dog I have brought does not eat from a potsherd,
neither can he be satisfied with any kind of light soup ; he must have
strong food, and that in a little open basket."
" All right," said the woman.
Soon after that the men went to beer-drinking.   The woman-folk
were left alone.   Then, Heaven help me! they cooked porridge,

[1] The Bu-Twa is the Abutwa of ancient geographers, the country of the
Ba-Twa.   These in Northern Rhodesia are fishermen who live mostly on the
Kafubwe (alias Kafue) and the swamps of its neighbourhood.   An interesting
article on the Ba-Twa of the Rukanga swamp may be seen in the Zambezi
Mission Record, April, 1913."
[2] The Ba-Sukulumbwe, who are intermixed with the Ba-Twa are particularly
fond of good dogs.   Once the compiler of these tales, was offered an ox for a
dog, because the dog had fought a leopard with success.
[3] The basket is for the more solid, the earthen vessel for the more liquid
food.   In most parts of Bantuland the ordinary food of a native consists of
nxima or nsima, " porridge," which is for the native what bread is for us,
and bucisa, or cisawi, a relish or sauce of some kind.

but without seasoning, and put it before the dog on a bit of broken pot. . . .

"Oh!" said the dog, "to-day they give me food on a potsherd, me who bring elephants! Well! now this very day I go back, and for good, to our own kraal."

And, without saying more, he is already on the road, while the woman says : "He is gone, is the foreign dog."

She goes after him at once : "Dear me! Be-thankful, come back."

Be-thankful only goes faster.

"Dear me! Be-thankful, come back."

Then over there he starts his song :

> "As I am Be-thankful, I go, I go back,"
> "As I am Be-thankful, I go, I go back."
> Solo : "I must go home."
> Chorus : "As I am Be-thankful, I go back."
> Solo : "To the river Wash-the-water-lilies." [4]
> Chorus : "As I am Be-thankful," etc.
> Solo : "Where the river forms deep waves."
> Chorus : "As I am Be-thankful," etc.
> Solo : "As I am Be-thankful."

"Dear me! No," says the woman, "my brother Be-thankful, come back."

Be-thankful goes every time faster and faster. He says : "At home, and nowhere else will I stop ; it was too bad of you to give me my food on a potsherd, me who bring elephants."

Ever faster, ever faster, ever faster, singing :

> "As I am Be-thankful," etc.

Before crossing the river he stopped in the shade.

. . . .

Meanwhile the husband coming home asked where his wife was.

"She has gone after the dog," was the answer. "She gave him food on a potsherd."

"Well!" he said, "I wish for her sake that some power may make me miss her."

And at once on her footsteps : "Let me go and thrust an assegai at her."

The dog then starts ahead once more ; he soon finds himself in view of his own kraal, then throws himself upon the water, while singing :

> "As I am Be-thankful," etc. (as above).

---

[4] An important article of the diet among the Ba-Twa are the roots of water-lilies, which abound in their swamps.

Just fancy! There he is on the shore taking long strides. At last he reaches the huts : " Look! " say the people, " here is the dog again! "

The man too is not long in showing himself. . . . " I want my dog," he says.

Then there is a fight with the wife. . . . " Stop that," say the Ba-Twa trying to separate them. " We will give you another dog. It was all your fault if you gave that one his food on a bit of a broken pot. Our dogs here do not eat from potsherds, but from baskets."

They at last succeeded in separating them. . . . " Give them another," said some one.

So the husband finally left his wife in peace.

I am CIBUTA.[5]

(IN BWINE-MUKUNI.)

'NAYA MARUMBE 'NABWERERA.

A bamwi bârubwesa.

Bê " Tunôya 'musansa."

Kulya nko bâkaya 'musansa, kuya kujaya bamwinjire : " O namata, mbo tujaya ñama, a tuporere ku Bu-Twa, tuye tukabone mbwa xâ ku Bu-Twa, tukasubule-wo."

Mbarya bâunka.

Kulya nko bâkaya, a mbwa bâula. . . . " Namata, mbwa nje mutôtora, pa kulya, ta iriti panxi, irarita mu ntumba. Kubwenjera 'mu rubiya, ta iriti mu cikaye. . . ."

A câro ono bâisubula. Mu nxira 'mo bâri kwǐsá, yaruma bamwinjire, yaruma nsofu. Nko bâkaamba ayi " Kwatemba mêja."

Bacu! A bêne a ku muxi. . . . " Ranga, mukaangu, ii mbwa indareta, pa kulita, ta iriti mu cikaye, ta iri rupere, una kwipakirira mu ntumba."

Mukaabo ayi " 'Mwece."

Basankwa bâya ku bwarwa. Nko bâkacara bârutundu, bacu! a kwipondaponda bo nxima, a pa cikaye. Mbwa " O! nebo sunu bâmpeta pa cikaye! Ne ntôreta nsofu! Ono sunu câ kuya nte kuya ku mixi yêsu.

A îne yawita mu nxira. A rakwe warutundu, " Yaunka mbwa ya bêne."

----

[5] This little tale, as well as the preceding, shows that a perfectly illiterate woman can be more natural in her style and more classical than most of the natives taught for long years at school. It is meant, of course, to impress upon masters that the blessing of a good servant should be duly appreciated.

A rakwe wawita-mo, " Bâna! Marumbe, bôra."
Marumbe a rubiro.
Tubiri ku nembo yarutatula :

'Na _ ya Ma _ ru _ mbe, 'na bwe-re — ra (bis) 'Na Ku-

-ya kwê - su Ma-ru - mbe 'na-bwe-re — ra....Ku rwa-pi -ra ma-

-ba Ma - ru - mbe 'na-bwe - re — ra, Ma - ru- mbe.

     " 'Naya,[6] Marumbe, 'nabwerera,[6]
     " 'Naya, Marumbe, 'nabwerera,
     " Na kuya kwêsu.   Chorus : **Marumbe, 'nabwerera**
     " Ku Sambe-nsaya.   „   „
     " Ku rwapira maba.   „   „
     " Marumbe! "
" Bâna! Akaka! Mukwêsu Marumbe, bôra."
Warutukula rubiro Marumbe ayi, " Nebo nkwece bo ku mixi
yêsu, mwakabixa [7] kumpeta pa cikaye, ne ndeta nsofu."
Yarutukula, yarutukula, yarutukula.
             " 'Naya, Marumbe, 'nabwerera," etc. (as above).
Yaimakana mu cimfwire. . . .

. . . .

Nkwakaxika ibaye ku muxi, ayi " Ino mukaangu nkwakaya ? "
Ayi " Bâkonkera mbwa. Bâkaipeta pa cikaye."
Ayi " Sombi mbule ku mujana-ko."
A rakwe mwisure, ayi " Nje nkamuyase risumo."
A yaro ku nembo, a kwine ku muxi wabo ku Bu-Twa, a îne a pa
manxi :
             " 'Naya, Marumbe, 'nabwerera," etc. (as above).
Bacu! a îne a pêtara.[8]
Bacu! a pa mânda.
" U! nji yabôra mbwa."

---

[6] *'Naya, 'nabwerera*, poetical for *ntôya, ntôbôrera*.
[7] *Mwakabixa*. More common *mwakabijixa*.
[8] *Pêtara*. In the record the true word is *pa citorobwi*, but I find no one who
understands it. I am advised to substitute *pêtara* for it.

A rakwe ibaye a rakwe wapora. . . . " Nebo mbwa yangu! "
Bârimbarwa a kulwa a mukaakwe. Mpa a kubapansanya Ba-
Twa. Bê " Bâna! A muleke kubatula, tulamupa imbi. Kubixa
nko mwabixa kuipeta pa cikaye. Swebo xinêsu ta xirî pa cikaye,
xirarita mu ntumba."
  Mpêce bâkabapansanya . . . " Babape imbi."
  Ndye a bêne a mukaabo te ndye bâkamuleka ?
  Ndime CIBUTA.

IV.—LET THE BIG DRUM ROLL.

This man was a young king. As he had gone with other people
to trade, his companions noted that he was bringing back a large
amount of goods. So, being mere blacks, they became quite jealous
and said : " Let us kill him."

In fact, they fell upon him and left him dead. After that they
threw his body into the bush.

He was then changed [1] into a little bird, with pretty colours and
cowries all over the body, which went and perched on the top of a
tree in front of the criminals. He then sang :

1. " Let the big drum roll! "—Chorus : " Let the big drum roll! "
    " It flaps the wings,
    " The little bird that has come out from the deep river,
    " From the great river of God.[2]   Let the big drum roll!
2. " Let the big drum roll! Let the big drum roll!
    " At the great river of beads and pearls
    " I have found fowls which pound,
    " Using mortars hewn from blood trees.[3]   Let the big drum roll!
3. " Let the big drum roll! Let the big drum roll!
    " Using mortars hewn from the blood-trees,
    " Their beaks are all white.
    " Here! Ñemba,[4] where are you ? Let the big drum roll!
4. " Let the big drum roll! Let the big drum roll!
    " Here! Ñemba, where are you ?
    " Start threading pearls,[5]
    " Brilliant pearls. Let the big drum roll!

[1] Var. " he flew into a little bird," *waulukira mu kayuni*. This variant shows
some difference of conception in the native minds regarding those mysterious
little birds of the Bantu lore which go about, when a crime has been com-
mitted, exposing the criminal. In the text here it is really the soul of the
man now winged by the imagination and transformed into a little bird. In
the variant it is the same soul, but migrating temporarily into a little bird
that happened to present itself there.
  [2] Lit. " of them."
  [3] That is, " crying vengeance for the blood spilt." The *mulombe* " blood-
tree," when hit, lets out red sap like blood.
  [4] Ñemba is the sister of the dead chief, as mentioned further on.
  [5] Pearls to be put on as a token of mourning.

5. " Let the big drum roll!   Let the big drum roll!
" Start threading pearls,
" Brilliant pearls,
" From the land I-wash-the-wrongs.[6]   Let the big **drum roll!**
6. " Let the big drum roll!   Let the big drum roll!
" The land Where-I-wash-the-wrongs!
" It is far here where you have brought me,
" Me who have no feet.   Let the big drum roll! "

Ñemba was the sister of the dead chief.

When those people heard that song, they caught the little bird and killed it by beating it.

They had hardly resumed their march when they saw the little bird alive once more going ahead of them, and heard it sing :
" Let the big drum roll," etc. (as above).

Once more they caught it and killed it, then this time said : " Let us burn it to ashes."

So they put it on the fire, reduced it to a cinder, then ground it to ashes.

But it got up again, flew into the air, and went on singing as before :
" Let the big drum roll! " etc.
until it flew away in the direction of their kraal.

When it reached the place the people saw it come down on the top of the royal house and perch there.

" Come," they said, " and see what a pretty bird."

They just heard it sing as above :
" Let the big drum roll! " etc.

. . . .

Now those people are coming to the kraal : " You have re-appeared! "—" We have reappeared."

" And the king, where have you left him ? "

They answer : " On the road."

---

[6] This song gives a pretty exact idea of the notions which the Bantu natives that have not degenerated through slavery or semi-slavery entertain regarding a future life.   The souls, though " having no feet," are supposed to go to a deep river of God far away, not a simple *mulonga* " river," but a *ri-ronga*, " big deep river," where God washes the wrongs clean, and where birds, with beaks all white, that is, innocent souls, cry vengeance against the spilling of blood. *Cinsambya-pyororo* or *Cinsambya-nsororo* is explained as meaning literally " The land where I wash the wrongs," but I find no one who can explain the exact meaning of *pyororo* or *nsororo*.   It is supposed to be a land far away somewhere in the East, whence come beads (*bulungu*), pearls (*nungu*) and other fineries.   In a sense it is a sort of paradise.
Note that the little bird sings on the spot, though it says they have brought it far.   This shows some notion of the agility, if not the quasi-ubiquity of the spirits.

Then : " Really ? On the road! Come and see a little bird which is on the roof of the royal house."

They at once said : " Let us kill it."

Meanwhile some people are digging a hole in the ground.

Then Ñemba says : " No, don't kill it. Let us hear the news first."

Just then the little bird started its song again :

" Let the big drum roll! " etc.

" Go into the hut, that you may explain to us exactly what the little bird sings."

They went and sat down in the hut on the mat spread there, but then *pŏwŏwŏwŏ*, they tumbled down into the hole. Boiling water was brought at once and poured on top of them. That is how they died.

I am MUMBA.[7]

(IN BWINE-MUKUNI.)

A IRIRE NTINGINI.[8]

Uyu ngo mwami. Uko nko bâkari kuya cisambara, babone wareta buboni bunji. Mpêce buboni bwabacisa bantu baxiya, bê " A tumujaye."

Mpêce bâmujaya jaye jaye. Bamane ku mujaya, bâmusowa bulyo mu rundu. Mpêce waba kayuni kâ mabara kafwete mpande mubiri ônse, kâya mu kwikara ku nembo ryabo kujulu rya cisamo, ayi :

A i-ri-re nti-ngi-ni! A i-ri-re nti-ngi-ni! Ka-ra-te-re-nte-nta kô-ni kâ-ka-swa kwi-ro-nga, kwi-ro-nga rya-bo A i-ri-re nti-ngi-ni!

---

[7] Mumba is a woman living in Cikwampu's kraal, Kasisi Mission Station. Some of the following tales are also from her. Here two or three insignificant details have been inserted from versions by Munje and a boy whose name I have forgotten.

Little birds revealing crimes and crying vengeance for them are quite common in the Bantu lore. But they have not the monopoly of such revelations. In some tales the revealer is a little dog. As seen above, in our tales *M'umbidluxe Katubi* and *Tata mpembe*, the revealers were babies. In all

1. " A irire ntingini! A irire nti-ngi-ni!
   " Karaterententa[9]
   " Kôni [10] kâkaswa kwironga,
   " Kwironga ryabo. A irire ntingini!
2. " A irire ntingini! A irire ntingini!
   " Kwironga rya bulungu
   " Ndasanga nkuku xiratwa
   " Xiracirika mirombe.[11] A irire ntingini!
3. " A irire ntingini! A irire ntingini!
   " Xiracirika mirombe,
   " Xiratubixa miromo.
   " Ano! Ñemba, mwaya pi? [12] A irire ntingini!
4. " A irire ntingini! A irire ntingini!
   " Ano! Ñemba, mwaya pi?
   " Mutungire nungu,[13]
   " Nungu yeci yeci. A irire ntingini!
5. " A irire ntingini! A irire ntingini!
   " Mutungire nungu,
   " Nungu yeci yeci,
   " Ya Cinsambya-pyororo.[14] A irire ntingini.
6. " A irire ntingini! A irire ntingini!
   " Cinsambya-pyororo,
   " Kutari kuno mwandeta
   " Ne cibula-maulu! A irire ntingini "[15]

Ñemba ngo mukwabo mwami wakafwa.

Mpêce bâkabwesa kayuni, bâkajaya mpu mpu.

Ingayi " tukumbuluke," bajane kâbuka kare, kâya kare ku nembo, bañumfwe ayi :

> " A irire ntingini," etc. (as above).

cases the revealer is a little being which might have been thought to have no notion of right or wrong.

[8] Vars. : *Wa irire ntingini, ma irire ntingini.*
[9] Var. *karaterenteja* or *karaterentexa.*
[10] *Kôni,* poetical for *ka-yuni.*
[11] *Mirombe,* from sing. *mulombe.*
[12] *Mwaya pi ?* Poetical for *Mwaya kuli ?*
[13] *Nungu* is said to mean things like beads, but much more precious. I suppose them to be " pearls."
[14] Var. *Cinsambya-nsororo.*
[15] The march followed in this song is common to a number of others, particularly in the Lower Zambezi (Tete, Sena, Kelimane). The end of a complete verse (less the chorus) is repeated with at most insignificant alterations, to serve as the beginning of the following verse, as :

> *kwironga ryabo . . . kwironga rya bulungu*
> *xiracirika mirombe . . . xiracirika mirombe*

Our songs *Bwenjebwe* (No. XI.) and *Ndime Tembwe* (No. XII.) are of the same kind.

When she reaches the place, she rushes into the hut, calling
" *Nambo*," but Nambo her daughter is no longer there. Does she
then make haste! As she is going to overtake the runaways, she
utters her own incantation, as follows :—

" Is this what my children do ?
" I shall stitch you with a big needle,
" I shall stitch you, stitch! stitch !
" I shall stitch you, my children,
" I shall stitch you ; is this what they do ? "

Great Lord! She shouts to the daughter, and brings her back.

When they reach the place where the mushroom umbrella was
before, she first shuts the girl in the hut, then fixes the umbrella again.
There she is now over there going back to her mat. . . .

At the court : " Dear me, Rumba ; and the woman! Where have
you left her! "

" I have left her on the road."

" Go and bring your sister. I want to marry her."

There he is gone. When he reaches the place, he hears again :

" *Pya!* Burn! Stitch! Sweep! Let me sweep the court " (three
times).

And he repeats his song :

" *Njerenjere !* " (as above).
" At the court let royalty be respected!
" At the court let riches be respected! "
etc. (as above).

Once more he is back at the town over there : " Come on!
Brother-in-law Rumba, have you brought my wife? "

" Great Lord! If I am your brother, first divide your herd of cattle
in two."

" Be red with riches," says the king, " it all belongs to my
brother-in-law."

.   .   .   .

Listen! The song is heard again :

" *Njerenjere !* " etc. (as above).

This time everything goes smoothly. . . .

When the mother reached the court, cattle were given her without
number. Also the brother of the bride received a herd of cattle,
and slaves besides. Also her other brother Rumba, the child of my
father, who had gone to bring her, he also received a herd of cattle.
And the other children of the little old woman, the very ones that
were opposed to the marriage, they too simply swam in riches.

Then the mother took out that tooth which was of that length
And the little story ends there.

I am MUMBA.[7]

(IN BWINE-MUKUNI).

NJERENJERE.

Bacu! Bê " Rumba! "
Ayi " Nkambo-Rêsa! "
Bê " Sá, ukandetere mwanakaxi? '
Mbo bâamba uku.
Bacu! bâbika-ko.
Kuli bañoko kulya nko bâkaya, ajane bo mu câpa câ bôwa mutô-
rira bo ntumba, kuli bo ntwé ntwé :

> " Pyá! Mpyayirire bwaro!
> " Pyá! Mpyayirire bwaro!
> " Pyá! Mpyayirire bwaro!

Kaca, mpa akaringa, warukanka :

> " Njerenjere! Njerenjere!
> " Njerenjere! Kasuwa Yombwe, ne mukwanu.
> " Njerenjere! Undumine nsaru, O mwendo-má.
> " Njerenjere! A bwaro buyani ka buyoxa!
> " Njerenjere! A bwaro bubire ka buyoxa!
> " Njerenjere! Kôtwara [8] Marambo, O mwendo-má.
> " Njerenjere! Undumine nsaru, O mukwêsu."

Bacu! Babone pwá.
Bacu! Mpêce a kulitumuna-wo rya parya bôwa.
Ingayi kuya mu kuxika, bacu! ajane bo bakwabo kutôrira bo-
mikunga " Mawe! ", kuli bo ntwé. Ajane parya pari combwe mpo
pari inongo, bacu! ajane bantu batôbaruluka bo mabara mabara.
Bañina bâbo barixite pa mporwe, rîno riritene okulya.
Wabika-ko :

> " Njerenjere! " etc. (as above).

Bacu! Kangañina wabo akaro kârikunkumuna.
Bacu! Kangañina wabo kulya kê kaxike bo, bâna bangu bañumfwe bo muwo ayi te te te te te. Sombi kâtukula nkoro xâ kâko.
Kê kaxike, a kêne kunkuru mu manda " Nambo! ", ajane mwana
tâmo. Sombi kâbika-ko rubiro, sombi kâbika-ko rubiro.

---

[7] At present the Bêne-Mukuni are an insignificant tribe, and are very poor.
Such stories may have been invented at a time when they had real kings or
queens. The first Mukuni herself, the woman who gave her name to the tribe,
is said to have been something of a potentate.
The Mumba to whom we owe this tale is the same as the reciter of the preceding story. A big book could be filled with the stories she knows by heart.
(As this is going to the press, I hear that the woman is now dead).
[8] *Kôtwala*, poet. for *kôtora*.

Ingayi kanôya mu kuxika, ayi :
      " Bâna bângu, nci bacita ?
      " Ndamutunga mu tungo.
      " Ndamutunga tungutungu.
      " Ndamutunga, bâna bângu.
      " Ndamutunga, nci bacita ? "
Bacu! A bêne sombi kâbakokorora, a bêne kâbabôxa-ko.
Ingayi kaxike mulya pari a bôwa, a bêne a kubênjixa, a bôwa a
kubutupika-ko. Bacu! nkarya katôya ku mporwe.
Bêne " Bâna! Rumba, bânakaxi nko wabaxiya nkuli ? "
Ayi " Ndabaxiya mu nxira."
Bê " Ukabarete bakwanu, tusé tukwate."
Wañamuka kare. Ingay' axike :
      " Pyá! Mpyayirire bwaro . . .
      " Njerenjere! Njerenjere! . . .
      " A bwaro bwami ka buyowekwa!
      " A bwaro bubire ka buyowexa! "
            Etc. (as above).

.   .   .   .   -   .

Ingayi baxike ku muxi kulya " Bacu! Wamuleta mukângu,
mweni [9] wangu Rumba ? "
    " Bacu! Sombi, ne mukwanu, sombi a kutimbula-ko cimpata câ
rrombe."
Ayi " Pyu! " Ayi " Cônse ncâ mweni wangu. . . ."
Bacu! A cimwi :
      " Njerenjere! ", etc. (as above).
Bacu! Mpêce awo.
Ingayi axike ñina, sombi rrombe wúuuu. A mukwabo cimpata
câ rrombe, sombi a kumupa baxa. A rakwe uyo waya kumuleta,
Rumba mukwabo, waringa kumuxara batá, a rakwe cimpata ca
rrombe. Sombi ajane bâna bâkwe bâkaringa kukaxa, ajane bâtan-
dabara kubira.
Eryo mpêce bañina abo a kukuxa bulyo a rîno riritene okulya.
Mpêce awo kêera.
Ndime MUMBA.

              ————

VI.—ALAS! FATHER! AT THE TEMPLE.

She said : " Come on, you my mates, and grind meal. The
chief has got up to go and hunt elephants."

    [9] *Mweni*, royal way of speaking for *mulamu*, " brother-in-law."

What ?   Did they grind meal ?

There the chief set out on his expedition with his slaves.   His two wives, the mother of Nsere and the mother of Cûma, remained at home.   Nsere's mother was also the mother of Ngoma (which means Drums), and was the big wife.

She was heard saying : " Let your child Cûma come here to sleep with us."

So the mother of Cûma said :   " My child, I must sweep the hut, go and sleep there in the hut where your other mother is." [1]

Well !   The little ones went out to go and sleep with the big wife.

Now during the night, what do you think ?   She simply put a big knife on the fire.   The little child of her mate saw it and looked fixedly :   " Well now," he thought, " that knife !   Where does my mother take it to ? "

Then, Heaven help me ! she made sure that the little child Cûma was in the middle and her own child at the back.   But Cûma, soon after that, without his movements being perceived, shifted to the side.

At the darkest time of the night the woman simply got up, then with the knife in her hand . . . cut! cut! cut ! at the throat. [2]

All of a sudden she utters a cry of distress : " Mother !   It is my own child that I have killed! "

Without waiting she puts it in a pot, pressing it down with her hands on its buttocks.

Next morning she asked : " Has not the chief come yet ? "

The answer was : " He has not."

Did she not play the spy during the day ?

One night the little child of her mate, the one she had wanted to kill, determined to go out.   He went to a fig-tree on the road which his father had followed.   There he got hold of a branch and tried to climb.   But, as he did so, what a sight ?   one of his armlets fell down and was changed into a spitting snake.

Never mind !   He went higher up and began to spy about.

When spying, he happened to see a line of Ba-Sukulumbwe

---

[1] In these parts children extend the name of mother not only to their maternal aunts, but also to all their father's wives, and even to their maternal uncles.   Likewise they extend the name of father to their paternal uncles and aunts.

[2] In a tonga version of this tale, the woman, the better to conceal her crime, thrusts the red-hot iron into the anus of the child.   Farmers in Northern Rhodesia not unfrequently find cows or oxen killed in this way, when their cattle-herds fear the cane more than God.

marching along in the distance.[3]   He then started his song :
    " It is far where my father has gone,
    " Away out, away out,
    " A little woman bore a child, bore a child, then killed it,
    " Away out, away out."
Here they are : " Give us some figs," they say, " thou who art singing up there."

He threw them figs and they went on.

Another line of men appeared.   So he resumed his song :
    " It is far where my father," etc. (as above).

Here they are in their turn.   He gives them figs, and on they go.

At last, after much spying about, there he sees his father appearing in the distance.   Shouts of joy, as of men who are coming back happily to their own abode, begin to be heard.   The number of elephants they have killed is not counted . . . " Great Lord! " they say, " let us go and have a rest under that fig-tree.   We may leave our loads there, and go and have a wash."

The slaves of the chief go to fetch water for him.   He comes and sits down under the tree.   Other slaves cook porridge.   Meanwhile the chief counts the tusks.

Over there, in the kraal, already people say : " Listen there to the west, hear the shouts of joy."

" They must be the hunters that had gone to the forest," say others.

" Well!   At last they have come," say others.

Now, here under the fig-tree, the hunters suddenly hear a song started above their heads :
  1. " Alas! Father, at the temple,[4]
     " While you were on your journey,
     " While you were on your journey,
     " We said : ' Forge, let us go, forge there.' "[5]
  2. " Alas! Father!   And at home
     " She has killed her own child,
     " The mother of Drums, for Cûma mistaking
     " Nsere.   O my mother!   O mother of Nsere! "

[3] This detail, with its song, is borrowed from the Tonga version of this tale.
[4] The place where the Bêne-Mukuni assemble to pray for rains are called by them *mirenda*, in Tonga and in Sori *marende*.   We translate by " temples." They are all places where some old chiefs are supposed to be buried.
[5] An elliptical way of saying : " You have been such a long time away that in your absence prayers were offered for rain."   The whole verse *fula, tende, fulo* " Forge, let us go, forge there " is borrowed, so I am told, from some old hymn praying for rain.   To understand it, one must know that the word *m-fûla*, " rain," is thought by the Bêne-Mukuni to be etymologically identical with *m-fûla* " I forge."   It is the Rain-Lord that is supposed to forge when it rains.   See the note [52] in the tale *Kapepe* (xviii.)

The people look at one another. . . . " What is that ? " they say.
" Listen to what is being said up there."

They add : " Let us spy it out." Then they see up there something like a little bird on the branches.

Again : " Hark! What does that song mean ? "

They just hear the bird, as it were, flapping its wings and singing :
" Alas! Father," etc. (as above).

Again : " Now look! It is a person that speaks up there. Cut
down the tree."

Some of them do, in fact, start cutting the tree at the bottom.
There is something like a rushing in the branches, but the song starts
again :
" Alas! Father," etc. (as above).

Now hear! " Let the tree fall down," says the chief.

The axes go on working at the big trunk, the men saying meanwhile : " We know how to lay low the giant trees."

Then all of a sudden : " It is thou, Cûma ; what art thou saying
up there about Nsere? "

" Rather go and ask my mother at home," said the child. " Nsere!
My mother has killed her, mistaking Nsere for Cûma. Then I bethought myself to come to the road which my father had followed,
in order to inform him, that he should not come home without
knowing the facts. Good gracious! She has put my sister in a pot."

" Say no more, child," said the father. " If at least she had
wrapped her in blankets! "

He then said to the carriers : " Let us go home."

A start was made at once.

When they reached the court-yard, shrill cries of welcome went
up into the air, but the chief said at once : " Bring my children."

From a distance a woman said : " I do not know where they have
gone."

" What! You did not see where the children went! Where is Nsere ?
Where is Cûma ? "

" Even Cûma we have not seen him for some time."

" Bring Cûma."

" We do not know which way he has gone."

They just keep on saying : " We have not seen them."

" Nonsense! " says the man, " bring me my children. They were
left here, and you have not seen them! "

He straightway goes to the pot, just lifts the lid a little, and
exclaims : " Why! This is Nsere. Nsere and no other! Cûma,
come here! "

You may see the mother rushing into the hut and saying : " I am
sick."

" Great heavens! " says the father, " come out of there, child of
a tendon.[6]   Now what is it that thou hast covered up in this pot ?
Let us see."

He now uncovers the pot altogether : " Is not this," he says, " my
very own child whom thy jealousy has killed ?   Why hast thou killed
my child ? "

Here now!   He says : " Go and carry that." [7]

He himself puts the pot on the woman's head.

" Let us go west," he says, " to the river."

There is no delay ; there they are going.

When they reach a certain distance, the woman says : " Father
of Mwinsa,[8] relieve me of my burden at this place."

" Nothing of the kind," says the man.   " My child shall be put
down where the river comes out from the west.   It cannot be put
down here."

She then wails :

> " Father of Mwinsa, relieve me ; it is heavy.
> " It was a little ant that bit her."

" Let us go as far as the river, not a step less," says the man.
" The child cannot be put down."

The woman staggers on, muttering :

> " Father of Mwinsa," etc. (as above).

" It cannot be put down," is the only answer.

The river is reached.   The woman goes on to the brink of a deep
pool, still singing as above, but receives only the same answer : " It
cannot be put down."

Now they are in water up to the neck.   The muttering goes on :

> " Father of Mwinsa," etc. (as above).

" It cannot be put down."

There she takes a false step.   Then the husband gives her a push
as well as to the pot which contains his child.   She disappears with

---

[6] See note [2] to the tale I. (How can I silence Katubi ?).

[7] In the Tonga version the pot is in the hut.   So, as the man comes in, he
says : " What is it that stinks in this hut ? "—" I do not know," answers the
woman, " perhaps a dead rat."   Then the man uncovers the pot and, seeing
the child in it, says : " Put it on the fire."   When the pot is quite hot, he puts
it on the head of the woman, saying : " Now carry it."

[8] " Father of Mwinsa," Bwine-Bukuni *Ixi-Mwinsa*, Tonga *Sya-Mwiza*, means
" a heartless man."   See further the Tonga tale *Wiriryo*, where the father of
Mwiza is described as killing his child in order to give it as meat to its own
mother.

it in the water, while the man says : " Go and beget more whelps,
thou child of a tendon who hast killed my children."
I am MUMBA.[9]

(IN BWINE-MUKUNI.)
BÂNA! TÁ, A MULENDA.

Ayi " Bâna! mo mata,[10] a mupere busu. Bâñamuka, batôya mu
nsofu."

Bacu! Bâpera busu.

Kulya bâbika-ko a baxa bâbo. Bâcara ba-makaabo, bêna-Nsere
a bêna-Cûma. Bêna-Nsere mbo bêna-Ngoma, bêna-bunene.

Kuñumfwa bêna-bunene ayi " Esé-wo mwana wanu Cûma tuna
koona akwe."

A bâro " Cûma, mpyayire, kôya oone mu manda umo muli
bañoko."

Bacu! A kuswa bacebace kuya mu koona a bêna-bunene.

Kwamba ayi ku maxiku, bacu! bâbika-wo bulyo cibexi pa
muliro. Bacu! A cîne cibexi kâna kâbo kâ bakaxiñina abo kuci-
rangirixa " Ino cibexi batôtora kuli bamá barya! "

Bacu! A kufukwita-wo mwana wabo Cûma pakati, mwana wa
manda waona mwisule.

Bacu! A rakwe Cûma a kuxinta kwisule.

Maxikuxiku bate kuñamuka bo, a cibexi! Sombi cééé pa
mulibu! . . .

Bacu! Kucita obulya " Mawe, ndajaya mwana wangu! "

Mpêce a kumuñamuna, bacu! a mu nongo! A mwine a kumuxi-
ndayira-mo, a ku matako.

Junsajunsa bê " Ta bana bêsa bamwene ? "

Bê " Ta bana."

Bacu! kusompa-ko.

Kwamba ayi bumwi buxiku, bacu! kâxikira kupula kâkacara-
wo kâna kâ bakaxiñina abo nko basuni bakajaye. Bacu! Kâpula
kuya ku bukuyu ku nxira nko bârangira bêxi.

A kêne sée a kuya mu kutanta.

Bacu! Kulya nko katanta, sombi bwansa butôroka bumwi, butôroka panxi bwaba makata.

Bacu! Kâbôra kâsompa-ko.

---

[9] The same Mumba to whom we owe the two preceding tales and some of the
following.

[10] The narrator says indifferently *mo mata* or *no mata*. It seems to have
nearly the same meaning as *namata* " youngsters, mates," literally, " children
of my mother and father," something like the Cape Dutch " Jong! "

Kwamba ayi kasompe-ko, kabone ngu mulongo wa Ba-Donga wapora. Ndy' arutatula :
    " Tata nkwakaya kwakarampa,
    " Ku runsense.
    " Kâxara mwana, kâxara mwana, kâmuxina,
    " Ku runsense."
Bâxika, bê " Twabire nkuyu, o wimba kujulu."
Kâbaabira nkuyu, bâinda.
Wabona a umwi mulongo kupora. Ayi :
    " Tata nkwakaya," etc. (as above).
Bâxika, kâbaabira nkuyu, bâinda.
Kwamba ayi kasompe-ko, kabone ono baixi mbarya bâpora.
Kañumfwe kwairira bo minkweru. Acu! Sombi nsofu bâjaya bo cimbi. " Bacu! A tuye toocexe mu bukuyu, tuye tutule mu bukuyu mulya tusambe."
    Kuya mu kuleta manxi baxa bâbo. Ayi kwĭsá mu kwĭkara.
Bacu! Bamwi citôponda. Bacu! A bâro bamwene bâbara mêja baixi.
    Sombi bâcara ku muxi ayi ' A musuwe-wo kumbo uku, a mu-ñumfwe bo minkweru."
    Bê " Mbaximusansa."
    Bacu! Bañumfwe kârutatula :

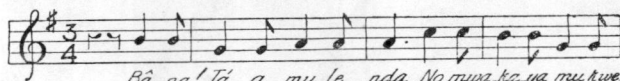

Bâ_na! Tá, a mu_le_nda, No mwa_ka_ya mu_kwe_nda, No mwa_ka_ya mu kwe_nda, Ay': Fû _ la_ tende_ fû_lo.

    1. " Bâna! Tá, a mulenda,
       " No mwakaya mu kwenda,
       " No mwakaya mu kwenda,
       " Ay' : Fula, tende,[11] fulo.
    2. " Bâna! Tá, a ku muxi
       " Bâjaya mwana wabo
       " Ay' ' Ngu Cûma ' Nangoma
       " Nsere, mama, Na-Nsere! "

Bâborerana " Bacu! A musuwe-mo mute kwamba kujulu."
    Ingayi " tusompe-ko," bajane karya kari anga nkayuni kujulu ku misampi.

----

[11] *Tende*, from Ñungwe, for Mukuni *twende* " let us go."

Kuñumfwa ayi " A muñumfwe bo mbo kate kwimba."
Bacu! Bañumfwe kâripampa :
    " Bâna! Tá, a mulenda," etc. (as above).
Bê " A mubone-wo muntu ute kwamba kujulu. A muciteme."
Sombi bamwi a kubujata bukuyu kunxi, sombi té té té té té.
Bañumfwe kujulu waripampa :
        " Bâna! Tá, a mulenda," etc. (as above).
Bacu! Bê " A mubuwixe."
Bacu! A bwine sombi rukutu. Bacu! babone " Sombi twaka-
yara masamo."
Bêne " Cûma, ncinxi utôcita oburya ' Nsere ' ? "
Ayi " Sombi bamá ku muxi. Nsere ngo bâkaxina bo bamá.
Bâka-mujaya ayi ' Cûma ngo Nsere.' Mpêce a nebo nko kwamba
ayi ' A nje ku nxira kwakaita batá, nje nkabarwite batá, batane
kwisá buryo. Macu! Mukwêsu wakamulongera mu nongo."
" Bacu! A mumuleke. Sombi, bacu! A kumubwesa a kumupe-
terexa mu makumbesa."
Bê " Ka tuya kuya ku muxi."
Bâbika-ko.
Ingayi baxike bo pa rubansa xâsokora ngubi. Ayi " A mubarete
bâna bângu'"
Mpo ayi bamwi, mpo bâringa-wo, ayi " Nxibabwene nko bâka
ranga."
" A! Tamubabwene nko bâbaranga! Ino Nsere a Cûma ! "
Ayi " A Cûma wonse ta tumubwene-wo."
" A mumulete."
" Ino ta tubabwene-wo nko bâranga."
Bacu! Bê " Ta tubabwene! "
Ayi " Bâna! A mundetere bâna. Mwacara bâna bângu tamu-
babwene! "
Kucita obulya kufwekula-wo " Ncite " . . . " Ngu Nsere uyu,
ngu Nsere! "
Ayi " Bâna! Cûma! "
Bacu! Babone bañina bârinjixa kare mu manda, ayi " Nebo
ndi murwaxi."
Ayi " Bâna! O mwana wa mukaxi, swá tubone. . . . Ino ku
muliri wafweka-ko nxi ? "
Kwisá mu kufwekula-ko, " Têxi mwanângu ngo bwajaya busuba
bwako ? Nce wajayira mwanângu ncinxi ? "
Bacu! " Kwesá umuyumune."
Bacu! A mwine a kumutwika.

Bacu! Bê " Katuya kulya kumbo ku mulonga."
Bacu! Ayi, bâbika-ko. Mbarya bate kuya.
Ayi " Ixi-Mwinsa, ntule pano."
" Ta atulwa. Mwana wangu uya kutulwa nko ruswá kumbo.
Ta atulwa."
Ayi :

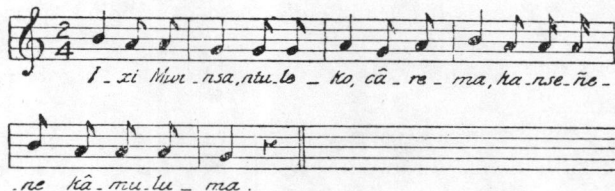

*I - xi Mwi - nsa, ntu-le — ko, câ - re — ma, ha - nse - ñe -
- ne kâ - mu-lu — ma.*

" Ixi-Mwinsa, ntule-ko, cârema.
" Kanseñene kâmuluma."
" Ka tuya ku mulonga nkwêce. Ta atulwa."
Utôya mu kutunkarara. Ayi :
        " Ixi-Mwinsa," etc. (as above).
" Ta atulwa."
Bâxika ku mulonga, a mwine a pa rixiba :
        " Ixi-Mwinsa," etc
" Ta atulwa."
Axika manxi mu nxingo.
        " I xi-Mwinsa," etc.
" Ta atulwa."
Watingama. Mpêce a bêne kubaxindikira a nongo ya mwana
wabo. A bêne puwuwu pa manxi " Kôya ukaxare, o mwana wa
mukaxi, wancayira bâna.
Ndime MUMBA.[12]

VII.—WHAT DO YOU MEAN, BLOCK OF WOOD ? [1]

How now ? " You, my mates," said a girl, " let us go and have a
look at the village yonder, where lives the man Kasere."
There is no delay. They already perceive the man there at a dis-

[12] For the Tonga version of this tale see the Zambesi *Mission Record*, 1907.
[1] A Tonga version of this tale may be seen in the Zambesi *Mission Record*,
No. 35, p. 142. Another version, but in which the hero is a hare, has been
published by Jacottet in *Textes Louyi*, pp. 8–11. The substitution of a hare
for a man seems hardly to improve the story. Here the name of the hero is
Kasere, that is, " the little dancer."

tance, and near him heaps of meat. " Yes, and no mistake," they say, " that is a husband worth having."

They come near : " You girls," says the man, " why don't you get married ? "

" Well now," they answer, " is a woman going to ask a man to marry her ? "

" All right," says the man, " just now we shall go and look for a wife."

And so he did. But as soon as he appeared in sight, the girls disappeared.

Their mother, too, would you believe it ? said : " No, you may come back another day."

The refusal was evident.

Another day he came again in the same direction, but a tree of the kind What-is-it-good-for [2] standing on the road caught his fancy. He set to work cutting it and stripping it of its branches, then began hewing it. He carved, carved, carved, and put it upright against a tree there in the forest. Then he went to buy a cowry, and came back to put it on the head of his block of wood. What do you think ? He finds it turned all of a sudden into a maiden : " Enough! mother! " he said, " I have found the wife they refused to give me."

On the following day he went to look for honey and brought some to his wife. When they had finished eating, they went to bed.

Next morning early, the man went out once more in search of honey. While he was away, people came and found the girl seated alone outside : " Give us fire and water," they said. She brought fire and handed it to them, she brought water and gave it to them. There they smoked and smoked again (admiring her silently), then went back to their kraal.

As they reached the place, they said : " Is she not a beauty, the girl we have seen over there ? "   .

The following day the king, having heard that, said : " Go and bring her here to me."

That day the man bethought himself of going once more in search of honey. The girl then said to him : " Some people were here yesterday, who asked for fire and water, and I gave both to them."

" To-day," said the man, " lock thyself in the hut." He went off.

When those people came they found her seated outside. They took her away.

[2] The Tonga version says " a euphorbia, *karundu-ngoma*," probably because the milk of the euphorbia associates itself in the Tonga mind with that of a woman.

There she goes crying : "*Mawe !* Mother! *Mawe !* They are taking me away."

The husband came home. . . . " Ugh! What! " he said, " they kept refusing me a wife, and now to-day they have taken this one! One whom I carved! "

He has soon made up his mind. Drums, that is the thing. He goes to cut them and adjust them. He loses no time : " Let us go," he says.

He goes beating the drums and singing on the way :
    " My wife made by carving! "
        Chorus.—" What do you mean, block of wood ? "
    " Stop that."—*Chorus.*
    " My husband, who gave them meat! "—*Chorus.*
    " My wife, who gave them fire and water! "—*Chorus.*
    " They were denying me a wife in the land."—*Chorus.*
    " The block that I carved! "—*Chorus.*

He came to a village occupied by common people. At once the principal woman of the place, good gracious, said : " Those who can accompany dances, come and see a dancer."

Good heavens! They heard the song falling down :
        " My wife made by carving," etc. (as above).

" Come on," says the woman, " throw presents to the man."

They are showered upon him. They make him quite red.

He then asks : " Have you not seen people passing this way and carrying away a woman ? "

" They have passed," is the answer. " They have gone further."

" What is she like ? " he asks.

" Beautiful," they say, " beautiful. She has a cowry on her head.

He then goes further, singing on the way :
        " My wife made by carving," etc. (as above).

He reaches another kraal. . . . " Come and see a man who beats the drum. . . ."

Then : " Come on, you who accompany the dance, throw presents to the man."

At last he stops for a little rest.

A little man then said to him : " Come near, I will tell you. . . . That kraal over there, that is where your wife is, in the big hut."

There goes the man, beating the drums once more :
        " My wife made by carving," etc. (as above).

Good Heavens! He is in view of the place . . . " Come and see a man who is on the road beating a drum."

As he comes near, he goes towards the king's house, as if to go and pay homage. Then he starts again :

" My wife made by carving! What do you mean, block of wood ?

" My wife who gave them fire and water! What do you mean, block of wood ? ", etc. (as above).

" Good gracious! " says the king himself, " come and throw presents to the man."

But he does not stop to receive any. He just goes on round the court-yard (beating the drum all the time).

A servant then says : " Shall we bring thy wife ? . . ."

He is already near the hut. Good Heavens! This is what he hears from within : " This is his wife, who has been carried away."

The drums then roll with full sound :

> " My wife, a gift for them!
> " What do you mean, block of wood ?
> " My wife made by carving!
> " What do you mean, block of wood ? "

" Come," say the people to the woman, " you too come and give presents to the man. All your mates have already thrown some to him."

" All right," says the woman, " go and throw him presents yourselves. I shall do nothing of the kind."

The drums are at last at the door :

> " My husband, the carver!
> " What do you mean, block of wood ?
> " My wife, a gift for them!
> " What do you mean, block of wood ? "

Great Lord! " Let us just peep, ' says the woman.

" Carry her out," say some people.

In fact, their hands are already on her.

Then they see the little man going on dancing like a fly all round the king himself, and singing :

> " The tree which I carved!
> " What do you mean, block of wood ?
> " They refused me a wife in the land.
> " What do you mean, block of wood ? "

" Let us look outside," she says at last. And she stands just at the door.

Heaven help me! Drum and song now sound and resound.

> " My husband, to give me to them ?
> " What do you mean, block of wood ? "

She now just lets her head appear with the cowry on it. By a rapid movement of the hand the husband takes this off. . . . Great

Heavens! She is already transformed into a simple block of wood, no, she has become but a bush standing at the door. . . . Then the little husband comes home humming his own tune, while the king and those who had seized the woman remain there with their shame.

I am MUMBA.[3]

(IN BWINE-MUKUNI.)

KANXI! CITANXI!

Bacu! Bârutundu ayi " Mo mata, a tuye tu kabone pa muxi parya, pari Kasere.

Acu! Babone bâpora kare basankwa, bajane ñama xiribungene, xiri bo mirwi . . . " E! manto, mbo bânarumi."

Bacu! " Mwebo no bânakaxi ta mukwatwa ? "

A bâro " Ino mwanakaxi a rakwe ajate musankwa ? "

Ayi " Cino cîndi tula kwĭsá tukeebe."

Bacu! Kwĭsá mu kweba.

Bacu! Kujana pwá . . . , bacu! kupuru.

Bacu! A mwine mwanakaxi, bacu! bê " Tawu, mulâ kubôrako."

Bacu! Bâbaima.

Bacu! Kwamba junsa angayi banôsá, bacu! bajane bo mu nxira bajane citanxi ciri imfwi. Bacu! a cîne a kucikankata, a rimwi a kucibesa bese bese, a kucitentekera mu musansa, a kuya mu kuula mpande, a kwĭsá mu kumubika pa mutwi, bacu! bajane ngu môye . . . " Mbubo, má, ndabona-wo mwanakaxi ngo bate kunjima."

Cûnsa waya ku bûci, a kumuletera mukaakwe. Ayi bamane kulya, bâona.

Bwaca, musankwa wafuma a rimwi ku bûci. Bâxika bantu, mwanakaxi bâmujana ulixite ênka pansengwe. Bê " Tupe muliro a manxi." Wareta muliro wabapa, wareta manxi, wabapa. Bâfwepa, bâfweba, bâunka ku mixi yabo.

Bê baxike, ayi " Kubota mwanakaxi uli kooko! "

Cûnsa bâmi bê " A muye mukamulete."

A rimwi musankwa wayeya kufuma ku bûci. Mukaakwe wamwambira ayi " Mpo bari bantu bâxika. Bâamba ayi ' Tupe muliro a manxi,' ndabapa."

Ibaye ayi " Kôrijarira sunu mu manda." Waunka.

---

[3] The Mumba of the preceding tales.

Ingayi baxike bantu abo, bacu! bamujane urixite pansengwe. Bâmutora.

Ngulya utôya cirira "Mawe! Mawe! Bântora."

Ingay' axike ibaye mu manda. . . . "U! Ka bâri kunjima mwanakaxi, a rimwi sunu bânjipira mwanakaxi! A mwine ngwa kubesa!"

Bacu! A pa ngoma xâbo, a kuya mu kuxikankata, a xîne a kuxitimbaula. Bacu! Bâbika-ko. Bacu! "Ka tuya."

Utôya ciimba :

> "Mukaxi wanji [4] wa kubesa!—Kanxi! [5] citanxi!
> "Ka mwera-ko.—Kanxi! citanxi!
> "Murume wanji [6] wa kubapa!—Kanxi! citanxi!
> "Mukaxi wanji wa kubapa!—Kanxi! citanxi !
> "Bâri kunjima mu cixi.—Kanxi! citanxi !
> "Cisamu nce ndabesa!—Kanxi! citanxi !"

Ay' axike ku muxi wa bantu, a bâro bêna-bunene, bacu! ayi "Baxi kuxaninina, a musé mubone muntu utôxana."

Bacu! bañumfwe rwaroka :

> "Mukaxi wanji wa kubesa!" etc. (as above).

Bacu! A mutayire muntu."

Bacu! Sombi babone ayi pyú.

Waipuxa "No bênsuma, ta bakwe kwinda pano bacite mwanakaxi?"

Bê "Bâinda, bâindirira."

Ayi "Uli buyani?"

Bê "Mubotu, mubotu, ulicite mpande pa mutwi."

Wainda a rakwe. Utôya ciimba :

> "Mukaxi wanji wa kubesa!" etc. (as above).

Ay' axike ku muxi umwi . . . "A musé mubone ucite ngoma. . ."

"Bacu! Baxikuxaninina, a mutayire muntu."

Sombi bâpumuna.

Bacu! A kamwi kamuntu pano . . . "Ka musena pafwifwi, ngo ulya muxi, ngo ucite bakaanu, mu manda inene."

Ngulya utôya ciimba :

> "Mukaxi wanji wa kubesa!" etc. (as above).

Bacu! Kwamba ay' axike . . . "A musé mubone utôsa xingoma."

---

[4] *Mukaxi wanji*, Ramba for Mukuni *mwanakaxi wangu* or *mukaangu*.

[5] *Kanxi!* "What do you mean?", Sori for Mukuni *Anu!* *Citanxi* is also pronounced *citaxi*.

[6] *Murume wanji*, Ramba for Mukuni *mwanarumi wangu* or *ibangu*.

Macu! Sombi kunôya mu kuxika, macu! kuya mu kwimakana, ayi :

"Mukaxi wanji wa kubesa!" etc. (as above).

Bacu! "Bâna! ayi, a musé mutayire muntu."

Bacu! Ajane kabaya bulyo.

Kâamba ayi kantu kamwi "Tukarete mukâko?"

Ingayi unôya mu kuxika, bacu! bañumfwe bo mu manda "Mba bakaabo mbo bâjata."

Bañumfwe waroxa :

"Mukaxi wanji wa kubapa!
"Kanxi! citanxi !
"Mukaxi wanji wa kubesa!
"Kanxi! citanxi!"

Bâamba ayi "A musé mumutayire, bônse babyanu bâmana kumu-tayira."

A bâro ayi "Mbubo, ono a muye mumutayire, nebo nxikwe."

Yaxika ngoma :

"Murume wanji wa kubesa!
"Kanxi! citanxi!
"Mukaxi wanji wakubapa!
"Kanxi! citanxi!"

Bacu! Angayi "Tusompe-ko."

A bamwi "A mubakuxe mubatembe."

Bacu! Baramubika pa mânsa.

Bacu! Bañumfwe karoncana katôya kuxana kuya kubaxinguluka bâmi :

"Cisamu nce ndabesa!
"Kanxi! citanxi!
"Bâri kunjima mu cixi!
"Kanxi! citanxi!"

Angayi "Tusompe pa nsengwe," a kwimakana.

Bacu! Bañumfwe kâroxa :

"Murume wanji wa kubapa!"

Ingayi unôya mu kuswa, a mpande pa mutwi, bacu! a bêne kukuxa-wo mpande! Bacu! Babone câpururuka bulyo cisamu, câba kare cisanswa pa mulyango. Mpêce awo . . . A kêne katôsa mu kulucancika kanga ibaye, bâba bulyo a nsoni a bâkamujata.

Kêera mpêce awo.

Ndime MUMBA.

VIII.—I AM CALLING YOU LOUD.

Some little girls went to gather wild fruit, but found the river full. Happening to meet some bigger girls, they asked : " Where is it that you gather wild figs ? "

" Over there, on the other side of the river," was the answer.

" Let us go," they said, " that you may give us some." (The bigger girls refused to go.)

The little ones had their baby sister with them. When they came quite close to the water, baby said : " Who is going to take us across ? See, the river is full."

While one of them was saying, " Just try to cross," they noticed the presence of a crocodile stretched at his ease on the bank : " Come," they said, " carry us on your back." And, as he agreed, they started singing :

" I am calling you loud, lord of the rivers."
    Chorus : " The paramour is gone, the paramour is gone there." [1]
" Come and carry me on your back."—" The paramour," etc.
" Climb on my back."—" The paramour," etc.

Bacu ! [2] They are on the water. There he is landing them across. They pluck their wild figs.

Bacu ! The crocodile is swimming over there in the river . . . " Now," they say, " who is going to take us back across the river ? Mates, let us call him."

So they came back to the water, and called :
" I am calling you loud, lord of the rivers," etc. (as above.)
He brought them across.

They went and found on the way other girls coming. They showed them the figs they had gathered and gave them some. These other girls, seeing that, went likewise to ride on the back of the crocodile, and sang just as their mates had done :
" I am calling you loud," etc. (as above).

So they also gathered their figs, came back to the river, and were taken across.

Now, when the girls reached the village, baby said : " Dear me!

---

[1] I translate *ñañari* by " paramour," but am not at all sure that such is the meaning. Anyhow the little explanation I can get of this chorus is that it threatens disaster to the foolish girls. The narrator says that *Ñañari* is a proper name. But. if that were correct, she should, it seems, say afterwards not *yaya* but *waya*.

[2] *Bacu !* We cannot always find an English equivalent for this interjection which comes so often to the lips of our story-tellers. As a rule, it expresses a surprise of some sort. Pronounce it *baachoo!* with the tonic accent on *baa*. The proper meaning seems to be " Superior Poweis! "

Mother, what takes us across! Why! It has hard swellings on the body, at the tail it is a knife. . . .''

" Now, child,'' interrupted the other children, " yes, tell us what takes us across! And the fruit we bring every time, do you forget it ? "

" Children,'' said the mother, " you may go back if you like. But, thou, my child, do not go to-morrow ; they would take thee to death.''

On the following day, a little after dawn, they said : " Let us go and gather wild figs.''

There they went, and this time they found there was only a little water in the river. So they went at once to eat at the trees. You might have heard the noise *té té té té té*. *Bacu !* Soon they are back near the water calling the crocodile (though they could cross quite well without him) :

Loud :   " I am calling you loud, lord of the rivers.''

        Chorus : " The paramour is gone, the paramour is gone there.''

Low :   " On a long tree.''—" The paramour,'' etc.

  ,,   " On the body hard lumps.''—" The paramour,'' etc.

  ,,   " At the head it is a crocodile.''—" The paramour,'' etc.

  ,   " At the tail it is a knife.''—" The paramour,'' etc.

Well! He was bringing them across. They thought that baby had told lies, and went on singing :

        " I am calling you loud, lord of the rivers

        " Rich lord, I am thy wife,'' etc.

Good gracious! As they were thus enjoying themselves, baby's sister said : " Let us go as far as the deep water.'' At this moment there was a diving, the beastly crocodile carried them down with him and there ate them all up.

That is where the story ends.[3]

I am MUMBA.

(IN BWINE-MUKUNI.)

NDAKUWAKUWA MWE.

Bâya mu kusepa xisepo, bajana mulonga uliswite. . . . " Mwebo cirembera nko muciyapa nkuli ? "

Ayi " Nko tusepa nkooko.''

------

[3] The crocodile is not, precisely, the most edifying character of the Bantu comedy. Representing, as he does, the unscrupulous kidnapper that used to go along the rivers of Africa carrying his wares in boats or canoes, he is constantly accused of enticing young girls away under the pretext of making them his wives. The foolish girls always suffer for it, and, if they ever reappear on land, it is only on the slave-market, yet he seems never to get any punishment.

Ingayi " A twende mukatupe-wo."

Ingayi kuya mu kuxika a kânike kâbo, ayi " Uti [4] amusubuxe ngani ? " Bê " Ino mulonga wêsula."

Ingay' " A musubuke," bajane ngu xitare, bajane ulixite. Ayi " Tubereke-ko. . . ."

"Ndakuwakuwa mwe bêne-mironga
" Ñañari yaya, ñañari yayo.
" Ka musá kuno mumbereke.—Ñañari, etc.
" A muntante.—Ñañari, etc."

Bacu! Mpêce bâsubuka. Bacu! Ngulya wabatora. Cirembera câbo bâyapa.

Bacu! Yabandarara ntare. . . . " Ino ngani atusubule? No mata, a tumwite."

Bacu! Bâbôra, bate kumwita :
" Ndakuwakuwa mwe," etc. (as above).
Wabasubula.

Bâbika-ko, bajane a bamwi, bacu! bâxika. Ingayi baxike, a xisepo kubonwa. Bâbapa. A bâro bâya mu kutanta-po pa musana wa ntare. . . .
" Ndakuwakuwa mwe," etc. (as above).
A bâro bâsepa, hâbôra, wabasubuxa.

Bacu! Nko bâkaya kuya ku muxi, kânike ayi " Bâna! Ma! citôtusubula, bâna! 'mapumba pa mubiri, ku mucira ncibexi."

Bâna bâbo " Ono, mwana, ayi, e! citôtusubula! Xisepo nxe tutôreta! "

Ayi " Bâna! A babôre. Sombi webo, mwanângu, cîro utayi-ko, baraya kukujayixa."

Kwamba ayi jûnsa bwaca kare . . . " A twende tukasepe cirembera."

Kulya bâbika-ko, bajane manxi ayuminina.

Nko bâkarya té té té té té té (nko kusepa). Bacu! bâimakana kare :

Nda-ku-wa-ku - wa mwe bê-ne-mi-ro-
nga Ña-ña-ri ya-ya, ña-ña-ri ya-

---

[4] *Uxi* is a more common form in Bwine-Mukuni.

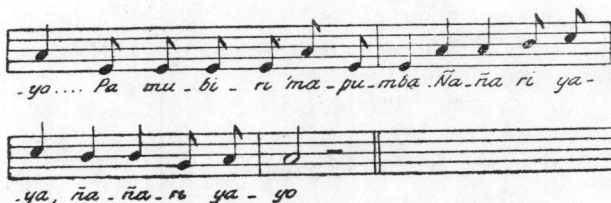

"-yo.... Pa mu-bi-ri 'ma-pu-mba. Ña-ña ri ya--ya, ña-ña-ri ya-yo"

" Ndakuwakuwa mwe bêne-mironga.
" Ñañari yaya, ñañari yayo.
" Ku muti wakuya.—Ñañari, etc.
" Pa mubiri 'mapumba.—Ñañari, etc.
" Ku mutwi ni ngwena.—Ñañari, etc.
" Ku mucira ncibexi.--Ñañari, etc."

Ayi, bacu! bâbika-ko. Ute kubasubula. Bajane kakwabo kâkabeja :

" Ndakuwakuwa mwe," etc. (as above).
" Ne, mutende, ne mukâko
" Ñañari yaya, ñañari yayo."

Bacu! Mpêce ingayi bacite boobo, a mukwabo kânike ayi " Tunôya mu kuxika pa rixiba," a bêne wuwuwuwu, a mwine wabatora cixitare,[5] a cîne câbarya câbamana.

Mpêce awo kêera.[6]

Ndime MUMBA.

IX.—OPEN, OPEN, LITTLE BIRD.

What do you think ? This is what they did. They went looking for wives, saying : " Let us go and try to marry."

One of them went looking for a wife here and there. Every one rejected him. At last he too succeeded in making a marriage, such as it was.

Well! He brought his wife into the house.

Now, when he married her, he said : " Look here, woman, you will eat porridge of small millet, and no other."—" All right,"

---

[5] *Cixitare.* The common form of this word is *xitare.* Here the prefix *ci* means " beastly."
[6] The number of words borrowed from Ñungwe or Ñanja for the songs of this tale, such as *muti* " tree," *wakuya* " deep, long," *kuwa* " shout, call loud," *mutende* " rich man," etc., show that either the tale itself has come from the East, or that those kidnappers represented here by the crocodile used to come from the East.

answered the woman.—" And I," added the man, " I will eat only Kafir corn porridge."—" All right," said the woman again.

So after that they simply ate porridge, the woman millet, the man Kafir corn.

Alas! One day the woman making a mistake, happened to eat the Kafir corn porridge. The man comes : " You have," he says, " eaten my porridge. Yet I told you to eat only millet porridge." Hereupon he just picks up an axe and strikes the woman. Then he drags her, drag! drag! drag! and goes and throws her away to the west.

After that the man used to go alone wandering about.

One day he said : " We are going for a ramble in the bush." There he went, and game was killed. He then remembered that one woman had been left in the village over there. So he said to himself : " Let us go and marry her."

He went, received her in marriage, brought her to his home, and said to her : " Look here! You know what killed your mate. . . . Now don't you ever dare to eat Kafir corn porridge ; you shall eat millet porridge, that's all."—" No fear," said the woman, " I shall eat no Kafir corn porridge."

The following day he thought of resuming his expedition to the bush. So, leaving alone in the hut his bride, the one just come, he said : " Now I shall have a walk into the bush." And there he went away.

Well! At night, when it was quite dark, the new bride hears the sound *kwé! kwé! kwé!* Drag! Drag! Drag! " That must be," she thinks, " the former wife, the one that was killed, struck with an axe."

There she is already at the door, drag! drag! drag! Now she knocks *nku! nku! nku!* Knock! Knock! Knock! Then a song in Ramba :

" Open, open, little bird.
" Open, open, little bird.
" O mother! Be satisfied with millet.
" A little porridge of Kafir corn is a little bird." [1]

The new bride went to open for her. So the old one dragged herself into the hut, and said :

---

[1] About the " little birds " of the Bantu tales, see note [1] to the tale " Let the big drum sound," No. IV. Here " little bird " may be rendered practically by " spirit," *i.e.*, " A little porridge of Kafir corn is a spirit, you will not catch it."

"Put it on the fire, put it on the fire, little bird (*bis*).
"O mother! Be satisfied with millet.
"A little porridge of Kafir corn is a spirit."

The old wife herself goes ahead and puts the pot on the fire. They both then remain quiet. Did you ever! The pot boils, the new bride then clearly recognises the old one, and hears :

"Stir the porridge, stir the porridge, little bird (*bis*).
"O mother! Be satisfied with millet.
"A little porridge of Kafir corn is a spirit."

The old bride then gets up herself to bring Kafir corn meal from the big jar, puts it with her own hands in the pot, and stirs and stirs her porridge, then puts it on a dish. Just imagine! She actually puts two fingers in it, saying :

"Let us eat, let us eat, little bird (*bis*).
"O mother! Be satisfied with millet.
"A little porridge of Kafir corn is a spirit.

She just eats alone. Her new mate goes so far as to put a finger on the porridge, but does not eat. So the woman repeats :

"Let us eat, let us eat, little bird (*bis*).
"O mother! Be satisfied with millet.
"A little porridge of Kafir corn is a spirit."

She finishes her porridge alone. Her mate has not said a word. The woman then moves away. There she is going. Drag thyself! Drag thyself! She just stops at the door to say :

"Shut behind me, shut behind me, little bird (*bis*).
"O mother! Be satisfied with millet.
"A little porridge of Kafir corn is a spirit."

Now she is out. There she goes towards her hole, and buries herself in it.

Next day the man came from the bush, and his wife came to meet him. "Dear me!" she said, "here in the hut where you have left me there is a thing which comes at night. It is impossible to sleep. It keeps one awake with songs.'

"What is it like ?" asked the man.

"You will see it to-night," answered the woman.

Night came : "Now," asked the man, "how about that thing you were speaking of ? "

"We shall see it, sure enough," said the woman.

Now it is dark. The woman is already there. The people inside hear *kwé! kwé! kwé!* Drag! Drag! There she is already knocking at the door :

"Open, open, little bird," etc. (as above).

Heaven help me! The present wife moves on to go and open.
The husband gets hold of her : " Do not go," he says.

" I will go," she says.

So the little woman gets away from his grip, and goes to open the
door. The late wife then comes in dragging herself :

" Put it on the fire, put it on the fire," etc. (as above).

She moves on, puts the pot on the fire, and just sits down. When
the pot boils, she says :

" Stir the porridge, stir the porridge," etc. (as above).

Then she stirs the porridge herself, takes it out of the pot, and puts
two fingers in it, singing :

" Let us eat, let us eat," etc. (as above).

Good gracious! She eats and eats her porridge herself. Then she
begins to drag herself again, but this time in the direction of the bed.
saying :

" Let us sleep, let us sleep, little bird.
" O mother! Be satisfied with millet.
" A little Kaffir corn porridge is a spirit."

She then begins to stretch herself on the bed in which is her husband
who struck her with an axe. Seeing that, the second little wife
rushed outside.

People came next morning ; they found in the hut only a corpse,
and this already swollen.

And this little story too, that's all, it ends there.

I am MWANA-MWENDERA.[2]

(IN BWINE-MURUNI.)

SARULA, SARULA, KAYUNI.

Bacu! Bâkacita. Bâkaya mu kweba. Ayi " A tuye tukeebe."

Umwi waya cêba, bâmana kumukaka. A kumwi nkwakaya, a
mwine wakwata.

Bacu! Kumuleta mu manda. Ayi, nkwakamukwata, ayi
" Webo, mwanakaxi, nxima yako una kulya ya mawo njece."

A rakwe ayi " E."

Bacu! A bâro basankwa ayi " A nebo nxima yangu njece ya
maira."

---

[2] Mwana-Mwendera is a Mukuni boy living on the Buyuni in the Bu-Sori.
In another version of this tale, by a boy called Kabwese, the head of the first
wife had been cut off by the husband. It was this head which then came
rolling several nights to the door of the hut. But the end of the story is quite
different from what we have here. There the murderer is described as making
expiation for his crime, and then being left in peace.

A rakwe ayi " Mbwece."

A! A mumene bararya bo nxima, wa-rutundu ya mawo, a bâro basankwa ya maira.

Bacu! Anu mumene mwanakaxi waruba bo, waxikira kulya ya maira. Ayi, nko batôsá basankwa bê " Webo wandita nxima yangu a rimwi. A rimwi ne ndakwambira ' Njece nxima yako ya mawo '! "

Ayi, a mwine bâbwesa apa kêmbe bâmuyasa. A mwine kwé kwé kwé kuya mu kumusowa kumbó.

Ayi, uko nko banôswá-ko bo bêne, barênda bo. Mumene bê " Tutôya mu rundu."

Uko nko bâkaya mu rundu, xâfwa ñama. Bacu! Kwakacara mwanakaxi ku muxi uko, i! " A rimwi tuye tukakwate a umwi."

Ayi, a rimwi nko bâkaya mu kukwata a umwi, bâmuleta. A rakwe ayi " Nce câkajaya mubyo ici. Ayi, a webo utakêrexa a kulya nxima ya maira, una kulya ya mawo njece."

A rakwe " Tawu kuna kulya nxima ya maira."

Ndye mumene ndye bâkabwesa rwendo rwa kuya mu rundu, mpo pa kumuxiya-mo ñabwinga wakêsá ono a rimwi umbi, ayi " Ono nebo nte kuya mu rundu." A bêne mbarya bâunka.

I ! Kwamba ayi maxiku, nkwakacara mwanakaxi ênka, bañumfwe bo maxikuxiku a mwine waxika ku cisasa kwé kwé kwé " Uyo ngo bâkêjaya, ngo bâkayasa a kêmbe, mutanxi."

A ku cisasa kwé kwé kwé waxika, a mwine, nkú nkú nkú ayi :

" Sarula,[3] sarula, kayuni.

" Sarula, sarula, kayuni.

" Mama! Werere mamawo,

" Kaxima kâ masaka [4] nkayuni."

Ndye wakaya mu kumujarwita, a mwine a kunjira mu manda, ayi :

" Teka-po,[5] teka-po, kayuni (*bis*).

" Mama! Werere mamawo.

" Kaxima kâ masaka nkayuni."

A mwine wainda wayambika-wo. Barixite bulyo. Bacu! A cîne citentu câbira. Wacibona kare mwine ngwece uyo, ayi :

" Kôponda, kôponda, kayuni (*bis*).

" Mama! Werere mamawo,

" Kaxima kâ masaka nkayuni."

A mwine mubye uyo wañamuka, waya mu kuleta busu ku nsansa, bwa maira, a mwine wabika-ko, waponda, waponda nxima yakwe

---

[3] *Sarula*, Ramba for Mukuni *carula* " open."
[4] *Masaka*, Ramba for Mukuni *maira* " Kafir corn."
[5] *Teka*, Ramba for Mukuni *yambika* " put the pot on the fire."

a mwine a kubika˘mu ntumba. Bacu! A mwine watintira-ko bulyo,
ayi :

> ·' Ka tulya, ka tulya, kayuni (*bis*).
> " Mama! Werere mamawo,
> " Kaxima kâ masaka nkayuni."

A mwine mubye uyo ute kulya bo ênka. Mpêce a rakwe watintira-
ko bo ryansa, kulya tawu. Ayi :

> " Ka tulya, ka tulya, kayuni," etc. (as above).

A îne nxima yakwe mubye waimana ênka. A rakwe tawo
ncâamba. Wafuruka bo. Ngulya utôya.
A mwine kwé kwé. Kutana ku mulyango waimakana ayi :

> " Sara-ko,[6] sara-ko, kayuni (*bis*).
> " Mama! Werere mamawo,
> " Kaxima kâ masaka nkayuni."

A mwine wapula. Ngulya utôya ku ciringo câkwe, waya kwïnjira.
Kwamba ayi mumene, basankwa bâringa mu rundu, a bêne bêsá
a bâro. Ayi " Bâna! Ku manda kuno nko mwakanxiya, bâna!
nko ciri cintu citôsá maxiku." Ayi " A kona tawu. Ciratongeka
bo kwimba."
Ayi " Ciri buyani ? "
Ayi " Mulacibona sunu."
A bwine bwaxiya kare. " A! Ino cîne ico cintu ciri buyani ? "
" Tulacibona."
A! Kwaxiya kare, a mwine wêsá kare. Bañumfwe bo kwé kwé,
wakonkaula kare ku cisasa :

> " Sarula, sarula, kayuni (*bis*).
> " Mama! Werere mamawo,
> " Kaxima kâ masaka nkayuni."

Bacu! Wainda mwanakaxi ayi " A nje njarule-ko." Kuya mu
kujarula-ko, basankwa bâmujata ayi " Webo utayi ukajarule."
A rakwe " Nte kuya bo."
A kêne kânakaxi kâpusumuka, kâya kucijarula cisasa. A mwine
kwé kwé wenjira :

> " Yambika, yambika, kayuni (*bis*).
> " Mama! Werere mamawo,
> " Kaxima kâ masaka nkayuni."

A mwine wainda, wayambika-wo a rimwi nxima. Bacu! Barixite
bo. A îne yabira :

> " Kôponda, kôponda, kayuni (*bis*).
> " Mama Werere mamawo
> " Kaxima kâ masaka nkayuni."

[6] *Sara=zara*, Ramba for Mukuni *cara* " shut."

A mwine mubye uyo waponda-ponda nxima yakwe. A kwipakira.
Watinta bo ryansa :
"Ka tulya, ka tulya, kayuni (*bis*).
"Mama! Werere mamawo,
"Kaxima kâ masaka nkayuni."
Bacu! A mwine mubye uyo kulya-alya nxima yakwe, waimana.
A mwine utôya kulikwerera a bulo, ayi :
"Kátôna, kátôna, kayuni (*bis*).
"Mama! Werere mamawo,
"Kaxima kâ masaka nkayuni."
A mwine kwé a bulo utôya mu koona a oyo ibaye wakamuyasa
kêmbe.
A karo kacibonene-wo kakaxi kâ onoono, a kâro katôya mu
kuconda kupula rubiro.
Bwaca bâxika bantu bâjana bo mu manda mubiri waximba kare.
A kâro nkêce ako kêera.
Ndime Mwana-Mwendera.

X.—LITTLE BEAD ! LITTLE BEAD !

Just then a man fixed his abode there.

Having fixed his abode there, he begat children and came into
possession of countless guinea-fowls.

As he thus had the place simply covered with guinea-fowls, he
said : These guinea-fowls of mine, you my children,[1] do not eat them.
If, perchance, you come to eat any of them, ah! mind you, you will
see me at the trial."

Those people remained at home.

Now, just listen! While the children remained there, the master
went rambling, just going round the little snares he had laid. Then,
being belated among his snares, he at last said : " Let me go back."
But, as he came home, fancy! he found his children had eaten one of
his guinea-fowls.

Seeing that, he said : " You, my children, all of you, come along
together, and let me too go and sing there."

Then it was that he went and stretched a string over the river
from bank to bank.

This being done, one of his children went and walked upon it,
while this was being sung :

---

[1] " Children " in the broad sense of the word, including brothers, sisters,
wives, servants.

1. " Little bead, little bead, perfectly balanced,[2]
   " Let us see who has eaten the guinea-fowls."
   Chorus after each verse : " Little bead, little bead, perfectly
      balanced."
   " My sister, it is thou who hast eaten the guinea-fowls."—
                                                    Chorus.
2. " Little bead, little bead, perfectly balanced!
   " Maiden, it is thou who hast eaten the guinea-fowls."—
                                                    Chorus.
   " (Swear by) the *funkwe*[3], lord of the rivers."—*Chorus.*
3. " Little bead, little bead, perfectly balanced!
   " Let the *funkwe* come and carry me off!—*Chorus.*
   " To the waters that resound and boil."—*Chorus.*
4. " Little bead, little bead, perfectly balanced!
   " Jump across!   Let him after this repay me with food." —
                                                    Chorus.

This one got across all right, then came another :
   " Little bead, little bead," etc. (as above).

He too got across, yet another mounted upon the string, the song
starting again :
   " Little bead, little bead," etc. (as above).

Then, as he was told to go as far as the middle of the stream, he of
his own accord jumped off the string, so that it nearly broke.

Good gracious!   At once the assegais were turned in one direction,
and he was killed on the spot.

And now I have left off for good.

I am XÂA-MINDA.[4]

———

(IN BWINE-MUKUNI.)

KARUNGU KARUNGU MUTENGEREXA.

Mpêce muntu nko wakêkara.

Ay'êkare waxara bâna.   Axare bâna, kâfuba nkanga xênka.

---

[2] As is well known, of all the beauties which nature and art can offer, none
can compare with beads in the eyes of the natives of Central Africa.   They
seem to tell them such a number of things.   The reason why a little bead is
here invoked as a sort of witness in a " judgment of God " must be that the
Bantu mind associates the beads with God.   In a number of Central African
languages, the word for " beads " is *bu-lungu*, which stands to *Mu-lungu*,
the word for " God " in a number of East African languages, in the same
relation as *bu-mbewa* " brood of field-rats " to *mbewa* " field-rats."   The beads,
in other words, are for the Central African native, who used to get them from
the East, something like " the brood of God."

[3] The *funkwe* is a fabulous snake, supposed to be miles and miles long.

[4] *Xâa-minda* was a man of Musabula's kraal on the Cârimbana.   I have
now lost sight of him.

Nkwari kufuba bo nkanga xênka, wâmba ayi " Ixi nkanga xângu, no bâna bângu, no mutôcara wano, kuxirya tawu. Cito kani [5] mukana kuxirya, o! manto! mulaya kumbona a cêbo.

Nko bâcara bantu abo.

Bacu! Bâna nko bâkacara oko, mwine waya ciindana, kuya mu tôse twakwe 'mwece.

Uko mu tôse twakwe 'mo akacara, waamba ayi " Mbôrere," jene bâna bâkwe imwi nkanga bârya-wo.

Uko nko bâkairya ayi " No bâna bângu nônse, mwebo a muyoboroke, nebo nje nkaimbe."

Uko nkwakaya mu kutantika rôxi pa mulonga, ayi, amane kulutantika-wo, umwi waya-wo. Ayi :

Ka.ru_ ngu Ka.ru_ngu mu_te_nge_re_xa, tu_bo_

_ne wa_rya ma.ka_ngu, ka_ru_ngu ka.ru_ngu mu.te nge_re_

_xa Mu.kwa.su, wa_rya ma.ka.nga ka.ru_ngu ka.ru ngu mu_

te_ nge_re_xa.

1. " Karungu, karungu, mutengerexa!
" Tubone warya makanga.
" Karungu, karungu, mutengerexa!
" Mukwasu,[6] warya makanga.
" Karungu, karungu, mutengerexa! "

2. " Karungu, karungu, mutengerexa!
" Môye, warya makanga.—Karungu, etc.
" Funkwe, mwine mulonga.—Karungu," etc.

3. " Karungu, karungu, mutengerexa!
" Funkwe êsé antware.[7]—Karungu, etc.
" Ku mênda [8] arira wawawa.—Karungu," etc.

[5] The Bêne-Mukuni say *pani* or *panxi* rather than *kani*.
[6] *Mukwasu*, Ramba for Mukuni *Mukwêsu* " my brother, my sister."
[7] *Antware*, Ramba for Mukuni *antore* " let him carry me off."
[8] *Mênda*, Ramba for Mukuni *manxi* " water."

4. " Karungu, karungu, mutengerexa!
   " Subwa! Akandipe [10] xiryo.
   " Karungu, karungu, mutengerexa! "
Wasubuka umwi, a umwi waxika :
   " Karungu, karungu," etc. (as above).
Waswa-wo a umwi, a umwi warokera-wo :
   " Karungu, karungu," etc. (as above).
Nde kwamba ayi " Akanôxika pakati," waswa mwine a rwine rôxi karuya mu kumuntuka.
Bacu! Mpêce a êne masumo bâbunganya-wo bantu. Mpêce bâmujaya.
A kuleka ndareka ono.
Ndime XÂA-MINDA.

XI.—HOW I SHALL BE ADMIRED!

This is what that man did.[1]

He went to the court to report : " Listen! " he said. " At the place where I come from I have found an enormous snake. I should say, my lords, that, if you had it brought here, all your honourable friends would assemble to come and look at it."

The king, hearing that, said : " I am going to call all the people of the land together."

He had them called, then held an assembly where he said : " I am the king, bring me the thing that is over there, that I too may come and see it with my own eyes in a hut."

Of course those people went. As they reached the place, they gathered together outside, trying to go and peep inside. Then, finding the thing still asleep, they started singing :

   " How I shall be admired!
         Chorus : " How I shall be admired!
   " Come out that we may look at thee.—(Chorus.)
   " That we may look at thee.—(Chorus.)
   " If I come out, you will be afraid of me.—(Chorus.)
   " By mother! You will be afraid of me.—(Chorus.)
   " That is what was done by your fathers,—(Chorus.)
   " By your fathers.—(Chorus.)

---

[10] *Akandipe*, from *ripa*, Ramba for Mukuni *riya* " pay."
[1] Among the Bêne-Mukuni every story is supposed to be the continuation of another.

" They left here even their bows,[2]—*Chorus.*
" Even their bows."—*Chorus.*

Those people ran away leaving their bows there and came and said : " As for us, Sire, that is more than we can do."

The king then said : " Go and give birth to children."

The following day, when they gave birth to children and these went, as soon as they reached the place, they too surrounded the hut, but said : " It is you, your very own self, that we have come for, you who are in the house."

Bacu ! They put the snake on their shoulders, the tail hanging behind. Then, having brought it outside, they dragged it along, singing the while :

" How I shall be admired! " etc. (as above).

Then, as they took that thing to the court and reached the place, the king said : " You my wives, all of you, go and fetch water to whitewash the hut."

So, having gone to fetch water, the women came and whitewashed the hut.

And, when they had finished whitewashing, the brute itself was brought in.

Then the king came over also to have a look at it. And, having seen it, he said : " You people of my realm, disperse and go away, all of you. I do not care in the least for such things. To me, such as I am, what have you brought but an ugly bit of a snake? "

I am XÂA-MINDA.[3]

(IN BWINE-MUKUNI.

MBWENJEBWE.

Mbwakacita muntu uyo.

Ay' aye ku bwaro, waya mu kuximika.

Nkwakaya mukuximika, ayi " Nebo nku ndaringa uku, ndajana cisoka cinene. Ingayi, no bâmi, kucireta muno cixi, bônse babyanu kabayoboroka kwïsá mu kucibona."

[2] A hill not far from here is called *Ka-xiya-mata* " the little-leave-the-bows," because once, so it is said, an army from the north that was coming south to plunder the Bêne-Futwe, saw there some mysterious portent and was seized with such a fright that the invaders left their bows on the spot and never reappeared.

[3] The conclusion of this tale refers, no doubt, to a means occasionally resorted to by African masters to get rid of the obligation of paying work done for them ; but, taken as a whole, it is simply one of the many Bantu tales invented to show that superstitious and ridiculous fears often make grown people incapable of performing quite simple feats, which do not present the least difficulty to children. See another tale of the same kind at No. XVI. (Mother, come back).

A rakwe uyo mwami ayi " Ndabayoborora cixi."

Ay' ayoborore cixi bantu, kwĭsá mu kubabunganya ayi : " Nebo mwami, a mundetere cintu ciri kooku, a nebo mwine nkana kwĭsá mu kwebera mu manda."

Ingayi bê baye bantu abo, ingayi baxike, bâbungana ansengwe a kuna kuya ku sondera-mo. Mpêce bajane ncâ koona kare, ayi :

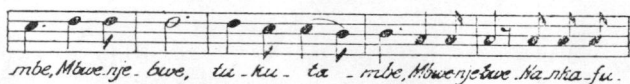

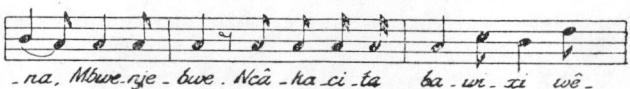

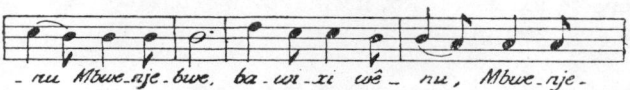

" Mbwenjebwe [3] ! Mbwenjebwe!

" Fuma [4] tukutambe,[5] Mbwenjebwe!

" Tukutambe, Mbwenjebwe!

" Na nka fuma,[6] mwakuntina,[7] mbwenjebwe!

" Ma! mwakuntina, Mbwenjebwe!

---

[3] *Njebwe*, let me admired, passive of -*eba*.

[4] *Fuma*, Ramba for Mukuni *swa* " come out."

[5] *Tamba*, Ramba for Mukuni *ebera* " look at."

[6] *Na nka Fuma*, Ramba for Mukuni *ndaswa* " if I come out."

[7] *Tina*, Ramba for Mukuni *yowa* " fear," flee from."

" Ncâkacita bawixi [8] wênu,[9] Mbwenjebwe
" Bawixi wênu, Mbwenjebwe!
" Bâkaxiya nâ mata [10] ônse, Mbwenjebwe
" Nâ mata ônse, Mbwenjebwe! " [11]

Bâronda bantu rubiro, bâxiya-ko a mata âbo.
Bâxika ayi " Swebo, mwami, câtwarira."
Ayi " A muye mukabaxare bâna."
Cûnsa nko bâkaxara bâna, bâna abo be baye, nko bâkaya uko, mbwêce a bâro bâxika ansengwe bâbungirira, bê " Webo ndwêce ndiwe twakonka uli mu manda.
Bacu! A bâro bâna bâkaciñamuna. Bê baciñamune, bâcikwenkwemfya :
" Mbwenjebwe! Mbwenjebwe! " etc. (as above).
Mpêce bê bacitore ku bwaro ico cintu, nko bâkacitora ku bwaro, bê bâxike " No ba-makaangu nônse, a muye mukateke manxi, muxibubule manda."
Bê baye mu kuteka manxi, bêsá kabaxibulula manda.
Nko bâkamana kuxibulula manda, a cîne mpo pa kucinjixa-mo.
Bê bacinjixe-mo, nko bâkacinjixa, bâmi kabaindirira kuya mu kwebera a bâro.
Mpêce " No bêne kwangu, ka mumwayika mumane kuya. Ono-ono nebo te nxibe-ko. Ne mwine mwandetera-ko cisoka."
Ndime XÂA-MINDA.[12]

XII.—I AM TEMBWE.[1]

They ground meal and went to clear new fields in the forest.
Where they went for that purpose they cut, and cut, and cut down trees till at last people said : " Now go back and bring fire from the shelter where we come from."

---

[8] *Bawixi*, Ramba for Mukuni *baixi* " fathers."
[9] *Wênu*, Ramba for Mukuni *bânu* " yours."
[10] *Nâ mata*, Ramba for Mukuni *a mata* " even the bows."
[11] About this kind of poetry see Note [10] of the tale No. IV. (Let the Big Drum roll!)
[12] This proper name has, it seems, a composition of its own. *Xâa* is Bwine-Mukuni for *xâna*=Tonga *syana* or *syaa* or *syâ*. *Minda* seems to be the Ñungwe word *mi-nda* " fields "=Mukuni and Tonga *my-unda*. So it seems that the name *Xâa-Minda* is half Mukuni, half Ñungwe, and means " the little master or keeper of the fields." A number of proper names thus refer to positions at something like a court, as *Xâa-mulyango* or *Syâ-mulyango* " the keeper of the gate," *Xâa-busu* or *Syâ-busu* " the keeper of the meal," *Xâa-maira* or *Sya-maira* or *Sya-namaira* " the keeper of the Kafir corn," etc.
[1] Already published, partly by A. C. Madan, *Lenje Handbook*, p. 57.

An old woman went and found something inside :
" Who art thou ? " he asked in Ramba, "thou who art in my house? "
Then a song came out, likewise in Ramba :

" I am Tembwe,[2]
" I am the Tembwe that lives in bamboos, let another come.
" Let another come, that we may disembowel him and throw him
    outside in the mud.
" In the mud, that cattle may trample him.   Are you not afraid ?
" Are you not afraid ?   To-day you will sleep outside."

The man [3] went away and came back to his companions.
" Well, friend, and the fire ?   Where hast thou left it ? "
" There is some one," answered the man, " who forbids me to take
it."

Then several said to another : " Go thou."

When he reached the place : " Give us fire," said he, " thou who
art in the house."   Then he added in Ramba : " Who art thou, who
art there in the house ? "

The answer was the same song as before :
        " I am Tembwe," etc.

Then : " Go."

So he too went away. . . . " Now the fire!   Where hast thou
left it ? "

" I have left it there," answered the man.   " There is some one who
forbids me to take it."

The chief then said : " Go, So-and-So, bring us fire."

He too went. . . .   " Come, come!   Give us fire."   The same song
again.   Meanwhile the beast finished the meal, finished it all clean.

At last the tortoise got up.   When he reached the shelter, he also
spoke in Ramba : "Who art thou," he said, " thou who art in the
house ?   Let us come out of it."

He heard the same song as above, but only repeated : " Let us
come out of our house, let us come out of our house."

While the creature was singing as before, he went into the house,
and got hold of the person he found there.

The song went on, but the tortoise got under the belly of the beast
and tore it, and tore it, and tore it, while the brute was beating him
with its wings and legs and still singing :
        " I am Tembwe," etc. (as above).

---

[2] *Tembwe* is said to be equivalent of *tembo*, which in Ramba means " a
hornet," but the giant hornet of this tale is, of course, purely fictitious.

[3] In the Bantu animal tales, the animals are treated as persons, and the
persons as animals.

Finally the tortoise picked it up, threw it outside, and made an end of it. Then he took the fire and brought it to his mates.

" Have you brought the fire ? " said they.

" I have brought it," he answered.

" Come, let us go," said the whole troop.

They got up, all of them, to go to their shelter.

As they came near it, they found the creature dead and stretched on the ground. . . . " Hurrah! " they said, " this is the creature that ate up our things and destroyed them. Hurrah! "

It was only then that they all got up and came near.

That is where the little record is complete.

I am Mwengwe.[4]

(IN BWINE-MUKUNI.)

NDIME TEMBWE.[5]

Bâpera masu. Bâya mu kutema.

Nko bâkaya mu kutema, be baye bateme, bâtema, bâtema, bâtema xisamo. Ayi " Ono mubôre muye mukarapule muliro ku musumba nko twaswa."

Mpêce ajane mwênjira kacembere . . . " Uwe nani we uli mu manda yanji ? "

Ayi :

" Ndime Tembwe,

" Ndime Tembwe rya mwĭkara nsununu, umbi êsé-mo.

" Umbi êsé-mo, tukaraule tupose pêsonde pa xinkumbi

" Pa xinkumbi xikumbire mombe, ta mwatina ?

" Ta mwatina ? Mba rero mwa kurara pêsonde."

Waunka wabôra.

Ay' abôre uko nkwakaya . . . " Ino, ndó, muliro wauxiya kuli ? "

Ayi " Nko ari muntu utôkaxa muliro."

A rimwi a bamwi " Kôya a webo."

---

[4] Mwengwe, now dead, was an old woman of Caxa's kraal, near the Kasisi Mission Station. The story is current on the Zambesi, and Mwengwe's account is inferior to those of most other narrators. It is an allegory explaining how the natives used, occasionally, to get rid of foreigners, when these without ceremony took possession of their springs or their fields. The compiler's reason for publishing Mwengwe's version, though inferior to others, is its song, a pretty good sample of Bantu poetry of a kind.

[5] This song has the same movement as the preceding (Mbwenjebwe). The end of a verse is taken up as the beginning of the following verse. In it Ramba words are *uwe* " thou," *nani?* " Who ?" —*anji* " mine," *nsununu* " bamboo," *posa* " throw," *pêsonde* " outside," *xinkumbi* " muddy places," *tina* " fear," *rara* " sleep," *rero* " to-day."

Ay' axike " Tupe muliro, o uli mu manda umo."
" Uwe nani we uli mu manda umo ? "
      " Ndime Tembwe," etc. (as above).
Bê " Kôya."
A rakwe waunka. Axike kulya nkwakaya " Ino muliro wauxiya kuli ? "
A rimwi " Wacara. Nko ari muntu wakaxa."
Bê " A muye-ko, ndaba, mukarete muliro."
Waunka waya. Ay' axike ayi " Bâna! Tupe muliro."
  " Uwe nani we uli mu manda umo ?
  " Tufumine mu manda.
  " Ndime Tembwe," etc (as above).
Warya masu ônse, wamana busu bônse pukutu pukutu.
A rimwi bâñamuka bafulwe. Bê baxike bê " Niwe nani uli mu manda umo? Tufumine-mo."
  " Ndine Tembwe," etc. (as above).
" Tufumine [6] mu manda yêsu. Tufumine mu manda yêsu."
  " Ndime Tembwe," etc. (as above).
Mpêce wênjira mu manda. 'Ay ênjire, wamwĭjata uyu muntu ngo wakêjana-mo :
      " Ndime Tembwe," etc. (as above).
Wênjira mu mara, wamwĭjayajaya. A mwine mpumpu wamu-pumpaula :
      " Ndime Tembwe," etc. (as above).
Wamubwesa, wamuwara pansengwe wamwĭjaya.[8] A muliro wañamuna, watora kulya ku bênxiñina.
Kulya ku babye nko wakaya " Wauleta muliro ? "
" Ndauleta."
" A musé twende."
Bônse bâñamuka kwĭsá ku musumba wabo.
Bê baxike, bêjana [9] " O! câfwa câtandabara. Ici nce câringa kutulita xintu. Mpêce câtumanina xintu nce ici. Olo! "
Mpêce apo bônse bâñamuka bêsá pwí.
Mpo kâkuma kêra mpêce apo.
Ndine Mwengwe.

---

[6] One may notice here how in the imperative one person is easily used for another. The normal form should be here the Ramba *fuma* " get out " (sing.) Instead of this the Baramba generally use the second person plural *fumêni*. But all through this tale the form used in the same meaning is the first person plural *tu-fume*. When the person addressed is a chief the same idea is expressed by the third person plural *ba-fume*.

[7] *Wamwjiata*. More common form wamujata.

[8] *Wamwjiaya*. More common form wamujaya.

[9] *Bêjana*. More common form bâjana.

XIII.—FIRST, LET ME HAND OVER.

Just then there was a double marriage with both a superior and an inferior wife. The inferior one then prepared a drug and caused the death of her mate, the owner of the place.

When she was dead, the people said : " Let us bury her in the village."

But the guilty woman said : " No, not in the village. That would not do. Rather at the back of it. I feel too much the loss of my mate."

The mourning was kept up for a long while.

At last the chief said : " Let them eat, otherwise they will die."

When this word was uttered, the woman-folk said : " Let us go to do field-work."

So they dispersed in order to go to the fields. But the guilty woman went up to the granary and took out some ears of corn. She then called the dead woman, saying : " Come and thrash this." So saying she went and dug her mate out until she came forth from the grave, in which she had been covered with earth, in order to go and thrash the corn.

When she had finished thrashing it, she winnowed and sifted it, then took it to the grinding-stone and began to prepare this stone for use by beating it with a small one.

Meanwhile in the hut the living woman was cooking porridge. When she had finished stirring it, she said : " Come and have some food."

Go into the hut! That is what her mate will not do. So she says : "Then go and grind. You are a fool."

So the dead woman goes to the stone and grinds, singing all the while :

" First let me hand over to you little things, my lady.

" Lady Rows,[1] let me hand over little things,

" Rows, I have left you the husband ; break me in two, yes.[2]

" Rows, I have left you the cowries ; break me in two, yes.

" Rows, I have left you the children ; break me in two, yes.

" Rows, I have left you the slaves ; break me in two, yes.

" Rows, I have left you the cotton goods ; break me in two, yes.

" Rows, I have left you the fowls ; break me in two, yes.

" Rows, I have left you the guinea-fowls ; break me in two, yes.

" Rows, I have left you the baskets ; break me in two, yes.

---

[1] *Mirongo* " rows " is the name of the living woman.

[2] " Break me in two." That is, probably, " yet you cannot leave me in peace even after death."

" Rows, I have left you the fire ; break me in two, yes.
" Rows, I have left you everything; break me in two, yes.
" Let me hand over all the rows."
(She disappeared before the people came to the village.) . . . .

Once more the following day the people dispersed in order to go to the fields. The woman went too, but soon came back, then went to the granary, and began to take out grain. All of a sudden she started towards the place where she had covered her mate with earth, saying : " Now, now ! Come, thrash, and grind ; the sun is sinking." So she went and dug her out.

The dead woman thrashed and thrashed. When she had finished thrashing, she took the grain to the grinding-stone, then once more began to beat it with another stone.

" Come along ! said her mate, " come and have some food."

" No," she said " I do not want any. Food is not what is on my heart."

" Well ! " said the other, " where are the people who are going to look at you the whole day long ? You died long ago."

Then she added : " What, eat ! that is what she will not do. . . . Then go and grind, dear, the sun is sinking."

Then the dead woman bent herself over the stone and began to grind, singing :

" First let me hand over," etc. (as above).

Meanwhile everyone left the fields and came back to the village.

Next morning people said : " Let us go to the fields, the sun is sinking . . . ." After having gone to the field, the woman once more came back before the sun was high and went up to the granary. After that her mate thrashed, took the grain to the stone, and began to grind, singing the same song as on the previous days.

Next morning at dawn people said once more : " Now let us go to work." But this time a number of people remained hidden in the grass. Then, fancy their surprise ! they saw the woman go up to the granary, start taking some ears of corn, and, on coming down, go and unearth her mate. Seeing that, they said : " This time it is plain, this is the woman that killed her mate."

Then, as they saw the dead woman thrash the grain and go and bend over the millstone, and heard her saying : " Let me begin to grind," then, good gracious ! when they further heard the song " First let me hand over . . . ", then, by the ghosts ! they were all in suspense. . . .

" Now," said the dead woman, " let me move away from the stone."

At this moment they got hold of the murderer . . . " Let me go," she said, " first hold a court of enquiry."

But they just went and dug up a poison and mixed it, and made her drink it by force. Meanwhile her mate had vanished.

Heaven help me ! There they made a heap of firewood, dug her heart out, and burned her over the fire.[3]

Now, little iron,[4] my little story stops. Little iron, that's all. I am MUNJE.[5]

(IN BWINE-MUKUNI.)

NTANJE NTUNTULE.

Mpêce awo bâkaparikira, a inabunene, a inabwanike. Inabwanike wapanda musamu wajaya mukaxiñina, mwine manda.

Ayi, uko nko wakamujaya, babye ayi " Tubike mu muxi."

Ayi " Mu muxi ta mwĭxi, sombi ku mafutire. Mwensuma ute kuncisa."

Bârira-rira.

Nko bâkamana kulira, ayi " Barafwa, kabarya."

Uko nko bâkaamba " Barafwa, kabarya," babye " Tukarime."

Bâmweta kuya mu kulima. Waya kutanta a butara, wa bansa-bansa. Ay' amane ku bansa, ayi " Kwesá ulupule." Waunka waya mu kumufukulula. Mubye waswa-mo mu cirindi 'mo bâka-mufumbika kwĭsá mu kulupula.

Ay' amane kulupula, wêsá wayula wapupuruxa. Wabuula wan-jixa mu ribwe, warimba kukunka ribwe.

Mu manda nxima waponda. Ay' amane kuponda " Kwesá ulye."

Mubye kunjira mu manda wakaka. Ayi " Bâna ! Kôya ukapere, uli muluya."

Waunka ku ribwe, wapera :

" Ntanje ntuntule tuntu, mwene, e !

" Mirongo, ntuntule tuntu, mwene, e !

" O Mirongo, mulume 'nakuxiyira, ntyoré, e !

" O Mirongo, mpande 'nakuxiyira, ntyoré, e !

" O Mirongo, bâna 'nakuxiyira, ntyoré, e !

" O Mirongo, baxa 'nakuxiyira, ntyoré, e !

" O Mirongo, nsaru 'nakuxiyira, ntyoré, e !

" O Mirongo, nkuku 'nakuxiyira, ntyoré, e !

---

[3] The natives say that when an execution of that kind took place they used first to poison the convicted witch, then take the heart out, burn it to a cinder, grind it, and throw the ashes to the wind, the body, meanwhile, being also reduced to ashes.

[4] The little iron is the phonograph, to which Munje has been telling her story.

[5] Munje is a woman of Cikonkoto's kraal, near the Kasisi mission station.

" O Mirongo, nkanga 'nakuxiyira, ntyoré, e !
" O Mirongo, nsengwa 'nakuxiyira, ntyoré, e !
" O Mirongo, manda 'nakuxiyira, ntyoré, e !
" O Mirongo, muliro 'nakuxiyira, ntyoré, e !
" O Mirongo, xônse 'nakuxiyira, ntyoré, e !
" Ntuntule mirongo."

.   .   .   .

A rimwi bâunka, bâya mu kulima. Wabôra waya kutanta a
butara, warimba kubansa. Waunka nkwakafumbira mubye
" Bâna ! Kwesá ulupule upere, risuba ryaunka." Waunka waya
mu kumufumbula.
Warupularupula. Ay' amane kulupula, wênjixa mu ribwe.
Mpêce, wakênjixa mu ribwe, a rimwi warimba kukunka.
" Bâna ! Kwesá ulye."
Ayi " Nxiyandi. Ta cikwe ku môyo câ kulya."
" Ino bê bakwebere mba bani ryonse ? Wakafwa kare."
Ayi " Kulya ta ari . . . Ka muya mupere, bâna ! ryaunka."
Mpêce wênjira mu ribwe, warimba kupera ayi :
          " Ntanje ntuntule," etc. (as above).
Mpêce bâkaunka. Bwe buce, bê " A twende tukarime, risuba
ryaunka."
Uko nko bâkaya mu kurima, bâbôra, bêsa bwaca, bâya kutanta
a butara. Bê batante a butara, mubye walupula, wênjixa mu
ribwe, warimba kupera ayi :
          " Ntanje ntuntule," etc. (as above).
Cûnsa bwe buce, bê " A twende tukarime." Ano bênji [6] câkara
kare mu cisuwa, câberamaberama. Babone, bacu ! utôya butanta
a butara, warimba kubansa, ay' aseruke, waya mu kufumbula mubye.
Wakaya, kâfumbula mubiye " Anu ! Ngo woyu, ngo wakajaya
mukaxiñina."
Uko nko wakalupula maira, ano ênjire mu ribwe " N'imbe kupera,"
bacu ! :
          " Ntanje ntuntule," etc. (as above).
Bacu ! Uko nko bâkacita boobo " Ono nkapûle " wakajaya
mubye a rakwe bâmujata. Uko nko bâkamujata, bê " A mundece
muloborore."
Mpo pa kukaba musamu kumunwixa. Ajane mubye waon-
domoka.
Bacu ! Mubye bâmuxita bâmutenta.
Mpêce, cêra, kâreka. Mpêce apo, cêra.
Ndime MUNJE.
          [6] The common form is *banji*.

XIV.—LITTLE OLD WOMAN THERE !

Another man had also taken two wives, the mother of the superior children, and the mother of the inferior children. Both of them gave birth. But the child of the inferior wife was constantly crying

One day, as she went to the field to dig, her child seemed to say: "Why bring me as far as this?" Well! There it was already changed to a spring of tears.

She then happened to see an old woman from the bush, who said : " Come along now ! Bring the child to me to nurse it. Are you a child who does not know how to say : Come and nurse my baby for me ? "

She said : " Alas ! Where shall I find a mother, little woman from the forest ? . . . Here it is." And she gave her the child.

She dug and dug, dug and dug, until she had enough of it. Then she sang :

"Little old woman there !
"Bring me my child.
"The people of the village have already come back.
"Bring me my child."

(The old woman answered with this other song.)

"I am coming.
"I am still picking the herb baby-nurse-me, oh ! "
"I am still picking the herb baby-nurse-me, oh ! "

What do you think? Next morning at dawn she had already gone to the field. She had scarcely arrived and was just making the first marks with the hoe on the ground when, don't swear ! the child was already crying.

She then saw the little old woman from the bush putting in an appearance. Here she is : " Child, you seem to be calling me to come and nurse the baby for you."

The mother said : " Be so good as to come, if you like, mother." There is the child over there being taken away."

Well ! Well ! The woman dug and dug and dug. When she had enough of it : " Now," she said, " I am tired, let her bring me the child, I must go."

So she called and called, singing as before :

"Little old woman there ! " etc. (as above).

No answer coming, she went on digging and digging and digging : "Well now ! " she said, "what is the matter with the little old woman ? Not bring me the child ! And I am so tired ! "

She called again :

"Little old woman there ! " etc. (as above).

At last the old woman came and brought the child. There then is the mother going home.

Bacu ! How she hurried on the cooking when she reached the place !

Meanwhile the people came home, and night fell. . . .

Dawn had already cleared up. They all went to dig in the fields. . . . What a bother ! The child is crying. The little woman from the bush comes once more to nurse it. There she is over there taking it away.

Bacu ! The mother has come back to the hoe, and she digs, and digs, and digs. At last she says : " I am tired, I cannot do any more, I must go home."

There she is calling the little woman :
" Little old woman there," etc. (as above).
No answer. Again :
" Little old woman there," etc. (as above).
At last she says : " She has killed it." And she goes home.

" Goodness gracious ! " say the people there. What has happened ? "

" Rather ask," she says, " the old woman from the bush. . . .''

Next morning, as she said : " Let me go to the old woman's abode," she found there some porridge, and said : " Show me my child. My child is dead ! "

Then the little woman went and cut off the head of the child and brought something wrapped on her back to the mother.

" Give me my child," cried the young woman.

" First eat your porridge," said the old one.

" I do not want to eat porridge," said the mother. " First give me my child (which you have on your back)."

" No," said the old woman, " first eat your porridge."

Meanwhile in the cloth on her back she had nothing but the head.

At last the mother said : " All right ! Let me eat a little porridge." But, as she took some to her mouth, it fell down before reaching it. At this moment the old woman said : " Here is your child." And the mother hastened to stretch her arms to receive it, but what she saw was only a head without a trunk. She dropped it down.

" O mother ! " she cried in despair, " she has already eaten my child ! "

Home she went. " Goodness gracious ! " said the people, " what has happened ? "

" Rather ask," she answered, " the little old woman who was

nursing for me, who lives in the bush. . . . Hurry up ! Make some drums."

When the drums were ready, the people began to beat them hard, making them sound far and wide, singing :

"Let the little old woman mourn Sere ! [1]
"I will call thy nurse to the dance, o Sere !
"O Sere, thy nurse I will call to the dance."

My goodness ! In truth, the little old woman was seen herself coming from a distance, dancing on the road, and singing in Ramba :

"I am coming to-day to dance,
"I am coming to the sound of the drum,
"I am coming to-day and I shall dance.
"Thou little one that art being mourned in the dance."

Meanwhile the people were repeating :

"Let the little old woman mourn Sere," etc. (as above).

Goodness me ! Talk of the scene when the little old woman joined the group of the dancers ! She had scarcely entered the ring when she was seized. Then in one instant she was already bathed in blood and tumbled on to the fire.

Bacu ! This little story too is finished, ripe, ending here. I am MUNJE.[2]

(IN BWINE-MUKUNI.)
KACEMBERE-WO !

A bamwi bâkaparikira, a bêna-bunene, a bêna-bwanike. Bâxara bâna.

Ino waxara ina-bwanike mwana wa kupika.

Ay' ainde ku mûnda "Nje nkarime," mwana ayi "Nkuno nkowacireta ? " Sombi mwana wasansayika kulira.

Abone bo kacembere kâ mu nxitu,[3] ayi : Bâna ! Kôreta nkurerere-ko. Ta acîxi kwita mwanike : A musé munderere-ko ? "

Ayi "Bacu ! Mbabone kuli bamá, kacembere kâ mu nxitu ? . . . Ngú." A kubapa mwana.

Warima, warima, wacimwa. Ayi :

Ka-ce-mbere-wo, ndete-re mwanawa ngu. Basi kumu.
zi bâ-bo-o-ra, Ade-te re mwana na wa-ngu.

---

[1] A Tonga version of this tale calls the child Ha-Nserere.
[2] The Munje of the preceding tale.
[3] *Nxitu* for Tete *m'situ* "forest."

" Kacembere-wo !
" Ndeteré mwana wangu.[4]
" Bari ku muxi bâbôra,
" Ndeteré mwana wangu
" Nte kwĭsá
" Nciyapa kâna-mundere-é
" Nciyapa kâna-mundere-wo."

Bacu ! Cûnsa bwaca, bâya kare. Ay' axike " Nkanke bo rise panxi," bacu ! mwana warira kare.
Abone kâpora kacembere kâ mu nxitu. Nká ano " O mwana, inga kônjita nkakulerere-ko mwana."
Ayi " Munana kwĭsá no bêne, má."
Mwana ngulya bâtora.
Bacu ! Warima, warima, warima. Ce cimucime " Ndarema ono, andetere mwana, 'na kuya."
Bacu ! Sombi kâita ayi :
" Kacembere-wo ! " etc. (as above).
Bacu ! kârima, kârima, kârima . . . " Ano ! A kacembere kari buyani ? Kutandetera mwana ! Ne mwine ndarema :
" Kacembere-wo ! " etc. (as above).
Bacu ! Kâxika kacembere. A mwana kâmuleta. Ke kamuletere mwana, ngulya utôya ku muxi.
Bacu ! Waxika, watakataka xâ kulya.
Bâbôra, bâona, kwaxiya. . . .
A bwine bwaca kare. Bâya ku mûnda kuya mu kulima. Bacu !
Mwana warira. Kâbôra kacembere kwĭsá mu kulera mwana. Nkarya kâtora.
Bacu ! Wabôra warima, warima, warima. Ayi " Ono ndarema, ono ndacimwa, 'na kuya ku muxi."
Ngayi kukaita :
" Kacembere-wo ! ", etc. (as above).
A rimwi :
" Kacembere-wo ! " etc. (as above).
Ayi " Kâmujaya."
Bacu ! Kuya ku muxi " Bâna ! Mbuyani ? "
Ayi " Sombi kacembere kâ mu nxitu. . . ."
Ngayi cûnsa ayi " Njise," [5] ajane-ko nxima, ayi " Njuburwite mwana. Mwanângu wafwa ! "

---

[4] The Tonga version says here : *Reta Ha-Nserere añonke* " Bring Master Nserere to suck the breast."
[5] Ramba *njise* placed in the mouth of the woman for Mukuni *nsé* " let me come."

Nko kâmutimbula mutwi mwana. Kê kamutimbule mutwi,
kuletera ñina.
" Ampe mwanângu."
Ayi " Tanguna ulye nxima."
Ayi " Nxiyandi kulya nxima. A mutangune mumpe mwana
wangu."
Ayi " Tanguna ulye nxima."
Mutwi 'mo bâkaberekera.
" Ono ndye nxima " yaroka pa mulomo.
Bacu ! Ayi " Ngú mwana wako."
Ngayi [6] " Nkatambule bo mwana," abone ncitwi, pumputu ! "
" Mawé ! Mwana wangu bârya kare."
Kuya ku muxi " Bâna ! Mbuyani ? "
" Sombi kacembere kâri kunderera kâikara mu nxitu. . . .
" Bâna ! A mubese ngoma."
Bê baxibese ngoma, kuumaula-wo, kulixa :
    " Kacembere karire Sere !
    " Ndakaita mu ngoma, Sere ya . . . [7]
    " Sere ! Yaya ! Ndakaita mu ngoma."
Bacu ! Sombi kate kwǐsá kacembere, ayi :
    " Naisa rero ncinde [8]
    " Naisa mu ngoma
    " Naisa rero nxane,
    " Karirwa mu ngoma.
    " Kacembere karire Sere !
    " Ndakaita mu ngoma, Sere ya . . .
    " Sere ! Yaya ! Ndakaita mu ngoma."
Bacu ! Sombi a kêne kâxika.
Bacu ! A kwindirira bo nko kukajata. Cino cîndi, bacu !
kwatekwa kare, kari mu muliro.
Bacu ! A kâro ako kêera, mpêce apo kâkuma, nko kêera.
Ndime MUNJE.

[6] Munje thus says *Ngayi*, meaning " she seemed to say," where other people
would say *Ingayi*, and she pretends that *they* do not speak correctly Bwine-
Mukuni.
[7] *Ya* . . . left incomplete, for *yaya* " nurse," a word of the Ñungwe
language.
[8] *Naisa rero ncinde*, Ramba for Mukuni *Nte kwǐsá sunu nxane*. The verb
" come " is pronounced *isa* in Ramba, *isá* in Bwine-Mukuni.

XV.—TO BE MARKED !

Note.—The natives of the Kafue region were accustomed till recently to notch, or file, or knock out a greater or lesser number of the upper front teeth of their children. The Ba-Sukulumbwe used to notch as many as six, and many of them still do so. The Ba-Renje notched only two. This notching was called *ku-bangwa* " to be marked." The following story was, it may be supposed, invented to make the children submit willingly to the operation by describing it as a source of untold blessings, when accepted in the genuine spirit of obedience. Such stories teaching obedience are not uncommon in the Zambezi region.

This is what a girl did.

Her mates said : " Let us go and have our teeth marked."

But she remained behind, her mother forbidding her to go and saying : " Remain thou, go and bring corn from the bin." This she brought.

The mother then said : " Go and fetch water." She went and brought water.

The mother said : " Come and grind." She came and ground, and put the pot on the fire.

The mother said : " Stir the porridge." She stirred the porridge.

When it was ready, the mother said : " Take thy food." The girl remarked : " My mates meanwhile will be far away." " Just take thy time," said the mother, " thou wilt catch them all right."

When she had finished eating, the mother said : " Now go."

She went, but could not find out where her mates had gone. They had taken one road, while she had taken another.

The path she followed took her where she found a little old woman, who said : " Now what have you come to do here ? "

" I wanted," she said, " to have my teeth marked. I intended to go with some mates of mine, but apparently they have gone by another way, for the one I have taken has brought me here, where I do not see them."

" Never mind," said the little old woman, " I too know how to notch the teeth. First go and fetch water for me, my child."

As the girl got up to go to the water, the woman offered her a coil to steady the pot on her head, saying : " Put this coil on your head."

" But," said the girl," " what sort of coil is that ? "

" Just put it on your head, it is a coiled snake," said the woman.

" What ? " said the girl, " how can I put a snake on my head ? "

Those little old women of the Bantu tales behave in many cases more or less like the fairies of our own. Those from the forest are bad, the others are good.

A frog was near.[2] It whispered to the girl : " No, just put that snake on your head. And, in general, do all what the little old woman tells you. Take that snake and simply go and fetch the water."

She went and brought some water. The old woman then told her to grind corn, she ground the corn. The old woman told her to come and extract some worms there on an ulcer, she extracted the worms from the ulcer. The old woman told her to fry them, she fried them and put salt on them. When she had done that, the old woman said : " Here is meal, make some porridge." She cooked the porridge.

The woman then gave her a little porridge, and presented her also with some of the fried grubs, saying : " Take this as a relish." But the frog appeared again, and this time to say : " No, do not use those worms as a relish, just eat your porridge as it is." So, when she had finished the porridge, she went and threw the grubs outside.

The woman then said : " Now come into the hut, and go up to the loft ; for I have a boy who eats people. To-morrow I shall notch your teeth without fail. By the way, my child, have you had any relish ? "

" I have," answered the girl .

The woman then made her go up.

The girl stayed up there until, the night beginning to clear, the woman went out to meet her boy coming and carrying on his shoulders a zebra which he had killed. He came to put down his load outside, and then entered the hut.

" There is a smell of something human," said he. " There is something that smells."

" Nonsense ! " said the old woman. " There is no particular smell here."

" Yes," rejoined he, " I perceive distinctly something that smells. I want to eat it."

" You are wrong, child," said the woman, " what goes to your nostrils, is it, perchance, my ulcer ? It is it that smells."

" That is not the smell I perceive."

Meanwhile the girl up there is shaking all over.

The boy then says : " Let me go up," and up he goes, but on the way he spills the salt, which was on a stand. So the mother says :

---

[2] The frog appears here as recommending obedience. In fact, its name, *bombwe*, reminds the natives of *bomba-we* " be obedient," but one should be slow to infer that this is the correct derivation. It scarcely agrees with the laws which Bwine-Mukuni follows in the formation of its words.

" O my child, what have you done ?   You have spilt my salt.   To-day what shall I put in that meat you have brought ?   Go away."
And she drove him away.

When he went off again to the bush, she notched the girl's teeth. Then, when daylight came, she put in the gap everything that can be seen here outside, cattle, fowls, goats, everything.   She made her eat all that.

When she had finished feeding her thus, she let her go back home. The girl just goes singing along the road.

The mother who had nursed her, saw her coming from a distance and said :   " That is my child coming."

And the girl had scarcely caught sight of her mother when she started this song :
" To be marked !—
Chorus.—" Doubly !   Doubly ! " [3] (repeated after each verse).
" She said :   Come and grind corn, Mother of Drums . . .
" She said :   Go and fetch water, Mother of Drums . . .
" She said :   Come and press here, Mother of Drums . . .
" She said :   Come and cook the porridge, Mother of Drums . . .
" She said :   Come and eat, Mother of Drums . . .
" I had found my mates gone . . .
" To be marked !—Doubly !   Doubly ! "

As she moves about singing her songs thus, her mother says :
" Now, my child, the porridge is ready."
But she refuses to eat.
" No," says the mother, " just eat a little porridge."
She will not take any.   She does not eat at all.

A day and a night pass thus without eating, then another day and night, then a third day and night.   At last the girl says to her grandmother :   " To-day I will sing a different song.   At night just take me to the bush."

" What is that ? " said the mother.   " Have they bewitched thee there where thou hast been ? "

" That is no bewitching," says the girl.   " I shall tell you where I have been."

" What hast thou brought ? " asks the mother.

" I went to have my teeth marked, that's all."

" But what hast thou brought ?   Hast thou gone for nothing ? "

" No," that is her only word.

When the night began to be dark, everyone in the village went to sleep.   So they could not hear her.   She then started her new song

[3] See note 4.

in her grandmother's hut where she was. In fact, nobody else heard. The song was as follows :

" (Up there) they said : Bite, bite, mother, mother !
" They said : Bite, bite, mother, mother !
" They said : Bite at our abode above the clouds.
" When the Lord above the clouds had sharpened my teeth,
" (He said) : Thou art Songore (*i.e.* : sharpen)
" *Woyeye !* Lord above the clouds, *thou* art Songo (*i.e.* : be sharp)." [4]

The grandmother said : " What art thou singing there ? "

" Don't ask," she answered, " just listen to what I sing. Let us go on singing."

She simply mingles tears with her song : " I pray you," she says, " let us go, let us go to the bush. Take me there and bring a hoe with you."

The grandmother then called the mother, saying : " Let us go with her."

So the mother took a hoe, and the grandmother too. . . . Coming to the bush, they clean away the grass, they make a floor. . . . Oh ! there she begins to vomit clothes. When she has finished, go on ! she vomits men. Then with her song :

" (Up there) they said : Bite, bite," etc. (as above).

She vomits cattle, she vomits goats, she vomits fowls. Everything that is here outside she vomits, vomits, vomits.

The people she has vomited then start building huts, others make kraals for the cattle, others build stables for the goats.

At the village no one hears anything. They are all asleep. But she is on foot with her grandmother, and they sing together :

" (Up there) they said : Bite, bite," etc. (as above).

Her people go on building huts and huts, while she sings. The cattle are grazing, boys are cleaning the milk-pails, the goat-herds herd the goats, those in charge of the fowls feed them. Other people go to fetch water. Everyone is occupied, but she is all in her song.

---

[4] This song explains the " Doubly ! Doubly," or, perhaps better, " In two places ! In two places ! *Kuwiri ! Kuwiri !* " of the preceding song. The earthly marking has been done by the old woman, but a celestial marking has been done at the same time " in our abode above the clouds." Soon it will be found that the other girls had received only the earthly marking. The notion of marking the women " below and above " is represented among the Ba-Sukulumbwe by notching not only their upper, but also their lower front teeth. *Woyeye !* is said to be simply an exclamation of satisfaction.

We may notice incidentally that, as early as the 10th century, the sharp teeth of some Bantu tribes were mentioned by Mas'oudi ; the Arab traveller who came several times to Kilwa of the Zendj

In the village everyone is still asleep. At last there appear some streaks of light. Then they say to one another : " Listen, there are people singing in the bush." Others say : " Yes, listen attentively."

As they listen they discover in the distance a number of fires, fires darting flames into the air from many places : " Great Heavens ! " say some of them, " Run away, it is war."

Others say : " No, no ! Let there be light first. Now, where could an army come from ? Besides, these really are songs. Well ! people who come to kill, do they sing ? "

As they listen more attentively, they hear distinctly the song : " (Up there) they said : Bite, bite," etc. (as above).

Now there is light in the village. The common people run away. Soon no more girls are to be seen there. A number of boys run away too. The girl from the bush there sees them and says : " What is it that makes them run away ? They do not know what has happened. Where I went to have my teeth notched, they say that probably it was just like the notching of my mates. No, notching of their teeth was a different thing. I went to get riches. Let me go and tell my fathers and uncles, my mothers and aunts, not to go away to the bush."

She then gets up with her escort. On the way she goes on singing :

" (Up there) they said : Bite, bite," etc. (as above).

Then : " Come back, my aunt, I know you. Those are my father and uncles, those are my aunts. And all of you, I know you."

Then it was that the shrill cry of joy went into the air.

But there those whose wives had left the girl alone, now beat them, beat them hard : " You," they say, " you did not go to have your teeth notched. You have brought no goods. You went to be marked with what is no mark at all."

Then they add : " Bring nothing at all ! Where have you been, you ? Your mate has brought cattle, goats, fowls, from the place where she went. Now you also go where your mate went and get a notching of the teeth worth having. Do you see ? Now she is a queen and has built quite a large town. To-day her mother is rich and honoured."

They saw the cattle, they saw all the things which are here outside. . . . " You," they asked again, " where have you been ? There is not a single thing which you have brought."

They go on beating them.

At last their mothers say : " Leave them alone, stop beating them."
Then only the boys stop beating their wives.
So the girl became a great queen. She then killed cattle. The people whom she had vomited simply waded in the blood. Her former mates ran away, no one knows where.
Finished.
NSOMEKA.[5]

(IN BWINE-MUKUNI.)

KUBANGWA !

Ncâkacita bantu.
Bênxiñina bâamba ayi " A tuye tukabangwe mêno."
Kulya nkwakacara, bañina bâmukaxa, bâamba ayi " Webo cara.
Kôya ukabanse maira." Wabansa.
Bâamba ayi " Kôya ku manxi." Waya wateka manxi.
Bâamba ayi " Kwesá upere." Waya wapera, wayambika.
Bâamba ayi " Kôponda." Waponda.
Nkwakaponda, bâamba ayi " Kôrya." A rakwe " Bênsuma baranxiya." Bâamba ayi " Kôxite bulyo, ulabajana."
Nkwakamana kulya, bâamba ayi " Ono kôya."
Kulya nkwakaya wajana bênxiñina tâbaboni tawu. Bênxiñina bâya nxira imbi, a rakwe watora imbi."
Kulya nkwakatora nxira imbi, wajana kacembere. Kacembere kâamba ayi " Ino wakonka-nxi ? "
" Ndayanda kubangwa mêno. Ndakaringa a bênsuma, bâkaya nxira imbi, a nebo ndêsá nenka kuno, nxibaboni tawu."
Kâamba " A ! kôxite, a nebo kuno ndicîxi kubanga. Kôya ukateke manxi, mwanângu."
Kulya nkwakañamuka kuya mu kuteka manxi, a nkata wamupa, waamba " Kôyumuna nkata."
" Ino nkata iri buyani ? "
Ayi " A ! kôyumuna bulyo nkata ya nsoka."
" A ! Nebo nxiyumuni nsoka tawu."
" O ! " kaamba kabombwe, " Tawu, kôyumuna bulyo nsoka iyo. 'Mwakwambira mucembere uyo utakaki. Iyo nsoka iyumune Kôya bulyo ukateke manxi."

<hr>

[5] This story, though typical enough, should not be taken as a perfect sample of the Mukuni language. The narrator, a man who has lived in different places, is apt to mix up several dialects. At present he lives at Kalulu's kraal in the Bu-Sori. His style shows, to a certain extent, how the old way of narrating once current among the Bêne-Mukuni is being transformed. In some respects it is an improvement. At any rate, the wearisome *bacu* ! is not iterated in every sentence.

Waya wateka manxi. Kâamba " Kôpera, wapera. Kâamba " Kwesá
ukuxe mapira apa pa cironda," wakuxa mapira pa cironda. Waamba
" Kôkanga," wakanga wabika mwiño. Nkwakabika mwiño kulya
" A ! " bâamba, " rino [6] kôponda." Waponda. A rakwe wamupa
nxima a mapira, waamba ayi " Kôbwenga mapira aya."
Nkwakaya wêsa bombwe. " A ! " bombwe ulamukaxa ku-
bwenga mapira, waamba " Tawu, utabwengi mapira ayo ; kôbuya
bulyo."
Amane kulya, mpêce waya mu kusowa mapira pansengwe.
Bacembere bâamba " Kwesá ono, kwesá mu manda, utante
pêjulu. Nko ari mwana wangu ulya bantu. Cîro ndaya kuku-
banga. . . . O mwana wangu, wabwenga ? "
A rakwe ayi " Ndabwenga."
A ! wamutantika pêjulu.
Nkwakatanta pêjulu, buxiku busé mu kuca, kwasarara, wamu-
cinxa mwana wakwe, wayumuna a cibise ngo wakajaya.
Nkwakayumuna cibise ulêsá akwe kwisá mu kutula pansengwe.
Nko kwĭnjira mu manda.
Waamba ayi " Cânunka buntu buntu. 'Mo ciri cinunka."
Bañina barakaxa, bâamba ayi " Tawu, tamo citônunka muno."
Waamba " Tawu, cintu citônunka ndacitêrera. Ndayanda
kulya."
Bâamba " Tawu, mwana, mpani ulatêrera cironda cângu ici. Nce
cinunka."
" Ta cinunki citônunka tawu."
A rakwe uyu nkwaya kujulu uko, ulatutuma bulyo.
Mwana wakwe ayi " Ntante-ko," wapukula mwiño uli pa rupingwe.
Nkwakapukula, bañina bâamba " O mwana, wampukwita mwiño
wangu. Sunu mbike-nxi mu ñama umu ? Kôya bulyo."
Mpâ ku mutandanya mwana wakwe.
Mpâkaya a rimwi kuya mu rundu, mpo pa kumubanga.
Cûnsa ri bwakaca,[7] ndye wakamulongera xintu xônse xiri pano
pansengwe. Wabika mombe, wabika bantu, a nkuku xônse, a
mpongo xônse, xônse wabika. Wamurixa, wamurixa.
Nkwakamana kumurixa, nko wakaya ku muxi.
Ute kuya ciimba.
Bamubone bulyo ku muxi bañina bâkamulera, bâamba " Ngo
woyu mwanângu ute kwĭsá."
Arakwe abone bañina, ayi :

---

[6] *rino*, Tonga for Mukuni *ono*.
[7] *ri bwakaca*. More common form *bwe buce*.

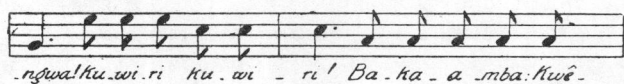

" Kubangwa ! Kuwiri ! Kuwiri !
" Bâkaamba : Kwesá upere, Nangoma. Kuwiri ! Kuwiri !
" Bâkaamba : Kôya ku mînxi, Nangoma. Kuwiri ! Kuwiri !
" Bâkaamba : Kwesá uxe-po, Nangoma. Kuwiri ! Kuwiri !
" Bâkaamba : Kwesá uponde, Nangoma. Kuwiri ! Kuwiri !
" Bâkaamba : Kwesá ulye-po, Nangoma. Kuwiri ! Kuwiri !
" Ndâkabajana basaama balayi. Kuwiri ! Kuwiri !
" Kubangwa ! Kuwiri ! Kuwiri ! " [8]

Aye a kuya, aimbe boobo ñimbo, bacu ! bañina baramwambira
" Ino, o mwana, ndaponda nxima."
Ta ari. Waikaka.
" Tawu, kôrya bulyo nxima."
Nxima wakaka, ta ari.
Waona buxiku bômwí. Cûnsa waona, xâba xôbiro. Cûnsa
wakaka, xâba xôtatwe. Cûnsa ulabaambira ba-nkambo yakwe,
ayi " Sunu ndaimba bulyo rwimbo rumbi. Maxiku tulaya,
mulantora ku rundu."
Bañina bâamba " A ! Sá, bâkakulowa nko wakaringa ? "
Waamba " Kundowa tawu. Ndamwambira nko ndakaringa
uku."
" Nxe wakareta nxinxi ? "
" Kuya mu kubangwa mêno bulyo."
" Ino wakareta-nxi ? Kuya bulyo ? "
Waamba " Tawu."
Bwe buxiye, bantu bôona. Ta batêreri tawu. Maxiku warub-
wesa rwimbo a ba-nkambo yakwe mu manda. Bantu bônse ku-

[8] This song is in Bu-Sori.   In Bwine-Mukuni it would run as follows :—
   " Kubangwa ! Kôbire ! Kôbire !
   " Bâkaamba : Kwesá upere, Nangoma. Kôbire ! Kôbire !
   " Bâkaamba : Kôya ku manxi, Nangoma. Kôbire ! Kôbire !
   " Bâkaamba : Kwesá utwe, Nangoma. Kôbire ! Kôbire !
   " Bâkaamba : Kwesá uponde, Nangoma. Kôbire ! Kôbire !
   " Bâkaamba : Kwesá ulye, Nangoma. Kôbire ! Kôbire !
   " Ndakabajana bênsuma bâunka. Kôbire ! Kôbire ! "

ñumfwa tawu. Ay' arurete rwimbo, waamba ayi :
" Bê : Suma,[9] suma, mama, mama !
" Bê : Suma, suma, mama, mama !
" Bê : Suma kwasu [10] ku mayoba.[11]
" Ku mayoba kwasu kwakam'anga mêno :
" Ndiwe Songole.
" Woyeye ! Kwa mayoba [11] ndiwe Songo."
Ba-nkambo yakwe ayi " Ulaimba buyani ? "
" Tawu, ka muñumfwa bulyo mbo ñimba. Ka twimba bulyo.
Ute kulira bulyo a rwimbo rwakwe. Ayi " Ka tuya bulyo, ka
tuya bulyo ku rundu. Kôntora bulyo, kôyumuna a rise."
Ba-nkambo yakwe bâita bañina ayi " Ka tuya akwe."
Bañina nko bâyumuna rise, a nkambo yakwe. Baraseba bulyo,
baraseba rubansa.
A ! Waruka citonje.
Nkwakaruka nsaru, " Sebenza ! " waruka bantu. A rwimbo
rwakwe :
" Bê : Suma, suma, mama, mama," etc. (as above).
Waruka mombe, waruka mpongo, waruka nkuku. Xônse xintu,
xônse xiri pano pansengwe, xônse waruka, waruka, waruka.
Bantu mbo waruka barayaka mânda, a bamwi barayaka citanga
câ mombe, a bamwi barayaka manda xâ mpongo.
Eryo bantu bônse bari mu muxi ta batêreri, baraona bulyo. Ulya
uli kooku uli imfwi a ba-nkambo yakwe. Bate kwimba :
" Bê : Suma, suma," etc. (as above)'
Eryo bantu batôyaka bulyo, batôyaka bulyo mânda. Mwine
rwimbo rwakwe ute kwimba. Mombe xite kulya, nsuwa xônse
bate kusuka, baximpongo bate kwembera mpongo. A baro baxiku-
langa nkuku bate kwembera nkuku. Bamwi batôya ku manxi.
Muxi wonse wêra kare. Eryo rwimbo rwenka :
" Bê : Suma, suma," etc. (as above).
Bari mu muxi barôna bulyo.
A buxiku butôsa mu kusarara. Nko bwasarara buxiku, bari mu
muxi bâamba " Ka mutêrera. Nko ciri cite kwimba mu rundu."
Bamwi basankwa bê " A musuwe."
Nko bâkasuwa, bâjana bulyo kuli miriro, iramwekauka
bulyo. Ayi " Bâna ! A mulonde, ni nkondo."

---

[9] *Suma*, Sori = Mukuni *ruma*. " *Cf.* in the tale *Njerenjere* (No. VIII.) the
expression ' Bite calico for me.' "
[10] *Kwasu*, Sori = Mukuni *kwêsu*.
[11] *Ku mayoba, kwa mayoba* " above the clouds." The Ba-Sori often use
these locatives in the sense of " God," just as for " king " they use the locative
ku-bwaro " at the court," and for " father-in-law " the locative *ku-makwe*, lit.
" at the affinities."

Bamwi bê " Bâna ! A buce. Ino baxinkondo bâswa kuli ? A kwimba ka baimba ! Sá, bêsá mu kujaya bantu baraimba ? "
Ino bâtêrera bo rwimbo rwenka :
" Bê : Suma, suma," etc. (as above).
Eryo a bari mu muxi a kuca bwaca. Bantu batôronda bulyo. A bârutundu ta bamo mu muxi. Basankwa bônse bâronda. A rakwe mwine " A ! Ncinxi câbarondexa ? Ta bakwe kucîxiba sunu. Nko ndakaya mu kubangwa mêno, bâkaamba bulyo 'Mpanxi mbwêce bwakabangwa benxiñina.' Ncômwi câkabangwa bênsuma, nebo ndakaya mu kuleta bubire. A nje mbabôxe batá, bataunki mu rundu, a bamá."
Bâñamuka bulyo, mwine a mulongo wakwe. A rwimbo rwakwe ute kuya ciimba :
" Be : Suma, suma," etc. (as above).
Ayi " Ka mubôra, má, ndamwïxiba. Abo mba batá, abo mba bamá. A mwebo ndamwïxiba."
Nko kuulubixa bulyo ngululu.
A ! Mbarya a ba-maka âbo bâkamuxiya mubyabo, barabauma bulyo, barabauma bulyo. Kwamba ayi " Mwebo ta mukwe kuya mu kubangwa mêno. Ta mukwe kuleta bubire tawu. Mwakaya mu kubangwa mêno â bulyo."
Kwamba ayi " A kuleta buboni tawu ! Ino mwebo mwakaringa kuli ? Kwakaringa mwenxiñoko, nko wakaya mu kubangwa mêno ; wareta rrombe, a mpongo, a nkuku. A mukonkere mwenxiñoko nkwakaya mu kubangwa mêno mabotu. Ino ngú waba mwami, wayaka muxi unene. A bañina sunu baxiye."
Bâbona rrombe, bâbona xintu xônse xiri pano pansengwe.
" Mwebo mwakaringa kuli ? Tawo nce mwakareta."
Barabauma bulyo ba-maka âbo.
A bañina bâbo a bâro " Ka mubareka, mutana kubauma. Ka baxite bêne."
Basankwa barabareka kubauma ba-maka âbo. Nko bâkareka, mwine waba mwami wajaya rrombe. Ajaye rrombe bâkaryata mu burowa bantu mbâkaruka, bamwi babye bâkamuronda, bâkaroboka.
Kêera.

NSOMEKA.[12]

<hr>

[12] When the boy Nsomeka came to tell this story to the compiler—which he did of his own accord—he was accompanied by a number of little boys from Kalulu's kraal, who came to do duty as a choir of angels to pick up the chorus at the end of each verse of the songs. The scene was quite animated.
Though this story reveals on the part of the Ba-Sori the great respect they had for their queens, whom they regarded as " sharpened from above," it did not prevent them from killing the last they had, a certain *Mukâmambo*. Two enormous mounds of ashes mark to this day the place where she lived.

XVI.—MOTHER, COME BACK.

This is what a woman did.

She was then living in the bush, never showing herself to anyone. She had living with her just one daughter, who used to pass the day in the fork of a tree, making baskets.

One day there appeared a man just when the mother had gone to kill game. He found the girl making baskets as usual : " Here now ! " he said, " there are people here in the bush ! And that girl, what a beauty ! Yet they leave her alone. If the king were to marry her, would not all the other queens leave the place ? "

Going back to the town, he went straight to the king's house and said : " Sire, I have discovered a woman of such beauty that, if you call her to this place, all the queens you have here will make haste to go away."

The following morning people were called together and set to grind their axes. Then they went. As they began to come in view of the place, they found the mother had once more gone to hunt.

Before going, she had cooked porridge for her daughter and hung meat for her. Then only she had started on her expedition.

They said : " Let us cut down the tree on which the girl is."

So they put the axes to it. The girl at once started this song :

" Mother, come back !
" Mother, here is a man cutting our shade-tree.
" Mother, come back !
" Mother, here is a man cutting our shade-tree.
" Cut ! Here is the tree falling in which I eat.
" Here it is falling."

The mother drops there as if from the sky :

" Many as you are, I shall stitch you with the big needle.
" Stitch ! Stitch! "

They at once sweep the ground. . . . The woman leaves just one to go and report [1] :

" Go," she says, " and tell the news." He goes. . . .

There at the town, when he came, the people asked : " What has happened ? "

" There," he said, " where we have been, I say, things are rather bad."

Likewise, when he stood [2] before the king, the king asked : " What

[1] The book of Job has in four different verses (I. 15–19) this detail of leaving just one man to go and report. It is common to a number of Bantu tales.

[2] It is rather noticeable that the Bêne-Mukuni of the tales, when appearing before a king, always stand, *imakana*. In some places the officials of the Chartered Company have tried to introduce the custom of making them

has happened ? "—" Sire," he said, " we are all undone. Your child alone has come back."

" Good Heavens ! You are all dead ! If that is so, to-morrow go to So-and-So's kraal over there and bring other people. To-morrow morning let them go and bring me the woman."

They slept their fill.

Next morning early, the men ground their axes and went to the place.

They too found the mother gone, while the porridge was ready there, and the meat was hanging on the tree. . . .

" Bring the axes." Forthwith they are at the shade-tree. But the song is already started :

    " Mother, come back," etc. (as above).

The mother drops down among them, singing in her turn :

    " Many as you are," etc. (as above).

They are dead. The woman and her daughter pick up the axes. . . .

" Halloo ! " said the king. " To-day let all those that are pregnant give birth to their children."

So one woman after another straightway brings forth her child. Soon there is a whole row of them.

There goes the whole band, making a confused noise.

When the girl sees that, she says : " There is no joke about it now. There comes a red army with the umbilical cords hanging on."

They find her at her own place in the fork of the tree.

" Let us give them some porridge," thinks the girl.

They just plaster the porridge on their heads, they do not eat it.

The last-born then climbs up the shade-tree, picks up the baskets which the girl was stitching, and says : " Now bring me an axe."

The girl shouts once more :

    " Mother, come back," etc. (as above).

The mother drops down among the crowd :

    " Many as you are," etc. (as above).

No, there is the troop already dragging the girl. They have tied her with their umbilical cords, yes, with their umbilical cords. The mother goes on with her incantation :

    " Many as you are," etc. (as above).

In vain. The troop is already in the fields and the *ngururu* [3] go

squat in their presence, as is done among other tribes. As far as I know, they have not succeeded. The Bêne-Mukuni will clap their hands readily enough, but to squatting they seem to have a rooted objection.

  [3] The *ngururu* or *ngululu*, or *ngubi*, are shrill sounds produced, generally by women, by moving the tongue rapidly right and left. They mean triumph or welcome.

up as far as God's abode, and soon the children are in the town.

As they reached it, the mother said : " Since you have carried away my child, I must tell you something. She is not to pound in the mortar, nor to go to fetch water at night. If you send her to do one of these things, mind you ! I shall know where to find you."

There is the mother going back to her abode in the bush.

The following day the king said : " Let us go a hunting." And to his mother he said : " My wife does not pound in the mortar. All she can do is to stitch baskets."

While the husband was away there in the open flat, the other wives as well as the mother-in-law said : " Why should not she also pound in the mortar ? "

When the girl was told to pound in the mortar, she said : " No." A basket of Kafir corn was brought to her.

The mother-in-law herself took away the meal from the mortar, and then the other women in their turn brought corn and put it all there.

So the little girl pounds, singing at the same time :

" Pound ! At home I do not pound,
" Here I pound to celebrate my wedding.
" Yepu ! Yepu ! [4]
" If I pound, I go to God's."

My little sister begins to sink into the ground. She goes on singing :

" Pound ! " etc. (as above).

She was in the ground as far as the hips, now she is as far as the chest.

" Pound ! ", etc. (as above).

Soon she is down as far as the neck. Now the mortar goes by itself pounding the grain on the ground, pounding on the ground. Finally the girl disappears altogether.

When nothing more of her is seen, the mortar still pounds as before on the ground.

The women then said : " Now what shall we do ? "

They went and called a crane, and said : " Go and break the news to her mother, but first let us know, what will you say ? "

The crane said : Wawani ! Wawani !

They said : " That has no meaning, go back."—" Let us send for the crow."

---

[4] Yepu is supposed to be an onomatopœa describing the efforts made by the girl, as if she were out of breath.

The crow was called : " Now what will you say ? "
The crow said : " *Kwá ! Kwá ! Kwá !*
" The crow does not know how to call. Go thou, quail. How wilt
thou do ? "
The quail said : *Kwalulu ! Kwalulu !*
" The quail does not know how to do it. Let us call the doves."
They said : " Let us hear, doves, what will you call her mother ? "
Then they heard :
    " *Kuku ! Ku !*
    " She-who-nurses-the-sun is gone,[5]
    " She-who-nurses-the-sun.
    " You who dig,
    " She-who-nurses-the-sun is gone,
    " She-who-nurses-the-sun." [6]
They said : " Go, you know how to do it, you."

.   .   .   .

The mother went. There she is going towards the town. She
carries medicines on a potsherd, also tails of animals (with which
she beats the air).
While she was on the road, she met a zebra :
    " Zebra, what art thou doing ?— *Chorus.—Nsenkenene* [7]
    " The wife of my father is dead. [8]   ,,
    " O mother ! You shall all die."   ,,
The zebra died. The woman went on, went on, went on, then
found people digging :
    " You who dig, what are you doing ?— *Nsenkenene.*
    " The wife of my father is dead.   ,,
    " O mother ! You shall die."   ,,
They also died. The woman went on and went on, then found a
man braying a skin :
    " Thou who brayest, what art thou doing ?—*Nsenkenene.*
    " The wife of my father is dead.   ,,
    " O mother ! You shall die."   ,,
When she reached the town there :
          1. " Let me gather, let me gather
             " The herd of my mother.
             " Mwinsa, get up.
             " Let me gather the herd.

[5] She-who-nurses-the-Sun is the proper name of the girl. A little further
she is called Mwinsa, and in another version " Child of God." The natives of
these parts have, generally, a number of names.
[6] Compare in my Compar. Gr. of Bantu, pp. 319, 320, the songs of the cock
announcing the disappearance of *Tanga-lo-mbibo* into the river. The two tales
are alike in some respects.
[7] *Nsenkenene*, meaning unknown.
[8] Here to call one's daughter " my mother " is found more endearing than
to call her " my child." A variant says : " The child of God is dead."

2. " Let me gather, let me gather
" The herd of my father
" Mwinsa, get up.
" Let me gather the herd."
She then heard the mortar still sounding right above the child.
So she sprayed one medicine, then another.
There is the child already pounding from under the ground.
Little by little the head comes out. Then the neck, and the song is
heard again :
" Pound ! At home I do not pound,
" Here I pound to celebrate my wedding," etc. (as above).
The child is now in full view. Finally she steps outside.
I have finished.
I am RUMBA. [9]

(IN BWINE-MUKUNI.)
MAMA, BWERA !

Ncâkacita muntu.
Mpêce kari mu rundu, kupora ku bantu tawu. Mwana uli umwí.
Uli ku cisamu, utôtunga ntumba.
Uko nkwakacita boobo, mpêce muntu nko kumuporera. Ajane
ñina waya mu kujaya ñama.
Nkwakaya mu kujaya ñama, ajane utôtunga ntumba . . . " Anu !
muno cixi muli bantu ! Uyu mwanakaxi mubotu obulya batô-
muleka ! Kumukwata bâmi, sá ? mu muxi mukare ba-mayoxa-
ñina ? "
Kulya nkwakabôrera ku muxi, kuya mu makarya, ayi " Nebo
ndabona-wo mwanakaxi, Nkambo, mwâ kubaita muno mu muxi,
bônse a bari-mo, bônse baraya ku-swa-mo."
Mumene nga kutamba bantu, a twembe bâkumba. Nga kuya
mu kumuporera, bajane ñina waya kare ku ñama.
Nkwakaya ku ñama ñina, a nxima wabapondera, a ñama wabaan-
gira, a kubika wabika.
Bê " Ono a tutebe cisamu ciri-ko warutundu."
A cîne a kucijata kuna kucitema :
" Mama, bwera.[10]
" Mama, nguno utema [11] muñumbiri wêsu.
" Mama, bwera.
" Mama, nguno utema muñumbiri, wawa.

---

[9] Rumba is a woman from somewhere near Broken Hill. Her language
differs a little from that of most of the Bêne-Mukuni.
[10] *Mama, bwera*, Sori for Mukuni *Má, bôra*.
[11] *tema*, Ñungwe for Mukuni *teba*.

" Mama, bwera.
" Tema, ngú wâ kuwa wakundira.
" Ngú wâ kuwa."
Waroka ñina :
    " Na mufuli, ndamutunga mu tungo
    " Tungu tungu ! "
A bêne pyá. Waxiya bulyo uli umwí wa kuya mu kuximika,
ayi " Kôyâ ukaximike." Waunka.
Kulya nkwakaya ku muxi, ayi " Mbuyani ? "
Ayi " Nko twaringa, ayi, nkubi uku."
Ayi aimakane, ayi " Mbuyani ? "
Ayi " Bâna ! Nkambo, swebo twamana. Mwana wako wabôra."
" Bacu ! Mwamana ! Ayi, sombi cîro kuli ba-Ndaba uku,
baye bakarete a bamwi bantu. Cîro mumene baye bakandetere
mwanakaxi."
Bâonenena.
Mumenemene bâkumba twembe kuya mu kutula-ko.
Bajane ñina waya kare, a nxima wabapondera, a ñama waba-
angira.
    " A mulete twembe."
Nko kujata muñumbiri . . .
    " Mama, bwera," etc. (as above).
Waroka ñina, ayi
    " Na mufuli," etc. (as above).
Bâfwa. A twembe bâtubwesaula. . . .
Ayi " Olo ! Sombi sunu bari a mafumo bônse a bamane kuxara."
Uli a rifumo wamutwa panxi, uli a rifumo wamutwa panxi.
Sombi mulongo kulya.
Kulya bwaunka bwaunka bwakokoma bwakokoma.
A kulanga-ko uyu mwanakaxi ayi " Sunu kwaretwa, kutôsa
bufubera, a nkowa."
Kumujana.
Ingayi " Tubape-wo nxima," nxima bâunga bulyo ku mutwi,
kuxirya tawu.
Mwanike watanta ku muñumbiri, wabwesa matumba âkwe ngo
utôtunga, ayi " A mubwese kêmbe " :
    " Mama, bwera," etc. (as above).
Waroka :
    " Na mufuli," etc. (as above).
Sobwe. Bwakaya kare. Bwakamuñantira rukowa, bwaka-
muñantira rukowa :
    " Na mufuli," etc. (as above).

A mu myunda bwaxika, a ngubi xâkata kwa Rêsa, a mu muxi bwaxika.

Kulya nko bâkaxika ku muxi, ñina ayi " Uko nko mutôtora mwana wangu, mwana wangu têxi kutwa, têxi kuteka manxi maxiku. Mwâ kumutuma mwana wangu, o ! nko ku kwanu." Ngulya ñina a kubôrera.

Cûnsa bânarumi ayi " Tukayare." A kubaambira bañina ayi " Mukaangu ta atwi, sombi kutunga ntumba."

Kulya nko bâkaya mu kuwesa bânarumi, mpêce bamwi bânakaxi-ñina a bênaxara-abo bê " A batwe-wo a bâro."

Nga bâkwinga kutwa-wo, " Sobwe."

A kumuletera katundu kâ maira.

A ñinaxara wabo a bwine busu wapakula, a kuleta-wo bakaxi ñina-abo, a kubika maira ônse mu nciri.

Watwa mwanike, watwa mwanike, ayi :

" Tu ! Kwêsu nxitwa

" Kuno 'natwira bwinga.

" Yepu ! Yepu !

" Ndatwa, ndaya kwa Rêsa."

Mwanike wangu utôya :

" Tu ! Kwêsu nxitwa," etc. (as above).

Waringa mu bukome, watana mu câmba :

" Tu ! Kwêsu nxitwa," etc. (as above).

Wari kutana mu câmba, watana mu nxingo.

Ono yenka nciri ite kuya cirundula panxi, yenka nciri ite kuya cirundula panxi.

A mwine mpinwa !

Uko nkwakaximangana mwanike, nciri ite kulira panxi : ayi " Ino tucite buyani ? "

Waya mu kwita kapomborwa " Kôya ukaximike kuli bañina, Ukaambe buyani ? "

Kapomborwa ayi ; Wawani ! Wawani !

Ayi " Tôcîxi, kôbora."

" A tutume cikwangara."

Waita cikwangara.

" Ino ucite buyani ? "

Bacikwangara : Kwá ! Kwá ! Kwá !

" Bacikwangara ta bacîxi kwita. Kôya, kancere. Ukacite buyani ? "

Kancere : Kwalulu ! Kwalulu !

" Kancere ta kacîxi. A mwite bacîba."

Ayi " Tuñumfwe, cîba, ukaite bañina buyani ? "

Bañumfwe ayi :

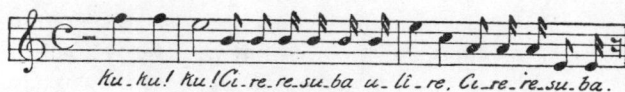

ku_ku! ku!Ci_re_re_su_ba u_li_re. Ci_re_re_su_ba.

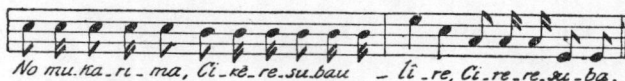

No mu_ka_ri_ma, Ci_ré_re_su_bau _ li_re. Ci_re_re_su_ba.

"Kuku ! Ku !
"Cirerêsuba ulîre,[12] Cirerêsuba.
"No mukarima,
"Cirerêsuba ulîre, Cirerêsuba."
Bâamba ayi "Kôya, ulicîxi webo."
. . . .
Bañina bâunka. Mbarya bâunka kuya ku muxi. A mânga
bâyumuna, a kubika pa cikaye, a micira.
Be baxike mu nxira, bâjana cibise :
"Cibise, ucita-nxi ? Nsenkenene.
"Wafwa mukâ tata. Nsenkenene
"Mawé ! Nônse mulafwa. Nsenkenene."
Wafwa cibise. Bêenda, bêenda, bêenda, bâjana bantu batôrima :
"No murima, mucita-nxi ? Nsenkenene.
"Wafwa mukâ tata. Nsenkenene.
"Mawé ! Nônse mulafwa. Nsenkenene."
Bâfwa a bâro. Bêenda, bêenda, bâjana uñuka cipaya :
"O uñuka, ucita-nxi ? Nsenkenene.
"Wafwa mukâ tata. Nsenkenene.
"Mawé ! Nônse mulafwa. Nsenkenene."
Bê baxike ku muxi kulya:

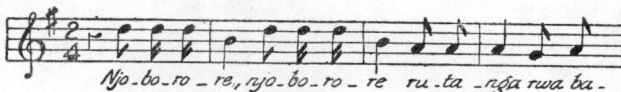

*Njo_bo_ro _ re, njo_bo_ro _ re ru_ta _ñga rwa ba_*

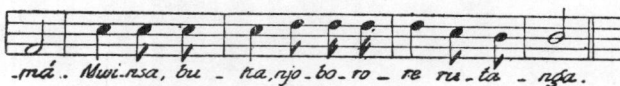

_má. Mwi_nsa, bu _ ka, njo_bo_ro _ re ru_ta _ ñga.

1. "Njoborere, njoborore
"Rutanga rwa bamá.
"Mwinsa, buka !
"Njoborore rutanga.

[12] *Ulîre=uli-yire*, Ramba and Sori for Mukuni *uli-ite* "he is gone."

2. " Njoborore, njoborore
" Rutanga rwa batá.
" Mwinsa, buka !
" Njoborore rutanga."
Bê baxike, bajane nciri yakarira kare pa mwana wabo.
Nga kuuguza-wo musamu, kuuguza-wo, kuuguza-wo.
" Njoborore, njoborore," etc. (as above).
Wakatwa kare mwana wabo, wakatwa kare mwana wabo, waka-swita mutwi pansengwe, ayi :
" Tu ! Kwêsu nxitwa,
" Kuno 'natwira bwinga."
A mwine mwana wabo wapula. A mwine mwana wabo a kuso-pokera pansengwe.
Ndamana.
Ndime RUMBA.

XVII.—BRANCH OFF, BLAZE OF FIRE.

At that time the king happened to cause friction between two wives, the mother of the superior children and the mother of the inferior children. When they were both pregnant, he went to the wilderness. And, when the girls had just been left behind, an order came to say : If one of them gives birth to a boy, she is my true wife ; but, if one of them gives birth to a girl, let her go and throw her child away."

At this very moment the big wife gave birth to a boy. . . . " It is a true child," she said, " that I have got."

The little wife also, soon after, was delivered, but the child was a girl : " Can it be," she said, " that I must go, mother, and throw her away."

As she was going round about at a little distance from the town, she found an old woman seated there. . . . " You now," she heard, " where are you going to ? "

" I am looking," she said, " for some one to bring up my daughter for me."

" Bring her here, mother. I will take care of her for you."

Now listen ! The man slept and slept again in the wilderness. At last he came back : " Have my wives," he asked, " been delivered ? "

" They have," he was told. " The queen has been delivered of a boy, and the little wife of a girl."

" And now," he asked, " where are they ? "

" The girl," they answered, " has been thrown away."

" Why," he asked again, " should they have thrown her away ? "

" What ! " they said. " Is it not you who said that the wife who should give birth to a girl had to go and throw her away ? "

.   .   .   .

Meanwhile the child is growing up at the place where we left her. In fact, she is of age already.

Then in the village some youngsters said : " Let us go where the grass has been burnt and set fire to the patches left there."

Then it was that the youngsters, among them one called Master Drums, were startled by Master Rabbit getting up all of a sudden and going into a hole. Said Drums : " Look, youngsters, here is Master Rabbit who has gone into a hole."

Cutting branches from a tree, they poked and poked into the hole. Then, did you ever ?, they heard this song :

" Branch off, branch off, blaze of fire.
          Chorus.—" What is it ?   What is it ? "
"That rabbits should get up for me.—*Chorus.*
" And come into my sleeping-place !—*Chorus.*
" You have hurt me, Drums.—*Chorus.*
" You have poked at me, poked at me,—*Chorus.*
" At me, a girl from your home.—*Chorus.*
" In that town of yours—*Chorus.*
" No girls go about,—*Chorus.*
" Only boys go about.—*Chorus.*
" Let them herd the cattle,—*Chorus.*
" Otherwise the cattle breed no calves." [1]—*Chorus.*

Then some one asked : " What do you say ? . . . Youngsters, let us poke again."

They came back to it and poked. Then again the song :

" You have hurt me, Drums,
          " Me, a girl from your home," etc. (as above).

They came back, cut the whole tree down, and poked with it. Again the same song. Would you believe it ? They came back : " Lads, let us poke once more." Again the same song. Now give it up. There they are going home.

The following morning Master Drums went to tell his uncle about the occurrence. " Believe me, uncle," he said, " my cousin is over there. She was singing to some people who had been where the grass has been burnt. This happened when, Master Rabbit having gone into a hole, we picked up a pole and started poking in that hole. Do not doubt, I say, your child is alive there, the one who was thrown away."

[1] That seems to mean " In that town of yours calves are preferred to girls."

The following morning, Great Heavens ! What a troop went together with the father ! And the very child they wanted they happened to find her outside. But just then she resolved to go in : " Poke in there with a pole," said the people. Then they heard : " Branch off, branch off, blaze of fire," etc. (as above). Meanwhile the father : " Let my child appear." His very own child then peeped out. . . . There ! . . . he got hold of her.

But the little woman there, why, bless me ! she was simply out of herself, tearing off her clothes and saying : " My child ! Where do you mean to take her to, the child you once drove away ? "

And the mother there, she literally flew into the air, saying : " Dear me ! Let her go. Here are all these cattle. Many as they are, and all that town too, we give it all to you and your people, old woman, you who have brought up the child for me."

There is the child now already at a distance. They are taking her to the town.

When they came there, what do you think ? At once they drove away the wife that had given birth to a boy, with her child following her as the tail follows the back. So she in her turn, there she is going, driven away, the great wife, who had caused the daughter of her mate to be rejected by deceiving the mother into throwing her child away.

Then Drums was the boy who married the girl, when she reached womanhood.

That is enough now. This little story too leaves the phonograph alone.[2]

I am MUNJE.

(IN BWINE-MUKUNI.)

SANDA, SANDA, RWANDO.

Mpêce bâparikira a bêna-bunene a bêna-bwanike. Bê bêmite mafumo, bâmi bâya mu rundu. Nko kwacara bârutundu, bê " Uyi akaxare musankwa, uyo ngo mwana wangu ; uyi akaxare warutundu, akaye akamusowe."

[2] In Northern Rhodesia one may hear a great variety of versions of this tale. Some were published in Anthropos (Vienna) in 1910, though with some alterations, even in the title, for which the compiler takes no responsibility.

In a Tonga version, which may be seen further (No. I. of the Tonga tales), instead of an old woman taking care of the child, we have a crocodile doing that good work.

Another version, in which, however, the rescued child is a boy, forms part of the long story " The Little Feather," which follows this one.

Cino cîndi bêna-bunene bâxara kare musankwa, bê " Ndaxara mwana."
A rakwe ina-bwanike, cê cînde-wo, wamuxara mwana, warutundu
. . . " Bacu ! Nje nkamusowe, ma ? "
Kuya cîndana, ajane kacembere karixite. . . . " Ino webo utôya kuli ? "
Ayi " Ntôya ciyanda baxikunderera mwana."
" Kôreta kuno, má, nkulerere-ko."
Bacu ! Bâona bâona mu rundu basankwa.   Cûnsa bâbôra. . . .
" Ba-makaangu bâkaxara ? "
Ayi " Bâkaxara. Ku câkwinda bâxara mwana musankwa, bêna-bwanike wa-rutundu."
Ayi " Ino mbari ? "
Ayi " Bâkamusowa."
Ayi " Bâkamusowera-nxi ? "
Ayi " A rimwi no mwakaamba : Uyi akaxare mwana warutundu akamusowe ! "

.   .   .   .

Nko kwakaya mwana ulakula, waba a cisungu.
Cûnsa ayi " A twende mu rwando kuya mu kutenta cisuwa."
Nko bari kwinda a ba-Xâa-Ngoma, bajane, bacu ! ngu Xâa-Sulwe wabuka kuya mu kwinjira, ku bulyango. Ba-Ngoma ayi " O ! Ngú Xâa-Sulwe wênjira ku bulyango, namata."
Kutema mu cisamu, bâcomya-ko, bâcomya-ko.   Bacu ! Bañumfwe-ko :
      " Sanda, Sanda, rwando.—*Niñi* ? *Niñi* ?
      " Basulwe kumbucira-n ! [3]   ,,   ,,
      " Bêsa kwïnjira kundara-n.[4]   ,,   ,,
      " Wancisa, Ngoma.   ,,   ,,
      " Wancomya-ncomya-n,   ,,   ,,
      " Ne musice wa kwanu.   ,,   ,,
      " Ku muxi wa kwanu   ,,   ,,
      " Ta mwendi baxikana,[5]   ,,   ,,
      " Muleenda barombwana.[5]   ,,   ,,
      " Beembere mombe,   ,,   ,,
      " Mombe xâpoowera.   ,,   ,,

[3] This final *n* here and in the following verses is not a characteristic of Bwine-Mukuni. It may be that in the mind of the narrator it stands for *–ne* " I, me."
[4] *ku-ndara-n*, from *lala* " sleep," Sori for Mukuni *ona*.
[5] *Baxikana, barombwana*, are not Mukuni words, but adaptations of Ñungwe *atsikana* " girls," *arombwana* " boys." Likewise the chorus *Niñi ? Niñi ?* is from Ñungwe. This tends to show that the story came originally from the Low Zambesi. The compiler, however, never heard it there, though at one time he collected there a large number of tales.

Ndye " Wo ! . . . Namata, a rimwi a tucomye-ko."
Bâbôra, bâcomya-ko :
" Wancisa, Ngoma," etc. (as above).
Bâbôra, bâciteba cisamu, bâcomya-ko :
" Sanda, sanda, rwando," etc. (as above).
Bacu ! Bâbôra . . . " A tucomye-ko a rimwi, namata." . . .
" Wancisa, Ngoma," etc. (as above).
Bacu ! Mbarya bâya ku muxi.
Cûnsa waunka Xâa-Ngoma, waya mu kwambira baixi : " Bâna !
Tá, mukwêsu uli kooku. Ute kwimbira bâkaringa ku rwando.
Mpêce Xâa-Sulwe wênjira ku bulyango, ndye twabwesa cisamu,
kucomya-ko. Mutaambi, ayi, mwana wanu bâkamusowa nko
ari."
Cûnsa kutambana, bacu ! a baixi. Bâjana a mwine uli
pansengwe . . . " Ono nkênjire."
Ayi " A mucomye-ko cisamu."
" Sanda, sanda, rwando," etc. (as above).
Sombi baixi " Mwana wangu a kaye mu kuboneka."
Sombi a mwine mwana . . . a kumujata.
Sombi parya, bacu ! kacembere kâparaya bulyo, ayi " Mwana
wangu, nkoxi aye ngo mwakatanda ? "
Sombi bañina parya bâulukira bo mujulu, bê " Bâna ! a muleke.
Nxi rrombe xônse na xifuli twamupa a muxi wonse ulya, kacem-
bere, o wanderera mwana."
Ngulya mwana kumutora ku muxi. Nko bâkamutora ku muxi
mwana, bacu ! bâkaxara musankwa mpêce a kubatanda, a mwana
wabo pa matako mucira. A bêne mbarya bâunka ; bâbatanda
bêna-bunene bâkamuñu ngaula mwana wa mubyabo ayi akamu-
sowe."
Mpêce mba-Ngoma bâkamukwata waba mwanakaxi.
Mpêce, kêera. A kâro aka kâreka cêra.
Ndime MUNJE.

XVIII.—*KAPEPE*, THE LITTLE FEATHER.

N.B.—This is one of the most popular stories all over the Zambesi region.
It was already published in 1908 in the Zambesi Mission Record. But
then several details were missing. Even now, no doubt, many are wanting.
A good many, however, borrowed from newly-secured versions have been added
to the one then published. As it is, it may be divided into fourteen songs.
Here the main text is from the mouth of a man called Mwana Mbirika, who
has given the whole story twice on the phonograph. Between brackets in
the Mukuni text are particulars supplied by three women who also know the
story quite well, viz., Munje, Mumba, and Rumba, whose names are familiar
from the preceding tales. All these contributors are illiterate. Mwana
Mbirika lives on the Buyuni stream in the Bu-Sori.
The story being rather long, we give the Bantu text on the same page as the
translation. This will make the references easier.

1st Song.

DRUMS, YOU HAVE HURT ME.

This is what was done at the home of a foreign chief.[1]

Those of his wives who were then pregnant remained at home while he himself went hunting elephants. The following words—who could believe it ?—were then given as having been uttered by him : " About these wives of mine who remain at home, this is my will, If one of them gives birth to a boy, she must throw him away. If a girl be born, that is the child I want to find here when I come back."

Bacu ! " O Mother ! Mother ! Mother ! Mother ! " said various women on hearing this piece of news, " Has he really uttered such words? Listen you, mates of ours, our husband, when going to the wilds, said that, if one of us gives birth to a boy, she must throw him away."

" Here now, that is a lie," said one woman.

" Great Heavens ! " said others, " we who are pregnant what shall we do ? "

Meanwhile the chief goes and goes an endless journey.

At this moment one of the wives finds she has given birth

WANCISA, NGOMA.

(Câkacitwa ku ba-mwene.

Ba-maka âbo â mafumo bâcara. Mpêce ibabo waya mu musansa. Ayi, bacu ! " Bamaka ângu abo bâcara, ndaya kujana uxi [2] axare musankwa akamusowe ; waxarwa warutundu, ngwexi [3] nkamujanemo."

Bacu ! Mbá bâxika bamwi bânakaxi " Má ! Má ! Má ! Bâamba boobo ! Bacu ! A muñumfwe, mo mata, bêbê su ndye bâri kuya mu rundu bâringa kwamba ayi : Uxi akaxare musankwa akamusowe."

" Anu ! nxâ kubeja."

" Bacu ! " bamwi, " so tuli a mafumo tukacite buyani ? "

Bacu ! Mu kwenda mu kwenda.

Cino cîndi wamutwa kare warutundu. A umwi wamutwa

---

[1] As a rule, a true national chief is called *mwami,* while a chief of foreign origin or self-imposed is more commonly called *mwene.* Such foreign chiefs are always supposed to be polygamous.

[2] *Uxi,* var. *uyi, uti, wexi,* Tonga *uzi* and *uti.*

[3] *Ngwexi,* var. *nguti.*

to a girl, while another has given birth to a boy.

" What is that ? " says the first. " Now what are you going to do with this boy to whom you have given birth ? Where are you going to take him ? "

" Nonsense ! " said a woman hearing that, " who ever, in the face of men,[4] said that he should be thrown away ? That is simply a lie invented by the excessive jealousy of the woman. How can she thus slander her husband, as if he had said such a thing ? "

Poor woman ! She put herself in movement. She took the child into what ? . . . into the reeds near the river, saying : " Can I throw away such a fine child ? No, by my mother ! Let me lay him down here, on what ? . . . on a piece of bark." [5] And there she got one and laid him gently on it.

Just then it happened that a little old woman, who was living in the bush, said to herself : " Mother ! I must go to look for something to eat." Heavens ! She hears a babyish cry like *mar̃ana*, and finds the baby asleep. Dear me ! Quick, she takes him in her arms, saying : " This is a child who

kare ngu musankwa.

" Bacu ! Ino uyu musankwa mucite buyani ngo mwaxara ? Mumutore kuli ? "

" Bacu ! Mba bani, mpa aringa bantu, ayi : A muye mumusowe. Anu ! Mbusuba bwakwe mwine bwalemenena. Abeje-bo ibaye a kwamba bo boobo ! "

A kubika-ko. Ku mutora mu yoyo, mu citete, ayi " Mwana wônse 'musowe ? A 'mwoneke, ma, a pa yoyo, pa cipande." A kumwoneka pa cipande.

Kulya nkwakamwoneka, bacu ! a kâro kacembere kaona mu rundu, a kâro ayi " Ma ! 'Nôya kusepa-wo, ma." Bacu ! Kañumfwe " Mar̃ana ! " kajane bo ngú ulirete. Bacu ! A kâro pimpituru " Ulaba mwana wonse uyu."

---

[4] That is " in the face of civilised people," opposed to savages living in the bush.

[5] In these parts there are trees whose bark is easily peeled off in cylinders or half-cylinders, which are used in the forest as dishes for porridge, honey, etc.. and are sometimes fashioned by children into small boats.

will become a genuine one, the whole of him."

You may fancy how she set to work. The child grew in no time, as people grow in stories only. The mother went regularly to deposit food (milk and porridge) there in the bush, while the old woman constantly took the milk to him to drink.

His mother used to call him Kalombe, but the little old woman changed his name to Mandu.[6]

One day it happened that his first cousin, a young girl called Drums,[7] said to her little mates : " Let us go and dig for field-rats where the grass has been burnt."

So the children went. Then they saw something like a rabbit start up and disappear into a cave in an ant-hill : " My mates," said Drums (*Ngoma*), " poke in there with a pole."

As they were poking they heard this :
" You have hurt me, Ngoma."
    Chorus.—" Let the drum roll."
" My mother is Mwinsa.[8]
                Chorus.
" She was the little wife.
                Chorus.
" She came to be pregnant.
                Chorus.

Bacu ! Bâbika-ko. Bacu ! Kwamba jûnsa wakula kare ngwa ku karabi. Mbañina kutora twa kulya pa cisuwa, kacembere aka kakamutorera akanwe mukaka kakamutorera.

Rìna ryakwe ryaringa Kalombe, kacembere kâmutumba rya Mandu.

Mpa a kwamba ayi mupyara wakwe, ngo Ngoma, ayi " A twende tukakabe mbeba mu rupya."

Mpa a kwamba ayi baye mu kukaba mbeba, babone wabundumuka anga ngu sulwe, kuya mu kunjira mu cicengo câ cûru. Ayi " Amutunke-ko cisamu, namata."
Mpa a kwamba ayi atunke-ko cisamu bañumfwe ayi :
" Wancisa, Ngoma."
                        A irire !
" Bamá mba-Mwinsa.   ,,
" Bâri mwanike.   ,,
" Bêsá kwĭmita.   ,,

---

[6] This introduction is due to Mumba, but it differs little from the introduction by other narrators.   What follows is from Mwana-Mbirika's version.

[7] Though the various versions of this tale do not agree regarding the name of the hero, they all give to his first cousin the name of *Ngoma* " Drum " or " Drums."

[8] *Mwinsa*, in Tonga *Mwiza*.   Another version says *Bêna-Mwinsa* " the mother of *Mwinsa*."   A variant of the whole verse is " My mother is in the town, *bamá bari mu muxi*."

" People came where I was born.
Chorus.
" Where, they said, is the child you have brought forth ?
Chorus.
" You have given birth to a boy. *Chorus.*
" Is it to herd cattle ? [9]
Chorus.
" You do not know how to bear children."
Chorus.
Ngoma said again : " You my mates, poke in another pole. Do you not hear how those things sing ? "
So they poked again, and heard again :
" You have hurt me, Ngoma," etc., (as above).
" Now," said Ngoma, " listen . . . . Bring another pole, but a long one."
So they poked with a long pole, but heard only the same song :
" You have hurt me," etc.

" Listen to that, mates."
At last they went home, then they said to their other mates : " Look here ! There where we have been we have heard a thing which was singing. To-morrow we must go again. . . ."
(Next morning) : " It is time to go. . . ." There they once more find something like a rabbit jumping into the cave.[10]

" Bêsá kunsemwa. A irire!

" Wasema mwana ciri ? "

" Wasema mwembexi. "

" Kucingula mombe ? "

" Tôcixi kuxara. "

A rimwi mpa a kwamba ayi " No basa, a mutunke-ko a cimwi cisamu. Ta muñumfwi mbo xite kwimbira xintu ixi ? "
Mpa a kwamba ayi atunke-ko cisamu bâñumfwa-wo :
" Wancisa, Ngoma," etc. (as above).
Ayi " No basa, a muñumfwe. Ka muleta cisamu, ka muleta ciramfo."
Batunke-ko ciramfo cisamu, bâñumfwa wo :
" Wancisa, Ngoma," etc. (as above).
" A muñumfwe, namata. . . ."
Mpêce pa kwamba ayi baye ku muxi, bê " Ayi, uko nko twaringa, namata, twañumfwa cintu câringa kwimbira. Cîro a rimwi tukana kuya."

" Bana kuya," bajane anga ngu sulwe wabundumuka.

---

[9] Some boys say that this verse means : " Is it to castrate cattle ? " The difficulty is in the somewhat uncommon word *cingula*, which some understand to mean " herd," while for others it means " castrate."

[10] In Mumba's version it is, all through, a cave in the rock, *cicengo câ ribwe*, but in the others it is either a hole in the ground, or a cave in the side of a big anthill. Mumba's version must be the oldest, considering that caves in rocks are unknown in this country.

Again they poke in it with a pole. The same song comes forth :
" You have hurt me, Ngoma." etc.

Then, instead of poking again, they pick up one of the hoes which they had brought to dig field-rats, and start digging. Dig ! Dig ! Dig ! What a surprise ! This is their brother. Quick ! They go and call the mother. But she says : " Do not tell his father when he comes back." They take oil to go and anoint him, they also take porridge to him.[11]

Abundumuke sulwe, bâtunkako cisamu :

" Wancisa, Ngoma," etc. (as above).

Mpêce mpa a kubwesa rise ndye bâkaringa kukabixa mbeba, kabu ! kabu ! kabu ! bajane ngú mukwabo.

Mpa a kuya a rubiro mu kwita bañina. A bâro ayi " Mutakabaambiri baixi bâbôra." A mafuta bâñamuna â kuya mu kumunanika, a nxima ka bamuretera.

2ND SONG.

AT MY FATHER'S ABODE.[12]

Well ! Well ! In no time the child was already a fine boy.

Some time after that the chief at length came back. They at once took to him the little girl that had been born during his absence, but she was not even able to walk, her eyes were covered with discharge, and her body was covered with itch.

MU MUXI MWA TATA.

(Bacu ! Cino cîndi mwana wabo waba kare musankwa.

Kwamba ayi cunsa, bacu ! bamwene bêsá bêbabo. Bâkalongera kare a kâna kâbo kâ rutundu, kâro a kwenda câara, a mu mênso koorofya,[13] a cipere câkatumba.

[11] The story of the wooer of the child of God is also well known at Sena on the Lower Zambezi, and, as told there, it has a number of episodes in common with our versions of the Upper Zambezi, but the beginning is quite different. There what the future son-in-law of God is most noted for is that he never allows himself to be deceived, much less to be deceived into doing anything wrong.   His father wants him to be called Manoel, a white man's name.   He says : No, my name is Zunguza, the name of my father."   The father changes himself into a leopard to see whether the son will throw a spear at him.   He says to the leopard : No, you are my father.   The father falls to the ground as if dead from the top of a high tree where he had gone to get honey, and the son is called to bury him.   But the child, though seeing the mangled bones there, refuses to bury them until he gets more convincing proofs of death, and then sees the father going back to his usual avocations, etc., etc.

[12] This particular song is only in Mumba's version.

[13] *Koorofya*, Ramba for Mukuni *bucere, macere* " discharge of the eyes." The whole expression in Bwine-Mukuni would be " *a mu mênso kujana koro a bungorobyo, ngo macere.*"

Now, at the little old woman's abode, the boy is already grown up. He has even hollowed out two drums.

When these were ready, he strung them on to his shoulders, and went with them as far as his father's town, but found that the people were still in the fields.

Dear me ! What a start he gave :

Wakula musankwa kuli ka-cembere. A kubesa ngoma wabesa xôbire.

Sombi a xîne ngoma a kuxi-pakata kuya mu kuxika ku muxi kuli bêxi, ajane baciri mu kulima.

Bacu ! Wabika-ko.:

Ndi ! Ndi ! Ndi ! Mu mu - xi mwa ta - ta, Ci - ri - ra mbi - ro ma - ri _mba, Ci - ri - ra mbi - ro. Ta mwe - nda Ka - lo - mbe, Ci - ri - ra mbi - ro ma - ri - mba, Ci - ri - ra mbi - ro .... Ci - ri - ra mbi - ro . —

" Ndi ! Ndi ! Ndi !
1. " At my father's abode,
" Chorus.—What wakes up speed is the sound of calabashes, what wakes up speed.
" There is no room for Kalombe.—Chorus.
2. " By mother ! O my little sister !—Chorus.
" Only for a maiden !—Chorus.
3. " My father said :—Chorus.
" If you give birth to a boy—Chorus.
4. " Go and throw him away !—Chorus.
" Nonsense ! You are telling lies."—Chorus.
" Ndi ! Ndi ! Ndi !
" Mu muxi mwa tata.[14]—Cirira mbiro marimba, cirira mbiro.[15]
" Ta mwenda Kalombe.—Chorus.

[14] Mwa tata, Sori=Mukuni wa batá.
[15] Mumba says that Cirira-mbiro-marimba is one of the names of the boy. As a variant she gives cirira-mbiro.

" *Mama ! Kakwasu,*[16]—*Chorus.*
" *Sombi kamware !*—*Chorus.*
" *Tata walawire :* [17]—*Chorus.*
" *Wafyara kalombe*[18]—*Chorus.*
" *Kóya ukapose*[19]—*Chorus.*
" *Kanxi ! Mwabepa.*[20]—*Chorus.*

Some one said : " Do you hear the drums that are being sounded over there ? "

Then the women and the slaves gathered into a heap together with the man, but found nobody there. So they went to hide themselves. Then they saw the boy come out and strike again :
" At my father's abode," etc (as above).

Bacu ! He has already disappeared in the bush and goes towards the old woman's abode carrying his drums.

The following day the people set out with the father to find out where the drum-beater had gone. All of a sudden some one said:
" Here he is ! " He had already brought out one of his drums.

" Now," they said, " to-day let us hide and see who he is who beats the drums."

Then they all made themselves as small as they could, including the father. No mis-

Bamwi ayi " A muñumfwe ngoma xitôrira kooku."

Bârundikira-ko bônse a ibaye, bajana tawo muntu. Bâyuba. A rimwi ayi bayube, babone waswa-ko. A rimwi watarika :

" Mu muxi mwa tata," etc.

Bacu ! Wacirukira kare pa cisuwa, a kuya mu kuxika pa kacembere a ngoma xâkwe.

Cûnsa bâswa a bêxi a kulanga kwakaita xikulixa ngoma. Bacu ! bajane ngú. Waisuxa kare ngoma yakwe.

" Ono sunu a muyube, tubone ute koomba ngoma."

Bacu ! A bêne a kubwantama, a bâro bêxi kubwantama. Bacu ! Babone bulyo ngu

---

[16] *Kakwasu,* Sori=Mukuni *kakwêsu.*
[17] *Tata walawire,* Sori=Mukuni *Catá bâkaamba.*
[18] *Wafyara kalombe,* Sori=Mukuni *waxara kasankwa. Kalombe* is here at the same time a common noun and a proper name.
[19] *Kóya ukapose,* Sori=Mukuni *kôya ukakasowe*
[20] *Kanxi I Mwabepa,* Sori=Mukuni *Ano ! Mwabeja.*

take that is his son, he recognizes him at first sight. Only he is buried in fine clothes.

Heaven help me ! He strings his drums on his body, then taps them. No delay, one drum already sounds.

" Assuredly ! " says the father, " that is my child. Have they deceived me thus ? And the little old woman herself thus practises deception on me ! There he is beating the drums. You, children of tendons, quick! Get hold of him."

No, they just remain hidden. They hear him then poking the fire.[21]

" At my father's abode," etc.

Good gracious ! They find themselves shivering with some ill-defined emotion, they simply shiver : " That will not do," says the father, " you spurious children, get hold of him."

At this moment the slaves fly at him and surround him. The father himself holds him in his arms : " Is not this my child ? " he says.

Heaven help me ! the little woman on her side springs like a wild beast, saying : " He is my grandson."

There is a real fight between the father and the little old woman, the man saying : " I tell you, he is my child."

mwana wabo kwé. Sombi bajane ulîpirite mu mînjira.

Bacu ! A mwine utôxipakata. Bacu ! Bañumfwe wômora-wo. Cino cîndi nje eyi yarira.

Mpo bâringa bêxi " U ! Ngu mwanângu ulya. Ano bâkancenjeka bo. A kacembere katôncenjeka bo. Anu uyu ngo utôrixa ngoma. Ka mwendexa, no bâna ba mikaxi mumujate."

A bêne a kuyuba, bacu ! bañumfwe wakunka-wo :

" Mu muxi mwa Tata," etc. (as above).

Bacu ! bajane batôtetema bulyo batôtetema. Mpo bâringa bêxi " Akaka ! No bâna ba bêne, a mumujate."

Bacu ! Cino cîndi ka bauruka bo baxa waá A bêne bâmujata kare . . . " Tê mwana wangu ? "

Sombi, mpâkaringa kacembere, kâaramuka bo ayi " Muxikulu wangu ! "

Macu ! Cino cîndi sombi câjatana kare a bêxi. Bacu ! Bê " Mwana wangu ! "

---

[21] " Poking the fire," metaphor for " beating the drum."

(Then, turning to his own people) : " And you, why did you deceive me thus ? "

" It was your queen," answered the people, " who said that the woman who gave birth to a boy should throw him away."

" Did I ever say such a thing ? " asked the man.

Then the little old woman, who had nursed and reared the child ! Talk of the presents in the shape of iron tools and heads of cattle which she received.

As to his child, the father dividing his town in two, gave him one half with a number of slaves and cattle.

Then the mother said to the boy : " You must go and marry the daughter of the Rain-Lord." [22]

" Ino mwebo mwakancenje-kera-nxi ? "

Ayi " Sombi ku câkwinda mbo bâkaamba ayi Mwakuxara musankwa, mukamusowe."

" Ndakaamba boobo ? "

Mpêce kacembere kâringa kumulera, sombi a xêra a Ꭓombe.

A bâro bêxi a mwana wabo bâmupaswita-ko muxi wakwe wa baxa bâkwe a Ꭓombe.

Mpêce bañina bâkacita ayi " A baye mu kukwata mwana wa Rêsa."

---

[22] " The Rain-Lord." Though in previous tales we have translated *Rêsa* simply by " God," here it seems more appropriate to translate it rather by " Rain-Lord," as it is principally in this character that God manifests Himself all through this tale. Besides, he is here supposed to have a wife and daughters, and this, even in fiction, hardly fits in with our notions of a pure spirit. The late A. C. Madan, the East African scholar, would have the difficulty solved by saying that throughout this tale " child of *Rêsa* " or " child of God " simply means " a Christian." According to him the wooer of the child of God would be simply a non-Christian wanting to marry a Christian, and the whole tale would be an echo of ancient Catholic missions. In my opinion, the tale, being better known precisely among the most independent nations of Central Africa than among those that were once under missionary influence must have a much more ancient origin. Besides, we shall see our hero " examined " precisely about laws unknown to most Christians, such as that of shunning the mother-in-law and that of working some time for the father-in-law.

3RD SONG.

PRETTY LITTLE BIRD, A FEATHER !	KÔNI KAWEME, NGARA !

So the boy said : "Lads, I am going to marry."

"Where," said the boys, " are you going to take your wife from ? "

" I ? " answered the boy, " no common woman will do for me, be she the daughter of a king ; the very child of the Rain-Lord, that is the one I am going to marry."

" Are you able to reach the place ? "

" I shall reach it."

Then : " Mother, cook some porridge for me, and put it in a pot."

She cooked some.

Then he said : " If ever this porridge cools, mother, you may say that your child is going to die." [24]

He got up. There he is taking long strides and falling into a path which leads him to a meadow.

Just as he was entering the meadow, he found there a little bird at rest, which allowed him to pass his hand on his back. " How nice it would be," he said, " to take a feather from

Ayi " Nebo, namata, ntôya mu kukwata."

Ayi " Utôya mu kukwata kuli ? ' '

Ayi " Nebo kukwata muntu bulyo tawu, na abi mwana wa mwami ; sombi mwana wa Rêsa ngwece ngo ntôya mu kukwata."

Ayi " Ukaxike uko ? "

Ayi " Ndaya nkaxike."

[Ayi " Ka muponda nxima, má, mukabike mu nongo."

Bâponda.

Ayi " Ito ikatontora, má, mula kaamba ayi : Ula kafwa."]

Wañamuka. Ngo woyu wasowayira-mo, wawita mu nxira kuya mu kupora [ku riwesa.

Nkwakapora ku riwesa ajane kayuni karixite, kukarambika ayi " Kâbota kayuni aka kukuxa-ko ngara ya kufwara nebo pa kuya mu kweba."

---

[23] *Kôni kaweme*, Ramba, Sori, etc., for Mukuni *kayuni kabotu*, pretty little bird.

[24] This interesting detail, from the narrative of the woman Munje, reminds the compiler of something of the same kind, which he read once in the *Contes Lorrains*. Unfortunately, having no longer the book at hand, he cannot give particulars. He just remembers that there the detail is compared with a similar one in an Egyptian tale.

such a beautiful bird, so as to put it on while I go courting! "

Now : " Let me get hold of it," the little bird slips away from his hand. Again : " Let me get hold of it," again it slips away. There it is taking him to a distance out of the way. . . . . " Well," he says, " I will not go back, I must get hold of this little bird, wherever he may be going to stop." He starts singing :

" Pretty little bird, a feather !
" For me who am exhausted, pretty little bird, a feather !
" For me who am exhausted, pretty little bird, listen !
" For me who am exhausted, that I may go with them,[25] listen !
" For me who am exhausted, that I may bring a feather thither !
" For me who am exhausted, that I may put it on when courting.
" For me who am exhausted, Ximukunkulu,[26] for me who am exhausted.
" Pretty little bird, a feather ! [27]

The feather kept at a distance, kept at a distance, kept at a distance. The song was resumed :
" Pretty   little   bird," etc.

Ino "Ncate" kâteximuka ; ino " Ncate," kâteximuka. Nka ako kâmutora ku muraxa mumbi. . . " Nebo kubôrako sobwe, sombi nkakajate aka kayuni, a kati kaye mu kwera." Ayi :

" *Kôni kaweme, ngara !*
" *Ne ngara, kôni kaweme, ngara !*
" *Ne ngara, kôni kaweme we !*
" *Ne ngara, 'na kuya nabo we !*
" *Ne ngara, tukarete-ko ngara.*
" *Ne ngara, tukafware pa kweba.*
" *Ne ngara, Ximukunkulu, ne ngara.*
" *Kôni kaweme, ngara ! "*

Yapereba, yapereba, yapereba :

" Kôni kaweme, ngara," etc. (as above).

---

[25] " With them," that is " with the divine protection."

[26] Mumba says that Ximukunkulu is the name of a young brother whom our hero has taken as a companion.

[27] Rumba says that the little bird was the very child of the Rain-Lord, thus transformed and sent by her father in order to try the wooer. This song is only in her version and in Mumba's.—In these verses the singer plays on the double meaning of *ngara*, viz. : (*a*) I can do no more, I am exhausted, (*b*) a feather, a mane, a charm.

The little bird fled, the little bird fled :
" Pretty little bird," etc.
The boy was tired. He said :
" Let us sleep here, to-morrow very early we shall try again."
When it dawned he made a fresh start :
" Pretty little bird," etc."
Then, as he happened to come in sight of a hut standing by itself, half-ruined, without grass on the roof, without so much as a doorway, belonging to a little old woman, there he found the little bird perched on the house itself.

As he came near the little old woman, she said : " You have put in an appearance, my child." [23]

" I have put in an appearance, mother."

" Now, where are you going to, my child ? "

" I was just following that little bird, as I wanted to take from it a feather, and to put it on where I am going to look for a wife."

" This little bird," said the woman, " is one that shows me my food ; it cannot be caught by anyone. Now, with regard to your marriage, where are you going to get a wife from ? "

" I am going," says he, " to marry the daughter of the Rain-Lord."

Kâronda, kâronda, kâronda :

" Kôni kaweme, ngara," etc.
Warema " A toone ano, a rimwi jûnsa tukafume."

Bwaca, wabika-ko :

" Kôni kaweme, ngara," etc.
Ingayi kuya mu kupora ku kânda kômwi kafwemukite kâ kacembere, katafumbitwe, kata-cite a mulyango wônse, ajane a karo kayuni nko kâya mu kwĭ-kara kujulu rya manda nkwece.

Ay' axike pa kacembere, ayi
" Waboneka, mwana wangu ? "

Ayi " Ndaboneka, má."

Ayi " Ino utôya kuli, o mwana ? '
Ayi " Ntôsa cikonkera kayuni ako, nkuxe-ko ngara, mfware pa kuya mu kweba."

Ayi " Aka kayuni nko kate kundwita xâ kulya xângu, ta kajatwa ku muntu bulyo tawu. Ino kukwata kwako utôya mu kukwata kuli ? "

Ayi " Ntôya mu kukwata mwana wa Resa."

---

[23] By the laws of Bantu politeness, the first greeting must come from the person visited.

" Well," she says, " if you are going to marry the daughter of the Rain Lord, first stay and sleep here to-night, my child ; you will go without fail to-morrow. Let me first cook some porridge for you to eat. Meanwhile get hold of that fowl there to make a relish for us." [29]

The boy caught the fowl and roasted it, while the old woman was stirring the porridge for him. He took his food.

When he had finished, he went to cut firewood for the little old woman and brought it to her : " Yes, that is right," she said, " you child, my brother, you have cut for me a little firewood."

Night came, they fell asleep.

As soon as the night cleared, the boy said : " Now I make a start."

" Before you go," said the woman, " let me give you the feather you want."

So she got hold of the little bird on the hut, plucked out one of his feathers, and gave it him, saying : " Now you have to go on your own account, and you shall find all sorts of difficulties on the road. It is God who will put those difficulties in your way. But just stick this feather in your hair. You will only have to speak exactly as this

Ayi " Mbo utôya mu kukwata mwana wa Rêsa, kôxite oone pano sunu, mwana wangu. Ulaya kuya cîro. Tanguna nkupondere nxima pano ulyewo. A nkuku irya cata tubwenge nxima."

Wajata nkuku a kukanga waikanga, kacembere kâmupondera nxima. Warya.

Ay' amane kulya, waya mu kuteba nkuni kutebera kacembere, wamuletera. " E, má ! mwana webo, mukwêsu, wantebera-wo tukuni."

Kwaxiya bâona..
Mbwe buce, ayi " Ono ntô-ñamuka."

Ayi " Tanguna nkupe ngara nje wari kwïsá cikonkera."

A bêne kukajata kayuni kari pa manda, a kunonkora-wo kapepe, a kumupa, ayi " Ono unôya mwine a kuya cibona mimpindikwe mu nxira. Mimpindikwe iyo mbêxi bana kucita ba-Rêsa. Iyi ngara njece fwara pa mutwi. Una kuya mu kwamba 'mwece umo ina kuya kukubuxa ngara îne. Kôya bulyo, ka rusarara bulyo, mwana

---

[29] At this point some narratives introduce the episode of the worms taken out of the leg of the old woman, as related above in the tale " To be Marked ! " As it seems decidedly more in place in the former story, we have omitted it here.

badge will suggest to you. Go
in peace, may your journey be
prosperous, my child."

So he stuck the feather on his
head, and said good-bye.[30]

wangu."

A kuikunga mu mutwi, a
kusowayira-mo.

4TH SONG.

| IS THIS THE ROAD ? | IYI NXIRA TUINDE ? |

As he went on his way, he
found the road covered with
excrements . . . [31] " Now this
filth ! " he said. " Where am I
going to tread ? "

Ingayi " Ñende-ko, ajane
fimatuxi mu nxira muliswite
. . . . " Ino utu tuxi ! Ndya-
tire kuli ? "

Ah ! He felt the little feather
fidgetting there on his head,
and at once started this song :

A ! Wañumfwa kapepe
kâkwe kuñañara-wo mu mutwi,
ndye pa kutatula rwimbo :

THE HERO : How now ! Little feather !

CHORUS : When I am eaten-eaten, I am bitterness, when I am
eaten-eaten.

THE FEATHER : These are ordinations of God.[32]   (*Chorus as above.*)

THE HERO : Is this the road we have to take ?—*Chorus.*

THE FEATHER : That is not the one, Master Mandu.—*Chorus.*

Rather go by this one.—*Chorus.*

These are ordinations of God.—*Chorus.*

In which he has intermixed charms.—*Chorus.*

When I was there.—*Chorus.*

---

[30] In the Sena tale of Zunguza, instead of the wonderful feather, we have
seven insignificant beings acting as guides to the hero, viz. ; a mouse, a reed-
rat, a wood-borer, an ant-bear, a spider, a crab, and a fire-fly.

[31] In the allegorical sense the excrements by which our hero finds himself
faced are, probably a coarse foreign language, something like what Kitchen
Kafir is for the Bêne-Mukuni a mixture of low English expletives and Dutch oaths.
In the Tonga tale *Nseyandi* (see further) a child sent from heaven is described
as unable to stand even the mention of the word " luck." The word used here
for " excrements " is *fi-ma-tu-xi*, made up of *ma-tu-xi* for Ñungwe *ma-tu-bzi*
with the deprecatory Ramba prefix *FI* (notion of filth).

[32] Var. " These are laws of God, *nga mâno â ba-Rêsa.*" The name of God
has here the prefix *BA* as a sign of respect. The Ba-Sara, who say " *ngo mâno
â ba-Reza* " also possess the whole of this song, but put it in the mouth of a
heroine in a tale apparently copied from this one. She is a woman going to
be married to the beast Rain-bow, who has already eaten several wives, because
they did not know the laws, *mâno*, of the place. But she, like our hero, has
got from an old woman a charm which brings her through every trial.
That charm is a cock's tail feather, *munimba wa kombwe.*

Bâna ! Kapepe !
Ka ndiwa-ndiwa, ndi bululu, ka ndiwa-ndiwa.[33]
Nga marere â ba-Rêsa.—Ka ndiwa-ndiwa, etc.
Iyi nxira twinde ?—Ka ndiwa-ndiwa, etc.
Iyi ta ixi, Xâ-Mandu.—Ka ndiwa-ndiwa, etc.
Ñga marere a ba-Rêsa.—Ka ndiwa-ndiwa, etc.
'Mo bâpandira mânga.—Ka ndiwa-ndiwa, etc.
Ka ndiwo.[34]

He saw the filth simply disappear, and passed on.

He went further. As he was saying : " Now let me go slowly," he saw in front of him the River Putu,[35] with no end on any side. So he stopped once more and sang :
" Come now ! Little Feather ! " etc.
" This river too, shall we cross it ?
" Cross it, Master Mandu," etc. (as above).

Well ! Well ! This river itself, even the Putu, he just went across.

The young boy went on taking long strides, until he saw him-

Abone tuxi mwá, wainda.

Wabika-ko. Ingayi " Ñendeko panini," ajane-ngu mulonga Putu, a 'mo wera ta muboneki. . . . A rimwi waimakana, ayi :

" Bâna ! Kapepe ! " etc.

" A waro mulonga twinde ?

" Ka mwinda, Xâ-Mandu," etc.

Bacu ! A wine mulonga a mwine Putu wainda.

Kâsowayira-mo kasankwa, kâwarayira-mo, kâwarayira-

---

[33] Var. in Ramba *Ka ndibwa-ndibwa*.

[34] Sutherland Rattray, in *Some Folk-Lore in Chinyanja*, p. 198, writes that the supreme Being recognised by the natives among whom he has been living " takes no concern whatever in the affairs of mankind as the spirits do." " He is," he says, " totally indifferent to good and evil." Is not this a rash assertion in the face of the above essentially Bantu song tracing distinctly to God the power of charms, and of a number of other positive facts, such as the ordeal poison *mwabvi* so graphically described by Sutherland Rattray himself, and those loud calls for vengeance, of which the *Ñanja* folklore is full, from little birds, little dogs, and little children ? Where is the M'ñanja who doubts that the supposed virtues of charms, of the *mwabvi*, etc., come from a God who keeps his eyes wide open ? For the generality of the Bantu God is essentially Providence, but he is also the Judge.

[35] When asked what is and where is the river *Putu*, the narrators point to the far north-north-east of Northern Rhodesia, and say that it is one of the *mironga ya kare kare* " rivers of old." They compare it to the Kafue (Kafubwe) when it is full, miles and miles broad. Must, perchance, our thoughts go to the Red Sea, or to the Nile ? Among the Western Bantu *Putu* has a somewhat different meaning. There it means Portugal. The old Bêne-Mukuni say that *Rucere*, a kind of demi-god, whom they credit with having brought the first Bantu to Central Africa in canoes coming from the North-West, was a brother of the original *Mwine-Putu* " the Lord of Putu."

self face to face with a herd of
elephants standing, looking at
him swinging heavy shoulders,
and no sign where it ended :
" Well, now ! " says he, " what
am I going to do ? "

This time he gets hold of his
little feather and sings :

" Come now ! Little feather ! "
etc.

" Here again shall we pass ?
" Let us pass, Master Mandu,"
etc. (as above).

Well ! Well,! The elephants
over there went out of the road.
There they are dispersing themselves, let them go.

He went on and on, until he
saw in front of him a big mountain built by God with wall
upon wall, all abrupt . . .
" Oh ! " he says, " this mountain ! Where are we going to
pass ? "

Once more he took hold of
his little feather, then sang :

" Friendly little feather! " etc.
" This road too ! Shall we get
over it ?
" You will pass, Master Mandu.
" These too are ordinations of
Providence," etc. (as above)

He saw the mountain vanish,
dispersing its rocks. So he
passed on. Good Heavens !
Did he not then put on speed,
and more speed ? But there he
found buffaloes. And those
horns, how twisted they were !
He sang :

" Friendly little feather ! " etc.
(as above).

mo, kajane nsofu xiri imfwi,
xitôñonga bulyo, a kuxêra ta
xiboneki. . . .   " U !   Ino
ncite buyani ? "

Wajata bo kapepe kâkwe :

" Bâna ! Kapepe ! " etc.

" A woawo twinde ?
" A twinde, Xâ-Mandu," etc. (as
above).

Bacu !   A xîne nsofuꝑa nko
xâringa xâswa-mo mu nxira.
Mbarya kumwayika bañama ka
baya.

Wênda-ko, wênda-ko ajane
ngu murundu wayaka wa-
ciyama . . .   " A !   Uyu
murundu !   Twinde kuli ? "

Waxikira   kujata   kapepe
kâkwe :

" Ndó kapepe ! " etc.
" A yaro iyi nxira twinde ?

" Mulainda, Mandu,
" Aâro aya nga marere â ba-
Resa," etc. (as above).

Abone mwá wamwayika mu-
rundu mparampara. A mwine
wainda. Bacu !   Kubika-ko,
kubika-ko, ko, ajane ni ñati.
Sombi mapango câkonkobera.
Ayi :

" Ndó kapepe ! " etc. (as above)

Well ! Well ! The buffaloes themselves scraped the ground, and he went on.

He went on did the little boy, taking long strides once more, but without any particular difficulty, until he met lions, and these in such numbers that he saw no end of them. . . ' Ugh!''

Holding his little feather, he sang :

" Come now ! Little Feather! " etc. (as above).

He saw them too vanish. So he went quietly along, but he had not finished yet. There he now sees long, long snakes, a confused mass of them, and no end of them in view. . . .
" Ugh ! " says he, " Now these snakes ! Where am I going to pass ? "

He simply once more takes hold of his little feather and sings :

" Come now ! Little feather! ", etc.

" These snakes too !'' etc. (as above).

Like the rest they vanish. So he goes on throwing forward one leg after the other. . . .

And that over there is the city ! [36]

Bacu ! A xîne ñati xâparula wainda.

Kâsowayira-mo kasankwa a kusowayira-mo, eryo karukutixe eryo, kajane bo nkaramu, a kuxêra a kuxibona tawu. . . .
" U ! "

Wajata kapepe kâkwe :

Bâna ! Kapepe ! " etc. (as above).

Abone mwá xâmwayika. Wasowayira-mo, wasowayira-mo. Mpâ kwamba ayi asowayire bobulya, wajana bo nsoka xâtandabara xâpirinkana bo, a kuxêra kuxibona tawu. . .
" U ! " Ino ixi nsoka ! Ñindire kuli ? "

Wajata bo kapepe kâkwe :

" Bana ! Kapepe ! ", etc.

" A xâro ixi nsoka ! " etc. (as above).

Abone mwá xâmwayika. Warawayira-mo a kurawayira-mo. . . .

A ku muxi.

[36] The Zunguza of the Sena tale does not reach God's abode so easily as that. He has to find his way through a thick jungle, but the reed-rat is there to open it. He is stopped by big trees, the wood-borer cuts them down. He comes, as in the present story, to a deep river; fortunately the spider is there to spread a cobweb on it and take the hero across. When he finds himself in front of a big mountain, the ant-bear digs a tunnel for him from side to side. Thus it seems that, as one goes from the interior towards the coast, the supernatural element of this tale is replaced by the fantastic. When at last Zunguza reaches God's abode, God says : " Just let him alone, he has come to die." And all sorts of trials are invented, as if to lead him to death. This apparent intention to kill the hero is foreign to the Mukuni tale, which mentions only harmless trials.

5TH SONG.

SHALL WE GO INTO THIS HUT ?	IYI MANDA TUNJIRE ?

On reaching the place, he goes and sits down under a tree with his arms folded over his knees.[37]

THEY [38] said : " Over there is a man that has arrived. Go and put to him the questions of welcome."[39]

People came and, after putting to him the usual questions, said : " Now you, man, what have you come for ? "

" I have," he said, " come for the lady daughter of the Rain-Lord."

" You have come to wed the daughter of the Rain-Lord ? "

" Yes," he said.

So these people went back and said : " He has come for the lady daughter of the Rain-Lord, wishing to wed her."

" Sweep," said THEY, " the hut of his intended mother-in-law, that we may see what sort of man he is." [40]

Ay' axike kunxi rya muxi, a kuñokomana. Bê " Nko ari muntu wêsá kokulya. A muye mukamwipuxe."

Kwïsá mu kumwipuxa, ayi " Ino webo, muntu, wakonka-nxi ? "

Ayi " Nebo ndakonka ba-mwana wa Rêsa."

Wêsa mu kukwata mwana wa Rêsa ? "

Ayi " E !"

Ayi " Wakonka ba-mwana wa Rêsa, ayi Nje nkakwate."

Bê " A mupyange manda ya kubukwe bwakwe, tubone uyu muntu."

---

[37] " Arms folded over his knees." This is the attitude taken by boys when they go courting.

[38] " THEY." Reverence is marked in Bwine-Mukuni by the use of the various forms of the plural pronoun THEY (*BA, BO, BENE*) instead of the singular, as in *BA-mwana wa Resa*, the lady daughter of God. And one often hears with the meaning of " God " not only the singular HE, but still oftener the plural THEY without any mention of Him having been made before, as is the case here.

[39] " The questions of welcome." Among the Bêne-Mukuni the first of these questions are : " Are you awake ? " Answer : " I am awake." Then : " Did you awake all right ? " Answer : " All right." Then : " Have you awakened yourself ? " Answer : " I have awakened myself." Among the new christians the custom is taking root of answering : " It is the Son of God that has awakened me."

[40] The most stringent marriage-law for a man in Northern Rhodesia is the prohibition to enter the hut of his mother-in-law. Likewise a woman is prohibited to enter the hut of her father-in-law.

They swept, then came and said to him : " Now get up and go into the hut over there."

He just got hold of his little feather and sang :

" Friendly little feather !

Chorus.—" When I am eaten," etc.

" Shall we go into this hut ?

" That is no hut for you, Master Mandu.

" It is your mother-in-law's.

" These are ordinations of Providence,

" Wherein He has mixed charms

" When I was there."

So the messenger came and said : " He does not want it, he says it is the house of his mother-in-law."

The people then swept the house of one of THEIR (God's) slaves, a spinster. When it was ready, they said to him : " Now this time come and enter here."

He just got hold of his little feather, and sang :

" Friendly little feather !

" What about that hut ? Shall we go in ?

" It belongs to a female-slave of THEIRS.

" They do not allow anyone to approach their slave," etc. (as above).

" He refuses," said the messenger, " he says it is the hut of THEIR slave."

" Oh ! " This man who has come here ! He beats us. Go and sweep this hut here."

They swept the hut of THEIR niece. Then HE said : " Go and call him."

Bâpyanga. Mpa a kwamba ayi imane ayi " A muñamuke muye mu manda mulya."

Wajata bo kapepe kâkwe ayi :

" Ndó kapepe !

" Ka ndiwa-ndiwa," etc.

" Iyi manda tunjire ?

" Ta ixi manda yako, Xâ-Mandu.

" Nje ya bañoko-xara.

" Nga marere â ba-Rêsa.

" 'Mo bâpandira mânga

" Kandiwo."

Ayi " Wakaka ayi nje ya kubukwe bwakwe "

Bâpyanga manda ya muxa waBO. Mpâ kuamba ayi bapyange boobo manda ya muxice waBO ayi " Ino ono a bêsé bênjire moomo."

Wajata bo kapepe kâkwe :

" Ndó kapepe !

" A mwaro mulya mu manda tunjire ?

" Nja muxakaxi waBO

" Ta bêrexa muxa waBO, Mandu.' etc. (as above).

Ayi " Wakaka ayi nja muxa waBO."

" U ! Uyu muntu ulakataxa a rakwe wêsa kokuno. A mupyayire yeeyi."

Bâpyayira ya mwicwa waBO. Ayi " Ino a muye mukamwite."

So they called him saying:
" Come now ! Go into the
hut. . . ."
" Friendly little feather," etc.
" Is this my wife's hut ?
" No, Master Mandu.
" It is THEIR niece's (God's
niece," etc. (as above).
So once more : " No, he says
it is YOUR niece's hut."
" Oh ! For goodness' sake !
Take him there into the hut
that is in ruins."
There he goes this time, carry-
ing his assegais.
While the people are making
a little order in the ruined hut,
dear me ! The vermin ! It is
full of them, full of them ! He
sings :
" Friendly little feather ! " etc.
" Shall we go into this hut ?
" You may go in, Master
Mandu ;
" It is your wife's hut.
" These are ordinations," etc.
(as above).
Just fancy ! Now as he goes
in, all the vermin that were
there disappears.
" Say, has he agreed ! " asked
the Rain-Lord.
" He has agreed," was the
answer, " he is in already."

Kuya mu kumwita ayi
" Bâna ! A twende mukênjire
mu manda. . . ."
" Ndó kapepe ! " etc.
" Nje ya bakeesu iyi ?
" Tawu, Xâ-Mandu.
" Nje ya mwicwa waBO."
etc. (as above).
Ayi " Wakaka ayi nje ya
mwicwa waBO."
O ! Bacu ! A mumunjixe-
wo mulya mu manda ifwemu-
kite."
Ngulya utôya, a masumo
wañamuna.
Bê bamubambe mu manda
yakafwemuka, sombi barongoro-
nxi ajane muliswite, barongoro-
nxi ajane muliswite. Ayi :

" Ndó kapepe ! ", etc.
" Iyi manda tunjire ?
" Mulênjira, Xâ-Mandu

" Nje ya bakaanu iyi.
" Nga marere," etc.

Bacu ! Sombi a kunjira mu
manda a nko xâringa nxe ba-
kajana-mo xônse xâswa-mo.
Be " Sá, bâsumina ? "

Ayi " E, bâsumina bênjira."

6TH SONG.

SHALL WE SIT ON THIS MAT ?

As he entered the hut, a mat
was brought to him, his future
mother-in-law's, and it was
spread in front of him. But

UBU BULO TWIKARE ?

Mpâ kwamba ayi ênjire mu
manda, bâreta bulo bwa ku-
bukwe bwakwe bâyansa mbubo.
Wêkara panxi. Bâamba ayi

he sat on the ground. When asked to sit on the mat, he just got hold of his little feather and sang :

" Friendly little feather !
Chorus.—" When I am eaten,"
etc.
" Shall we sit upon this mat ?
" It is not the right one, Master Mandu,
" It is your mother-in-laws.
" These are ordinations," etc.[41]

The messenger said : " He refuses even the mat."

They took that one away, and went to bring the one belonging to the daughter of the Rain-

" A mwïkare pa bulo." Wajata bo kapepe :

" Ndó kapepe !
" Ka ndiwa-ndiwa," etc.

" Ubu bulo twïkare !
" Ta buxi, Xâ-Mandu,

" Mbwa bañokoxara.
" Nga marere," etc. (as above).

Ayi " Wakaka a bulo."

Bâñamuna-wo, bâya mu kuleta bwa mwana wa Rêsa mwine. A kubusansa bulo

[41] The Sena version is quite different from this. It is as follows :

" Then he got a hole dug in the ground, and spears put right at the bottom, and a mat was spread on the top, while he said : " When my son-in-law comes here to-morrow morning, he must sit here, so as to fall into the hole upon the spears." Then he sent a messenger to say : " The son-in-law must come early to-morrow." Zunguza answered : " All right." When Zunguza went early in the morning clapping his hands, he heard the Rain-Lord going *gidigidigidi* in answer to the clapping of the son-in-law's hands. The wind blew, the rain fell in torrents, the flashes of lightning crossed one another on the top of Zunguza's head. Zunguza said : " I don't mind. Where you pass I shall pass too." Then, just where Zunguza passed there was no rain, behind him it was all rain. The rat fell in at this moment : " Master," he said, " do not sit down near the mat, as spears have been put there. Above all things do not sit on it, otherwise you will die. But go and sit near the door." Zunguza came ; the Rain-Lord said : " Pass on as far as the mat so as to sit comfortably." Zunguza said : " No, I will sit here. Even at home I always sit near the door."

Pidakumbê mulindi, mbaika madipa pantsi gwebede, mbakwata bonde, mbaika padzulu, ati " N'kamwene akabesa kudza kuno, akhale kweneko, towera agwe m'mulindi, madipa amulase." Pidatumê mwanakati ati " N'kamwene mangwana mbabese," Zunguza ati " Ndapibva."

Pidabesê mangwana báabawbdabaw, anadzabva Mulungu gidigidigidi kutawira mânja â n'kamwene ace, mpepo bu, mulungu codo, ndiko kubvumba kwene ; njazi tanta pa n'solo pâ Zunguza. Ati " Tayu, padapitêwe inembo ndapita-po." Kunênda Zunguza Mulungu bvumba bi, 'nduli mwace mo kunabvumba mulungu. Cilu gwagwagwa ati " Mbuya, kuli bonde leka khala-ko, pantsi-po pâce pâikwa madipa, leka khala-po gopa unafa ; ndoko wakhale kunsuwo." Zunguza mbwé, Mulungu ati " Pitani ku bonde, mukhale padidi." Zunguza ati " Tayu, 'nakhala kuno. Na kwathu kwene 'nakhala ku nsuwo."

Lord. They shook it, then spread it. He sang again as above :
" Friendly little feather," etc.
" Shall we sit on this mat ?
" You may sit on it, Master Mandu.
" This is your wife's mat."
So he sat down on the mat with legs stretched at length, THEY leaving him in peace for some time.
The people then went to get some wine [42] for him. But what they brought was his own father-in-law and his mother-in-law transformed into wine. They put this down before him in a close-woven little basket, and said : " Drink this wine from the basket."
But he, looking at it : " Ye-e-es, is this truly wine ? "
He just got hold of his little feather, and sang :
" Friendly little feather," etc.
" Shall we drink this wine ?
" It is no wine at all, Master Mandu,
" That wine is your father-in-law and your mother-in-law," etc.
Then the father-in-law and the mother-in-law stand up. There they are going.
Porridge was cooked.
Heaven help me ! They changed themselves, the father-in-law into a roasted cock, the

bâyansa. Ayi :

" Ndó kapepe ! " etc.
" Ubu bulo twïkare ?
" Mulêkara, Xâ-Mandu.

" Mbwa baka anu ubu."
Wêkara pa bulo fwankaba, bacitentemene.

Bâya mu kuleta funku. Ku-bukwe bwabo bwaba funku. Kwïsa mu kutentekera mu ntumba. Bâamba ayi " A munwe-wo funku."

A kâro ayi " E-e-e ! Uyu funku uyu ? "

" Ndó kapepe !
" Uyu funku tunwe ?
" Uyu têxi, Mandu,

" Nko kubukwe bwako ubu. etc.

A bâro fukuruku ku-bukwe bwakwe mbarya bate kuya.

Bâponda nxima. Bacu ! Ku-bukwe bwakwe bwaba nkuku, bânakaxi bâba nxima. Bacu ! Kuxitantaula, a xîne

---

[42] " Some wine." The Bêne-Mukuni, the ba-Tonga, etc., make a beverage which is more like wine than beer by soaking crushed *munkoyo*-roots in beer still hot from the fire.

woman into porridge. Great
Heaven ! A boy carries them
on plates, brings them to the
wooer and says : " Eat this
porridge." He also brings water
for the wooer to wash his hands.
But the song begins again :
" Friendly little feather," etc.
" Shall we eat this porridge ?
" Do not eat it, Master Mandu.
" This is your mother-in-law,
" And this is your father-in-
law," etc.

Then what a picture ! The
mother-in-law who had become
porridge standing up, and the
father-in-law rushing out of the
dish crowing *kokoliko*. There
they are both of them running
as fast as they can.

Then it was that this word
went forth : " Come, come !
You are tiring the man for
nothing. Simply cook the
porridge."

So the porridge was stirred,
genuine porridge this time. It
was taken out of the pot, and
some relish was put beside it.
Then : " Come, child of the
Rain-Lord, and take that to
him."

So the child of the Rain-Lord
herself came quickly and went
to put the one and the other at
the feet of the boy. There she
is already out of the hut, while
he sings :

" Friendly little feather," etc.
" Shall we eat this porridge ?
" You may eat it, Master
Mandu.

kuxireta, ayi " Iyi nxima a
mulye." A manxi bâreta.

Ayi :
" Ndó kapepe," etc.
" Iyi nxima tulye ?
" Mutairi, Xâ-Mandu
" Mba bañokoxara
" Mba baisoxara," etc.

Abone ¡ku-bukwe bwakwe
fukuruku bâringa bâba nsima.
Abone ku-bukwe bwakwe
" kokoriko " bâswa. Mbarya
bate kuya rubiro.

Mpâkwamba ayi bacite boobo,
ayi " Bâna ! Muntu mute ku-
muremya. A muponde bo
nxima."

A îne a kwiponda. Anu ! ni
nxima bo. A kwipakira, a bucisa. Ayi " Kwesá utore,
mwana wa Rêsa."

A mwine mwana wa Rêsa wa-
katuka kwïsá mu kutentekera
nxima. Ngulya waswa. Ayi :

" Ndo kapepe," etc.
" Iyi nxima tulye ?
" Mularya, Xâ-Mandu.

" It is simple porridge," etc.
So he takes the porridge and
eats.[43]

" Ni nxima bulyo iyi," etc.
A îne nje bajata kulya.

7TH SONG.

IS THIS OUR WIFE ?

" Now," say THEY, " what
shall we do ? "
Then THEY said : " Let the
woman go. Take the child of
the Rain-Lord to her husband."
Now fancy this ! The
mother-in-law metamorphosed
herself once more, and went.
. . . . Then :
" Friendly little feather !
Chorus.—" When I am eaten,"
etc.
" Shall we marry the woman ?
" Don't, Master Mandu.
" She is your mother-in-law.
" These are ordinations," etc.
There she is going away.
" What has happened ? "
" He has refused."
Well ! They went to fetch
another woman, the young sister
of his mother-in-law, and began
to dress her. She was soon

MBO BACEESU ABA ?

Bê " Ino ono tucite buyani ?

Bê " Ono sombi mwanakaxi.
A mutore mwana a Resa uyo
kuli ibaye."
Bacu ! Bârisandula ku-
bukwe bwakwe mbomuña,
bâunka. . . .

" Ndó kapepe !
" Kandiwa-ndiwa," etc.

" Mwanakaxi tukwate ?
" Utakwati, Xâ-Mandu.
" Nko ku-bukwe bwako aba.
" Nga marere," etc.
Mbarya bâunka.
Ayi " Mbuyani ? "
Ayi " Wakaka."
A! Bâya mu kuleta a umwi,
mwanike wa ku-bukwe bwakwe,
bêsá kumufwarika. A mwine
rubemba wêsula, a mwine

---

[43] This is the episode of the porridge in the Sena tale :

" When clean porridge was cooked
he put poison in it. When bran
porridge was cooked, he put no
poison in it. The rat then fell in
and said : " Master, do not eat the
white porridge, it is poisoned ; the
bran porridge—yes, eat it. When
the porridge came, he ate the bran,
and threw away the white. The
Rain-Lord said : " Go and see how
he is getting on." When they had
seen him and withdrawn, he asked :
" Is he dead this time ? " The
answer was : " He is not dead yet."

*Pinaphika-wo ntsima ya kucena,
mbaika ufiti. Pinaphika-wontsima
ya gotye, kuika ufiti bi. Cilu gwa
gwa gwa ati. " Mbuya, ntsima
yôcena leka kudya, yaikwa ufiti, ya
gotye-yo idya. "Ntsima pinadza-dzo,
mbadya ya gotye, ya kucena mbataya.
Mulungu ati " Ndokoni mwamône."
Pidamôna-wo, pinênda-wo konto,
pinabvundze " Ati kufa ? "—" Kâti
Kufa."*

literally covered with brass
ornaments. Then she went with
great solemnity to enter into
the hut. As she came she sat
down on the mat. But he,
looking fixedly at her, got hold
of his little feather, and sang
as above. (The answer came) :
" She is not your wife, Master
    Mandu,
" She too is your mother-in-
    law, the young one." [44] etc.
There you may see her getting
up and going.
" What did he say ? "
" That she too is his mother-
in-law."
They then dressed the niece
of the Rain-Lord. But the
ornaments they put on her !
They could not be counted.
They made her move, and went
ahead showing the way. When
she comes, they see her sit down
at her ease on the mat. . . .
" Friendly little feather," etc.
" Is this our wife ?
" No, Master Mandu.
" She is thy future cousin," etc.
She, too, see her going.

" What has happened ? "
asked the Lord.
" He does not want her,"
answered the messenger. " He
says she is his cousin."

wa katauka kwĭsá mu kunjira
mu manda. Mpâ kwamba ayi
axike, wêkara pa bulo. Mpâ
kwamba ayi amulange, wajata
bo kapepe kâkwe. . . .

" Ta bêxi, Xâ-Mandu,

" Nko   ku - bukwe   bwako
    bânike," etc.
Abone ngulya mwine waña-
muka ute kuya.
Ayi " Wâmba buyani ? "
Ayi " Nko ku-bukwe bwabo
a bâro."
Bâfwarika   muntu   waBO.
Sombi bâmufwarika bo pambi
makaka. (Bâmubika-ko bâmu-
tangixa.)   Ndye ute kwĭsá,
babone   fwanka   wêkara   pa
bulo. . . .

" Ndó kapepe," etc.
" Mbo bacêsu aba ?
" Ta bêxi, Xâ-Mandu.
" Mbo bapyara bâko aba." etc.
A mwine ngulya waunka,
kuya kuunka.
Ayi " Mbuyani ? "

Ayi " Wakaka ayi ngu
mupyara wakwe."

[44] One of the difficulties of the languages of Northern Rhodesia is the
multitudinous meaning of the words " father, mother, mother-in-law, son,
brother, etc." Thus a man gives the title of " father, tá, or batá, or tata "
(1) to his real father, (2) to his paternal uncles, (3) to his paternal aunts (sic).
Likewise he gives the name of " mother, má, or bamá, or mama " (1) to his
true mother, (2) to his maternal aunts, (3) to his maternal uncles (sic), (4) to
the various wives of his father. From this let the reader reckon how many
mothers-in-law a man in this country may have and may be bound to shun.

" Now," said they, " dress a girl from another hut."

They went to adorn his future sister-in-law ; they simply covered her with cowries. She got up and, as the others had done, came and sat comfortably on the mat. . . . Same song and similar answer :

" This is not your wife, Master Mandu.

" She is your sister-in-law," etc.

He sees her getting up.

" The sun is gone," said the Lord. " Tell him that tomorrow we shall give him without fail the true lady daughter of the Rain-Lord."

Bê " Ono a mufwarike mwana wa mumbi mu manda."

A mwine bâmufwarika mulamu wakwe, kuya mu kumufwarika a mapande ônse. Wañamuka kwïsá mu kwïkara fwankaba. A ! Wajata kapepe kâkwe. . . . Kuñumfwa ayi :

" Ta bêxi, Xâ-Mandu,

" Mbo ba-maramu âko abo," etc.

Abone ngú wañamuka.

(Bê " Risuba ryaya. A mumwambire ayi junsa tulaya kumutorera kabotu bêne ba-Mwana wa Rêsa.")

8TH SONG.

PEEL OFF SOME FIBRE FOR ME.

The following day passed quietly. Only just when the sun was going down, these words were heard : " All they that wish to marry our child, let them appear together."

Two other young men then got up besides our own, who had his feather on his head and an axe in hand.

" My child," said the Rain-Lord, " is not for marriage, unless the suitor goes first to bring me fibre from the top of that baobab over there." [45]

MFUNDIRE KAROXI.

(Kwamba ayi junsa bêkara bulyo. Ingayi babone risuba ryaya mu kuwa, bâñumfwa ayi " Baxikusuni kukwata mwana wêsu kababoneka bônse, pantu pômwí."

Bâñamuka basankwa bôbire, a mwine a kapepe kâkwe mu mutwi a kêmbe mu ryansa.

Bê " Mwana wangu ta akwatwa. Uti ankwatire mwana sombi amfundire rôxi ruli ku mubuyu uku."

[45] According to Jacottet (Textes Soubiya, pp. 104, 105), the Ba-Subiya say that once upon a time Reza had his terrestrial abode under a big tree called

One of the men got up saying:
" Let us climb and peel off
some bark." He too had a
song, but in Bu-Sori :
" Come, come ! Father ! Peel off some fibre for me.
        Chorus.—" Slip ! Slip !
        " Go there !—Slip ! Slip !
        " Tumble down !—Slip ! Slip !
        " Oh ! Mother ! I cannot reach.—Slip! Slip ! "
        " Bâna ! Tata ! Umfundire karoxi.
        " Teremu ! Teremu !
        " Kôya owa !—Teremu ! Teremu !
        " Kulumuko !—Teremu ! Teremu !
        " A ! Mawe ! Ndarera.—Teremu ! Teremu ! "

Umwi ayi " A tutante tukaru-
funde." Ayi :

He fell on the ground. " Too
much for him." They left him
alone.

Waroka-ko. " Câara." Bâ-
muxiya.

The second one got up too,
and the song was repeated.

A umwi wañamuka ayi
" Bâna ! Tata ! Umfundire
karoxi," etc.

He too fell down.[46]

Waroka-ko.

Then the owner of the little
feather got up in his turn, and
with his own song :
" Friendly little feather,
" When I am eaten," etc.

Mpêce a rakwe mwine kapepe
wañamuka, a rakwe a rwimbo
rwakwe ayi :
" Ndó kapepe !
" Ka ndiwa-ndiwa, ndi bululu,"
        etc.

" Shall I climb up this baobab ?
" You will climb, Master
        Mandu," etc.

" Ku mubuyu uyu ntante-ko ?
" Ulatanta, Xâ-Mandu," etc.

He just fixed his axe in the
tree and went up, singing for
fun the song of the others :
" Come, come ! Father ! " etc.
(as above).

A kunjixa kêmbe mu cisamu,
a kutanta, a kuparamya babye,
ayi :
" Bâna ! Tata ! " etc.

He jumped from branch to
branch up to the top, pulled off
the bark, and came down.

Wauluka kare kujulu, a rôxi
walufunda, akuseruka waseruka,

---

ibozu, that people used to take thither quantities of sheep and goats for his
food, and that he occasionally showed himself there. As the baobab is called
mubuyu in Tonga, Mukuni, etc., mubuzu in Sara, Ila, etc., I strongly suspect that
Jacotter's ibozu is nothing else than an extraordinarily big baobab. Note that
the baobab is very slippery. In Mukuni the fruit of the baobab is called ri-
buyu. May be that this too is pronounced ibozu in Subiya.

[46] The failure of their songs is, perhaps, meant to show the difference between
a vain incantation and a real charm or a prayer.

When he was down, the word
uttered was : "Now *you* may
go, the one who has brought the
fibre is my son-in-law."
There they go away towards
their kraals, while the winner
comes back to his ruinous hut.

Nkwakaseruka, bê "Ono ka
muya, wafunda rôxi ngo mukwe
wangu."

Mbarya bâunka batôya ku
mixi yabo. Mwine wabôra waya
mu kunjira mu manda yakwe
ifwemukite.)

9TH SONG.

THIS IS THE CHILD OF THE RAIN-LORD.

When it was dark, this word
was heard : "Now let us take
to her husband the very child
of the Rain-Lord."
Would you believe it ? They
first shaved her hair close,
smeared her all over with ashes,
and even gave her for her dress
a shred of skin.
Her slave, on the contrary,
they dressed with all possible
finery ; on her head beads
strung with her hair, with all
sorts of ornaments and brilliants
for which only goldsmiths have
names ; on her ears rings ; on
her forehead a cowry ; on her
shoulders cowries, on her neck a
cowry, on her chest a cowry ;
on her wrists armlets ; on her
fingers rings ; at her waist red
beads and a fine belt ; under
her arms special ornaments ;
on her legs copper wires
clanking so as to beat time.
Her face and head were anointed
red.

MBA BA-MWANA WA RESA.

Kwe kuxiye, bañumfwe ayi
"Ono tuñamune mwana wa
Rêsa ngwece."

Bacu ! Bâmukulula-kulula,
sombi a mirota yonse bâmutu-
kweta, bâmupa a kapaya.

(Sombi muxa wabo ngo bâf-
warika fwarika, ku mutwi bulungu ka baosera kumwi a
misusu, a xikarunsuce, a mu-
tenta, a myompwe ; a ku matwi
mpete ; a pa nkumo mpande,
a pa mafuxi mapande, a mu
nxingo mpande, a pa câmba
mpande ; a ku mânsa bwansa
a makosa a nsaramu ; a ku
bukome bulungu bwa xitaraka
a rimwi a miñone ; a mu kwapa
mipakato ; a ku myendo rubemba rutôrira. A ku mênso
a ku mutwi bâmunanika ruxira.)

There she is going with an
escort ahead, and the true child
of the Rain-Lord behind gather-
ing up the skin to her body as
close as she can, as if shivering
with cold.

When the bridegroom looked
in the direction from which
they were coming, he saw
lightning upon lightning, lightning upon lightning : " This
time," he said, " she is coming."

Then, as they came near the
door, HE began to thunder, roll
of thunder upon roll of thunder,
rururu, rururu, rururu. This
time," says the boy, " it is her
own self."

They begin to enter the hut.
God help me ! It is all illumi-
nated, lightning upon lightning.

The woman buried in cowries
then sits down at her ease, but
he, getting hold of his little
feather, just sings :

" Friendly little feather,
" When I am eaten, I am
    bitter," etc.
" Is this our wife ? . . .
" This one, no, Master Mandu. . .
" She is her slave. . . .
" But the one that is behind. . .
" All besmeared with ashes . . .
" With her head clean-shaved . . .
" Having only a skin as a
    dress . . .
" That is THE LADY CHILD OF
    THE RAIN-LORD."

Mpêce ngulya kumutangixa,
a mwana wa Rêsa kwisule utô-
kokoñana bo mu kapaya.

Mpa a kwamba ayi arange-
ko musankwa nko bate kwïsá,
abone kuli bo mabyabya [47] ênka.
kuli bo mabyabya [47] ênka, ayi
" Ono ndye waxika."

Abone bo, pa kwamba ayı
bana kuxika bo mu mulyango,
a mwine warunduma, waruruma
a kururuma, a rururu, rururu,
rururu. A rakwe ayi " Ndye
bâxika bêne."

Mpa a kwamba ayi baxike
mu manda, ajane, bacu ! mwa-
fuberenkana kare, muli bo
mabebe ênka.

Abone muntu wïpirite mu
mapande wêkara bo fwankaba,
a ! wajata bo kapepe kâkwe :

" Ndó kapepe !
" Ka ndiwa-ndiwa, ndi bululu,"
    etc.
" Mbo bacêsu aba ? . . .
" Aba ta bêxi, Xâ-Mandu . . .
" Ngo muxa wabo. . . .
" Sombi uli kwisule . . .
" Watukwetwa mirota . . .
" Wakululwa misusu . . .
" Ufwete kapaya . . .

" Mba BA-MWANA WA RESA."

[47] Var. *mabebe.*

He just put his hands on her,
saying : " I know her, my wife,
with the shred of skin." [48]

The people then dispersed,
and the two of them went to
sleep.

A ku mujata ayi " Ndimûxi
muka wangu wa kapaya."

A bêne bâmwayika. A bâro
a ku tulo.

10TH SONG.

HOLD FOR ME MY SON-IN-LAW.

The marriage having thus
been celebrated, next morning
the Rain-Lord said : " Now
what am I going to do ? This
son-in-law of mine, to what
work shall I send him ? "

At last he said : " To-day I
am going to the hole to trample
mortar."

Good gracious ! There he is
in fact with a hoe in hand.

When the little son-in-law
saw him thus going to dig in the
hole, he stretched himself quick
enough, and coming up to him
said : " Let THEM give me the
hoe."

He took hold of it. . . . And
now there he is in the hole,
digging, digging, digging, turning up and turning up the soil.
Then he remembered his badge,
took it off and said : "Father-

NCATIRE MUKWE WANGU.

Nkwakakwatwa mwana wa
Rêsa, cûnsa bwe buce " Ino ono
ncite-wo buyani ? Uyu mukwe
wangu 'mutume-wo mulimo-
nxi ?

Bê " Nebo sunu ntôya ku
cikanda."

Bacu ! A rise ryabo.

Mpâ kwamba ayi baye mu
kukaba ku cikanda uko, a kâro
kakwe kâbo kâriorora, kuya mu
kuxika ayi " A bampe rise."

Kâxikira kulijata. A mu
cikanda mukati kabe, kabe,
kabe, kabe, 'mo mu kukaba
bulongo, 'mo mu kukaba
bulongo. Wañamuna ngara ayi
" Tataxara, a muncatire-ko

---

[48] In the Sena version the servants of God are represented as spitting on the
daughter of God disguised as a slave and covered with black mud. Zunguza
says : " Come near, you *bicu* (slave)."   Then he takes out a ring, passes it on
her ring finger, and says : " I want a poor consort like myself, the one on
whom you spit, that we may be faithful to each other."   On the whole, the
Sena version seems to be comparatively modernised.

in-law, kindly hold this little feather for me there where you are, lest it get dirty."

So he passed it to THEM, to the Rain-Lord himself, and THEY stuck it in their hair.

While they had it thus on their head, THEY bethought themselves of saying :

" Hole, hold for me my son-in-law."

This THEY said four times.

Hearing that, the little son-in-law from his hole said likewise four times :

" Little feather, hold for me my father-in-law."

" Ha ! " said the father-in-law.

The feather was already beginning to grow and to fix itself firmly on the skin, the roots going through.

Listen : " Little feather ! Ha ! " . . . " Then :

" Hole, give me back my son-in-law." (Four times.)

And at once the son-in-law moving from his place :

" Little feather, let go my father-in-law." (Four times.)

" Here ! " Take thy badge," said the Rain-Lord. And he did not take long to get rid of it.

He then said : " Let us go home."

So they went home and just sat down.

kapepe aka apo mpo [49] muxite, itabi a bulongo."

A kubapa bêne ba-Rêsa. A bâro kufwarika mu mutwi.

Mpâ kwamba ayi bafware boobo bâxikira ba-Rêsa bê :

" Cikanda, ncatire mukwe wangu " (tône).

Kâro kakwe kâbo mu cikanda umo ayi :

" Kapepe, ncatire ku-bukwe bwangu " (tône).
" A ! "

A ine ngara yaxikira kumena, yaya mu kujata mpêce pa rubwibwi ngá.

Kuñumfwa " Kapepe ! . . . A ! "
" Cikanda, mboxexe mukwe wangu " (tône).

A mwine a kutuntuka :

" Kapepe, ndekere ku-bukwe bwangu " (tône).

" A ! "　A bêne a ngara yaswa-mo.

Mpâ kwamba ayi iswe-mo, bê " A tuna kuya ku muxi."

Mpâ kwamba ayi baye mu kuxika ku muxi bêkara.

---

[49] *Mpo*, var. *mpa*.

The following day THEY said :
" To-day let us go and clear a
new field in the forest."

When they reached the place
where they had to cut trees, the
father-in-law said : " Thou,
my son-in-law, climb up to the
top of that thorn-tree there
and cut off its branches."

The son-in-law then remembered to take out his little
feather and to say : " Kindly
put this little feather of mine
on yourself."

There he is now going up to
the top of the tree.

Seeing him there the father-
in-law says :
" Take away my son-in-law,
tree." (Four times,)

The son-in-law says likewise :
" Take away my father-in-law,
little feather." (Four times.)

Soon the Rain-Lord said :
" Let us go home." [51]

The following day he said :
" To-day where shall we go to ?
We had best go to the heap of
dry wood."

Junsa bê " Sunu tuye tukateme cibibi." [50]

Nko bâkaya mu kutema
cibibi, kubukwe bwabo ayi
" Webo mukwe wangu, tanta
ku mukunkurwa uku uteme-
ko."

A rakwe waxikira kufûla
kapepe kâkwe ayi " A mum-
fwarire-ko kapepe kângu."

Ngo woyo waya mu kutanta
kujulu rya cisamu.

Mpâ kwamba ayi, nko wakaya
mu kutanta, ayi :
" Ntorere mukwe wangu, cisamu " (tône).

A rakwe mukwe :
" Ntorere batataxara, kapepe."
(tône).

Bâxikira bê " A tuye ku mixi
yêsu."

(Cûnsa bêne " Sunu tuye kuli ?
Sombi ku cibibi."

[50] Var. *tukateme nteme.*

[51] In the Sena version the episode of the tree to be cut is quite different from
the above, and presents the father-in-law somewhat as the lightning-lord.
" Here," he says, " when we fell a tree, we strike only once. That is how you
have to bring down that big tree there." The mouse at once said : " Master,
say that you will cut it down to-morrow, meanwhile during the night the wood-
borer will furrow it through and through." So he said : " All right, I shall
bring it down to-morrow, and that with this assegai which I am going to
sharpen for that purpose." He marked with charcoal for the woodborer the
place where he meant to strike and went home. The following morning many
people were there to laugh at him, some of them leaning against the tree.
He clapped his hands and said : " Kindly get out of the way, the tree is going
to fall." They only laughed at him, saying : " And that with an assegai ! "
He then with the assegai struck the tree at the place lined with charcoal, and
down it went, crushing the people that had been laughing. " It is no fault
of mine," he said, " did I not clap my hands and tell them to get out of the
way ? "

So they went to the heap of dry wood. Then the Rain-Lord said : " Go up, my son-in-law, here in the very middle of the ant-heap."

The son-in-law went up there, but first said : " Hold my little feather for me."

The father-in-law, the Rain-Lord, put it on. Then were heard, Heaven help me ! the following words :

" Fire, burn me my son-in-law." (Four times.)

But the son-in-law from the middle of the heap, said likewise :

" Little feather, burn my father-in-law." (Four times.)

And in fact the father-in-law really began to burn. So he said at once :

" Fire, let go my son-in-law." (Four times.)

And from the antheap came the words :

" Little feather, let go my father-in-law." (Four times.)

Well ! Well ! The father-in-law was left free by the little feather.

They came home.

The following day the Rain-Lord said : " I go to the forge." [52] There he is carrying the tools himself and going to the forge.

Be baye ku cibibi kulya, bê " Tanta, o mukwe wangu, pano pakati pa cûlu mpêce."

Mukwe wabo watanta. A rakwe ayi " A muncatire kapepe aka."

Ku-bukwe bwakwe bâfwara ba-Rêsa. Bacu ! baye bañumfwe bo ayi :

" Muliro, ntentere mukwe wangu " (tône).

A rakwe, mpa akaringa, ayi :

" Kapepe, ntentere batataxara" (tône).

Bâpya a kupya :

" Muliro, ndekere mukwe wangu " (tône).

Ayi :

" Kapepe, ndekere batataxara " (tône).

Bacu ! Mpa akaringa kapepe kâbareka bo bêxixara.

Bêsá ku muxi.

Mpâ kwamba ayi junsa bê " Ntôya mu kufula." A bêne bâñamuka kuya mu kufula.

---

[52] " To the forge," that is, to forge thunder and lightning. The Bêne-Mukuni connect *m-fula* " rain " with *m-fula* " I forge," but perhaps not correctly. Comparative studies show that *m-fula* " rain " is more closely connected with *m-fûla* " I undress," as in many languages the word for both " rain " and " I undress " is not *mfula*, but *mvula*, while *m-fula* " I forge " does not change to *m-vula*.

"I, too," said the son-in-law, "let me go and hold the bellows."

So he went to blow the bellows but just as he put his hand on them, he said : "Let THEM kindly hold for me this badge of mine." And he handed it to the father-in-law.

THEY then said :
"Hammer, take away my son-in law." (Four times.)
"Little feather, hold for me my father-in-law." (Four times.)
The Rain-Lord had no remedy but to say :
"Hammer, give me back my son-in-law." (Four times.)
Well ! The hammer just went and struck the ground.

THEY then said : "Now, let us work as friends. Thou, my son-in-law, give us water by shedding tears." [53]

"I, my revered friend," said the son-in-law, "for my own work I have here this pot of mine, but let all the sons-in-law of your abode come together to shed tears into it."

Would you believe it ? There they began to come together. But the father-in-law did not wait until they reached the forge.

He just said : "Heaven help me ! This son-in-law of mine, well ! he is one who is hard to beat. Let us go back."

A rakwe mukwe waBO "A mebo a nje ncate-ko mûba."

Kuya mu kufukuta. Waxi-kira kuujata mûba ayi "A bancatire-ko ngara yangu iyi." A kubapa [ngara ku-bukwe bwakwe.

Bê :
"Ñundo, ntorere mukwe wangu " (tône).
"Kapepe, ncatire ku--bukwe bwangu " (tône).
A bêne "A ! " Sombi :

"Ñundo, mboxexe mukwe wangu " (tône).
"A ! " A îne . . . panxi pum-putu (yaroka).
A bêne " Ono a tuye manto. Webo, mukwe wangu, reta manxi, una kulira minsonxi."

Ayi " Nebo, manto,[54] kufula kwangu nongo yangu iyi, bônse ba-makwâbânu bayoboroke bana kuririra-mo."

Bacu ! Bônse nko bâkaa-mba kuyoboroka. . . . Bâcireka.

Mpâ kwamba ayi bacite boobo " Bacu ! Uyu mukwe wangu tawu, 'mutaremya. Tu-bôrere bulyo."

---

[53] That is "Make rain."
[54] *Manto*, lit. "friends," plural of respect, perhaps from singular *ndó*.

132

So they both went home, and they left him in peace.

The following day THEY said : " Give us some bark that we may go and fix the roof."

Then THEY themselves went up the roof. Seeing that, the little son-in-law threw himself, also upon the roof. Then he said : " Let my father-in-law hold this badge for me and go down."

The father-in-law, having come down, said :

" Roof, take away my son-in-law."

(Then followed in succession):
" Little feather, hold my father-law."
" Roof, give me back my son-in-law."
" Little feather, release my father-in-law."

So the son-in-law came down.

Bâbôrera ku muxi. A bêne barixite.

Cûnsa bê " Kôtupa rôxi kuya mu kuximba ciruli."

A bêne kutanta.

Mpâ kwamba ayi kakwe kâbo kacibonene-wo, a kêne a ku ciruli kâriwara. Ayi " Ngara iyi bancatire ku-bukwe bwangu panxi."

Mpa a kwamba ayi bacibonene-wo ku-bukwe bwakwe, ayi :
" Ciruli, ntorere mukwe wangu."

" Kapepe, ncatire ku-bukwe bwangu."
" Ciruli, mboxexe mukwe wangu."
" Kapepe, ndekere ku-bukwe bwangu."

A mwine a panxi fulukutu.

11TH SONG.

BRING ME MY CAT-SKIN.

Heaven help us ! They said : " Now what shall we do ? "

But the son-in-law said : " Now all these days I have been on fire. To-morrow, by my mother, I go to our own home."

The mother-in-law said : " With thy wife ? "

He said : " With my wife."

NDETERE NJARUXI YANGU.

Bacu ! Bê " Ono ncite-wo buyani ? "

Mukwe wabo ayi " Ono nebo xino nxiku rwapya. Cûnsa ntôya ku mixi yêsu, má."

Ayi " A muka ako ? "

Ayi " A muka angu."

She said : " My child ! No, let her remain here."

Next morning he said : " My wife, let us make a start, that I may go and see my mother."

" Go by yourself," said the wife.

" Ha ! " said the boy.

He straightway got up. When the wife saw him going, she got up saying : " After all, I will follow my husband."

Well then ! The Rain-Lord himself, seeing that, began to fill baskets with provisions, together with his slaves. And these he gave to his daughter as an escort. Cattle too were added. There they are now on the road.

When they had gone only a little distance, the boy passed his little feather to his wife, and she put it on. She, besides, took from him his skin of the *nsimba* wild cat, and went away with it.

He then moves on ahead, moves on ahead. Seeing her follow at a little distance, he sings :

" Child of the Rain-Lord !
Chorus.—" Bring me my cat skin."
" I must go.
" I am coming, child of Wood-cutter.
" Make haste, child that comest with water from the clouds,[55] bring me my cat skin."

Ayi " Mwana wangu, nebo tawu, acare."

Cûnsa " Ono, muka angu, a tuna kuya, nkaye nkabone-wo bamá."

Bâkaamba baka akwe ayi " Ka muya bulyo."

" A ! "

Bâxikira kuñamuka.

Mpâ kwamba ay' añamuke boobo, a bâro baka abo bâxikira kuñamuka ayi " Nebo ntômu-konkera ibangu."

Bacu ! A bêne bate kulon-gera a baxa bâ mixi yabo. A bâro mulongo. A mombe bâtunka-ko. A bêne a mu nxira.

Mpâ kwamba ayi baxike mu nxira, a kumupa kapepe muka akwe, a kufwara. A njaruxi ya musankwa muka akwe wamufumuna, warondexa.

Mwine ku nxira, mwine ku nxira. Nko bâmukonkera, ayi :

" Mwana wa Resa,
" Ndetere njaruxi yangu.

" 'Na kwenda.
" Nte kwenda, mwana wa Ximutema-mbaro.
" Ka mwenda, mwana wa kuswa a manxi ku mayoba, ndetere njaruxi yangu."

[55] The children of the Rain-Lord are supposed to come with the rain from the sky. (See further on the Tonga tale *Nseyandi*, No. II). This observation

Meanwhile he takes long strides, long strides, long strides, while she lags behind with all the slaves. Then, giving a look back towards the city, she sings :

" My father has forsaken me.
" At home he has let rain fall.
" The rainfall has come, mother.
" It has come down in big drops."

That is enough to throw all the men down under a torrential rain.

The boy ahead, seeing that, says : " Now how has the woman, the child of the Rain-Lord, treated me ? " So he changes his song :

" At our abode it is all sunshine,
" All sunshine, all sunshine,
" All sunlight."

Behold ! The sun shines again. And the people are released from their spell, the cattle too.

Now they move on correctly.

However, after a time the boy, looking behind, sees the daughter of the Rain-Lord lagging once more. So he sings again :

A kêne kâwarayira-mo a kuwarayira-mo, kâwarayira-mo a kuwarayira-mo. (Kulya nko bâkacara a baxa bônse, bê barange ku muxi, ayi :

" Batá bânxiya,
" Kwêsu kwêroka
" Kwêroka kwêwa, má,
" Kwêwa mandondo."

Sombi a bêne bantu bâmana ku mfula.

A rakwe musankwa, mpa akaringa, ayi " Ino ono mwa-nakaxi wankataxa buyani, mwana wa Rêsa ? " Ayi :

" Kwêsu nko rubara,

" Nko rubara, nko rubara,
" Nko rubara myenje."

Bacu ! A rwine rumwi ! Sombi bantu bâpatamuka, bacu! a mombe xônse.

Bâbika-ko, bâbika-ko.

Mpâ kuamba ayi karange pêsure, kabone ba-mwana wa Rêsa bâcara-ko mumbi, ayi :

may be generalized by saying that, according to the Bantu view, God creates and generates through rain, just as he annihilates through fire and lightning. A certain approach to this Bantu conception may, perhaps, be noted in Genesis, where the Spirit of God viewed as creator is associated with " the waters " (Gen. i. 2).

By contraction Mwana Mbirika says *njaruxângu* instead of *njaruxi yangu.* Most of the natives I have consulted did not know what is a *njaruxi.* They only understood that it is some kind of belt. But Mumba explains that it is a skin of the *nsimba* wild cat, *mpaya ya nximba.* The right of wearing such an ornament is a prerogative of royalty. So it must be supposed that our hero, by becoming the son-in-law of the Rain-Lord, has entered the royal circle.

Instead of *Nte kwenda* " I am going," Mumba puts into the mouth of the bride the word *ndakaka* " I don't want."

" Child of the Rain-Lord,
" Bring me my cat skin," etc.
(as above.)

This time she also, there on the road, puts on speed.

But now she begins to climb up a hill, and there, looking behind, she finds that a servant is coming over there in the distance, loaded with brass ornaments for her. She then sings again :

" My father has forsaken me," etc. (as above).

Heaven help me ! The people are like dead men. At once the man sings) :

"At our place it is all sunshine," etc. (as above).

The people in a trice are up again and moving on.

The slaves are now on the declivity of the mountain. They actually swallow up the road. After a time the man finds that the neighbourhood of his own kraal begins to come into view far away in the plain. " Now," he says, " over there, that is where our kraal lies."

At that moment his wife joins him : " Now," he says, " we are going soon to reach the place. . .."

When he saw that the distance was not great, he despatched one of his wife's men, saying : " Now go towards our kraal to announce us, so that when the child of the Rain-Lord comes, she may not be put into

" Mwana wa Rêsa,
" Ndetere njaruxi yangu," etc.

A bêne a mu nxira yabo bâwarayira-mo.

Mpa a kuamba ayi baxike mu mulundu ômwi basompe-ko baka abo pêsule, bajane kañamuka kantu, rubemba rwenka rwakaremya, (ayi :

" Batata bânxiya," etc.

Bacu ! . . . .

" Kwêsu nko rubara," etc.

Sombi a bêne bantu pataka pataka bâmana kubuka. Bacu! bâkiba-ko.

Eryo baxa mulundu bâfunduka, bârukutixa a kurukutixa. Eryo bâjana a ku mixi yabo kwafumpuka. " Ino nko ku mixi yêsu."

Eryo a kwine eryo bâgumana.
" Ono tute kuya kuxika."

Mpâ kwamba ayi abone kwafwimpa ku muxi, waxikira kutuma muntu wabo umwi, ayi " Webo kôtantira ku muxi uye ukatwambe, mwana wa Rêsa ataxiki mu manda bulyo ya bwisu, sombi îne ya kubumba

a hut of grass, but into the
brick house, and let them whitewash it."
The servant went.
A little further, the man
looked behind, and again sang :
" Child of the Rain-Lord,
" Bring me my catskin," etc.
(as above).
Then longer strides than ever.
Then he sees that already a
great part of the neighbourhood
of his kraal comes out quite
clear. Then he sees even a
forest : " Now," he says, " that
is the forest which is on this
side of our kraal, now I am
assuredly near." Then :
" Child of the Rain-Lord," etc.
(as above).
The little man, then, good
gracious ! begins also to feel
really tired. Yet he swallows
up the distance more than ever.
Just when he reached the
forest, he found there a stream.
and near the stream a big tree :
" Now," he said, " this is the
very place where I sat down
the other day. To-day also
let me sit down a moment while
waiting for my wife."

ya kuxibulula, baye bakaxi-
bulule."

Kâxikira kantu kâkaya.
Mpâ kwamba ay' arange
pêsule, ayi :
" Mwana wa Rêsa,
" Ndetere njaruxi yangu," etc.

Eryo kâwarayira-mo a ku-
warayira-mo kasankwa. Eryo
kabone ku mixi yabo kwafumpuka a kufumpuka. Eryo, a !
kâubona a musansa.   " Ono
ulya ngo wa ku mixi yêsu, ono
ndananamina. . . ."

" Mwana wa Rêsa," etc.

A kêne eryo, bacu ! kâkaam-
ba kuñumfwa kulema kasankwa.
Eryo, bacu ! kâri kulukutixa
a kulukutixa. . . .
Kuya mu kuxika mu musansa,
ajane ngu mulonga.   A kuya
mukuxika pamwi pa cisamu,
ayi " Mpa ano mpo ndakêkara.
A sunu nkare-wo panini n'inde
muka angu."

12TH SONG.

MOTHER OF LOADS.[56]
When the child of the Rain-
Lord reached the stream, she
said : " Go ahead quietly, while
I take a bath here."

NAMITEMBO.
(Ay' axike mwana wa Rêsa
ku mulonga, ayi " Ka muya
kabotu, nebo nsambe pano."

[56] This particular episode, as far as the impostor is concerned, is due to
Mumba, the narrator of Njerenjere, No batá a murenda, etc. It is current all
over the Zambesi region, but is, generally, detached from the present tale.

The man went on with the slaves behind him.

When he had gone a little distance, he heard a honey-bird singing *ncé ncé ncé ncé.* " Let me go and dig out some honey," says the man, " while my wife is still at the stream."

He goes to the place where he has heard the bird singing, thinking it may still be there. . . . " No, he is gone."

Just then he hears it further on, calling *ncé ncé ncé ncé.* Here is the honey.

He extracts some, then comes back to the road, and finds there, as he thinks, his wife, but, good gracious ! she is an impostor with all the cattle and some of the slaves, and the cat skin.

She says : " Let us go, husband, you have already extracted the honey, let us go."

She puts the honey on her head, and they go.

The true bride, meanwhile, there far behind, is also coming at a good pace, accompanied by other slaves and singing :

" Mother of loads ! Mother of loads !
" On the road by which we go
" There is an impostor,
" With all the cattle
" All the slaves,
" All the herds,
" All the beads,

Bâinda a baxa pêsule.

Be baxike mu nxira bêbabo bajane ngu maimba. Ngú ncé ncé ncé ncé . . . " Nje nkapande bûci, muka angu ucisamba."

Bê baxike kulya, bañumfwe bo ku ntango nko bâkaya " Mpani mpo ari," tâpo.

Bañumfwe bo ncé ncé ncé ncé, bajane mbú bûci.

Bamane kupanda, bacu ! banôya bo mu kuxika mu nxira, bajane, bacu ! ngú cimparanya [57] waroka, a mombe xônse, a baxa bamwi, a njaruxi ya nximba.

Ayi : " A twende, mwapanda kare bûci, bêbêsu, ka tuya."

A bûci bâyumuna.

Nkwakacara ba-nabwinga kulya bâbika-ko. A bâro mwisule, a bâro a bamwi baxa bâbo. . . .

" Namitembo ! Namitembo !

" Mu nxira tuya
" Muli cimparanya
" A mombe xônse,
" Baxa bônse,
" Ñama xônse,
" Bulungu bônse,

In it the daughter of the Rain-Lord calls herself *Na-mitembo* " Mother-of-loads," probably to show sympathy with her slaves, who by this time feel the weight of their loads.

[57] Var. *cimparamya.*

" All the brass,
" All the goods,
" All the clothes.
" Wait for me, that I may undeceive thee,
" My husband,
" Wait for me, that I may undeceive thee,
" Mother-of-loads ! "
The young man then looked
behind, but saw his wife near.
He never suspected that it was
the impostor. Yet there at a
distance the song was going on.
" Wait for me that I may undeceive thee," etc. (as above).
At last they are on the out-
skirts of the village. People
from there come out to look in
the direction of the road and to
see over there coming with quick
steps not only their child, but
also the impostor behind. . . .
" The child of the Rain-Lord ! "
they say, " the child of the Rain-
Lord ! There she is on the point
of reaching our kraal. . . .
Quick ! sweep the house."
Good gracious ! How nicely
they have whitewashed it and
smeared it ! [58].
Meanwhile the husband puts
his foot into the precincts of
the village,
" Oh ! There is my child ! "

" Here I am, mother. The
porridge you cooked on that
day, has it cooled ? "
" No, it still steams."
They go to take the cover off,
and steam comes out.

" Rubemba rônse
" Bubire bônse,
" Ngubo xônse.
" Mpembe nkuraye,

" Mulume wangu,
" Mpembe nkuraye,

" Namitembo ! "
Eryo kâranga-ko kwisule
kasankwa, kâmubona muka
akwe ngú uli pafwifwi. A
rimwi ngu cimparanya. Sombi
mwisule :
" Mpembe kuraye," etc.

Eryo a kwine ku mbari ku
muxi. Ayi kusompa-ko bari
ku muxi, bajane mbarya
batôsa cikatauka mwana wabo
a cimparanya pêsule. Bê
" Mwana wa Rêsa ! Mwana wa
Rêsa ! Ngulya utôya kuxika
ku mixi yêsu. Bacu ! A mupyayire mu manda."

Bacu ! Bâkaixibulula.

Eryo a mu muxi a baro kunkuru kuli bañina.

(" U ! " Mwana wangu mpo
ari ! "
Ayi " Mpo ndi, má. Nxima i
mwakaponda yakaora ? "

Ayi : " Tawu, icisunta."
Ngayi baifwekule bajane a
bwixi bwasukuma kare.[59]

---

[58] The smearing is done on the floor with fresh cow dung, when it can be had.
[59] This detail of the porridge still steaming is from Munje's version.

He then finds that the house of bricks has been built for his wife.

But, as the impostor is going to step inside, the mother-in-law, looking closely, says : " Is this really the daughter of the Rain-Lord ? No, by my mother, it is not."

The man, too, looking at her : " O my wife," he says, " where is my badge ? "

" I have left it at the stream."

" Let me go and fetch it."

And he rushes out.

But, as he rushes out, a song is heard to the west of the road : " Mother of loads ! Mother of loads ! " etc. (as above).

" Now look ! " says the mother of the boy, " at the people coming from that direction and singing."

Meanwhile the song goes on : " There is an impostor . . .

" Wait for me that I may undeceive thee," etc. (as above).

Good gracious ! They just see, heaven help me ! What ! They see the impostor pack off as fast as she can, and into the bush ! Look for her !

Now here is the true child of the Rain-Lord reaching the place in her turn, and with the little feather on her head.

Mpâ kwamba ayi axike boobo mu muxi ajane bâbumba manda ya matafwari.

(Mpêce kuya mu kunjira cimparanya, kumulangirixa bañinaxara : " Ngu mwana wa Rêsa uyu ? Ayi " Têxi mwana wa Rêsa, má."

A rakwe ibaye " O muka angu, ngara yangu yacara kuli ? "

" Yacara ku mulonga."

Mpêce " Nje nkairete."

A kuswa a rubiro.

Nkwakaswa, bañumfwe kumbo rya nxira : " Namitembo ! Namitembo ! " etc. (as above).

" A musompe ono bantu batôsa bwimba kooku. . . ."

Kuñumfwa ayi : " Muli cimparanya . . . " Mpembe nkuraye," etc.

Bacu ! Babone bo, bacu ! kwá, babone bo cimparanya kutukutukutuku rubiro mu rundu purururu.

A rakwe mwana wa Rêsa ngú waxika kale, a kapepe mu mutwi.

13TH SONG.

LET US SIT DOWN.

When the child of the Rain-Lord came in front of the house-door, she sat down there outside.

KA TWǏKARA.

Kuxika ba-Mwana wa Rêsa pansengwe bêkara.

" What ! " said some one, " the lady child of the Rain-Lord remain thus outside ! Shame upon us ! Quick ! Bring something to make her step into the house."

" A ! Ino ba-mwana wa Rêsa abo, cut ! A mulete câ kubênjixa mu rranda."

They brought a cow, and, when presenting the girl with her, they said : " Now let THEM go in."

Bâya mu kureta mpwixi, ayi " Ono a bênjire."

She went into the house, but she remained there standing. Then her husband sang :

Bânjira, bari imfwi. Mpêce musankwa ayi :

" Child of God, give me my cat skin, with which I go about.
" I will not, child of Heavy-brain.[60]
" Then let us sit down, child coming with water from the clouds.
" Let us sit down, child of Wood-cutter.[55]
" *Mwana wa Rêsa, kômpa njaruxi yangu ya kwenda ayo.*
" *Ndakaka, mwana wa Côngo.*
" *Ka twïkara, mwana wa kuswa a manxi ku mayoba.*
" *Ka twïkara, mwana wa Ximutema-mbaro.*"

On the mat she sat, and her husband helped her to sit comfortably.

A pa bulo a bêne bêkara bâmwikarika.

Then they brought porridge and said : " Here is some food for the lady daughter of the Rain-Lord." But she just crossed her arms over her chest. . . . . Then :

A nxima bâreta. Mpâ kwamba ayi barete boobo nxima, ayi " A barye ba-mwana wa Rêsa." Sobwe, bârikumbata. . . .

" Child of God, give me my cat skin, with which I go about.
" I will not, child of Heavy-brain.
" Then let us eat, child coming with water from the clouds.
" We eat with the child of Wood-cutter."
" *Mwana wa Rêsa, kômpa njaruxi yangu ya kwenda ayo.*
" *Ndakaka, mwana wa Congo.*
" *Ka tulya, mwana wa kuswa a manxi ku mayoba.*
" *Tute kulya a mwana wa Ximutema-mbaro.*"

They then started eating, and the porridge was all finished.
And then cattle were killed.

A bêne bâjata kuna kulya. A îne nxima yamana. Sombi xâfwa mombe. Sombi

---

[60] Mumba says that *Congo* " Heavy-brain " was the name of the mother, and *Ximutemambaro* " Wood-cutter " the name of the father of the hero.

All the people ate to their fill.
Next morning the mother said : " Now to-day brew some beer for her." [61]
Beer was brewed and brought. . . .

bantu bârya câtamwa."
A bwine bwaca. Ayi " Ono sunu mukakumbire bwarwa."

A bwine bwarwa butôkumbwa. Mpâ kwamba ayi barete bwarwa, ayi :

" Child of God, give me my cat skin, with which I go about.
" It is enough to inhale this aroma with the child of Wood-cutter.
" You ought to drink, child coming with water from the clouds.
" I will not, child of Thick-brain.
" At least give me my cat skin.
" Here, take thy cat skin, my husband."
" Mwana wa Rêsa, kômpa njaruxi yangu, ya kwenda ayo.
" Bate kwema a mwana wa Ximutema-mbaro.
" Mulanwa, mwana wa kuswa a manxi ku mayoba.
" Ndakaka, mwana wa Congo.
" Kômpa bo njaruxi yangu.
" A ! Nji njaruxi yako, ibangu."

Of the beer itself at last she drinks just a little.

Bwine bate kubunwa a bwarwa.

14TH SONG.

I GO, I GO, MY LITTLE BROTHER.

She remained there ten days. Then she said : " Here everything is not all well. People get drunk every day.[62] Take me back to our own place. I do not feel here as if I were at the proper place. There are things looking like incest. I cannot bear it any longer. I, the daughter of the Rain-Lord."
" O my wife," says the man, " is that how you speak ? And

'NAYA, 'NAYA, KAKWASU.

Bêkara nxiku rikumi. Eryo bê " Ono kuno ta kuxi kubotu. (Batôkorwa bwarwa nxiku xônse). Nebo mukantore ku mixi yêsu. Nxikwe kubona-ko kabotu. Kuli marwêsa kuno. Ndapenga ne mwana wa Rêsa."

" A ! O muka angu, mbo wamba obo ! Baxikire bulyo,

---

[61] This is the beverage called *bwarwa* lit. " the weak have fought," much more intoxicating than the one called *funku*, which word in song No. VI. we have translated by " wine."

[62] This mention of the beer as an explanation of the bride's displeasure is due to Mumba.

only just arrived ! . . . Now what do you mean ? To go back to your own abode ! First get accustomed. When you are accustomed, then you will go back all right."

Next morning the husband said : " Let me just have a look." The woman at once said : " I am going."

" You, my wife, how will you go ? "

" I go as I am, alone, if need be."

She is up already . . . " My wife, where are you going to ? "

" To my father, to the Rain-Lord."

While the husband gets up, the wife has already disappeared.

There she is with her clothes flying against the wind, and the husband from behind just hears this song :

" I go, I go, little brother.
    Chorus.—" Sins have sucked me dry."
" Near pools, is it not where I sleep ? [63]—*Chorus.*
" Mother-in-law, did you want me to commit incest ? [64]—*Chorus.*
" *Naya, 'naya, kakwasu.—Mirandu yankunamina.*
" *Ku maxiba te koondara !*   ,,   ,,
" *Mamaxara, wambona marwesa ?* "   ,,

She simply goes on, her clothes continuing to fly against the wind, the husband following from a distance and calling : " Come back, come back,

ino ! anu ! kuya ku mixi yanu . . . ! Tanguna mwĭxibire. Mpâ kwamba ayi mwĭxibire, ndye mukaye kabotu."

Mpâ kwamba ayi ibabo mumene " Ntôxikira bo," ayi " Nebo nte kuya."

Ayi " Webo, o muka angu, utôya buyani ?"

Ayi " Ntôya bulyo, na mbi nênka."

Bâxikira kuñamuka . . . . .

" Webo, o muka angu, utôya kuli ?"

Ayi " Ntôya kuli batá, kuli, ba-Rêsa.

Mpâ kuxikira kuñamuka, muka abo waroboka.

Mpâ kwamba ayi akwempere akwempere, bâro bêbabo pêsule bañumfwe :

Eryo bâkwempera a kukwempera.

Eryo a bâro barumi mu mukonkero :   /
" Bwera, bwera,[65]

---

[63] Var. " Near dregs of beer is it not where I sleep, *ku maxiwa te koondara ?* " So the pools abhorred by the daughter of the Rain-Lord seem to be made from dregs of beer.

[64] Mumba says that this question refers to the beer which the mother-in-law had ordered to be given to the bride.

[65] *Bwera* " come back " is from Ñungwe for Mukuni *bôra.*

" Finder of cowries and beads,
" Finder of brass-coils."
Her clothes there are still flying. So again the husband on her track behind :
" Come back come back," etc.
" I go, I go, my little brother," etc.
She goes faster and faster with her clothes flying. At last she sees over there the rise on which stands their city. And then too lightning upon lightning. " Now," she says, " over there that is the true abode of my father. And his voice too, is it not thunder ? "
" Yes," she adds, " that truly is my father." [66]
She then was seen trotting. She sang again :
" I go, I go, little brother," etc.

The husband now sees the wife trotting and ever trotting, while he feels himself dying from exhaustion. Nevertheless, he calls :
" Come back, come back," etc.
He just hears :
" I go, I go, my little brother," etc.
He too then trots and trots without stopping. Then he too hears the thunder rolling. Though exhausted, he calls again from behind :
" Come back, come back," etc.
" I go, I go, my little brother," etc.

" Rubona-mpande na marungu,
" Rubona-nsambo.
Eryo bâkwempera a kukwempera. Eryo a bâro bânarumi mu mukonkero :
" Bwera, bwera,
" 'Naya, 'naya, kakwasu," etc.

Bâkwempera a kukwempera eryo. Eryo ka babona a kulya ku mixi yabo kwatuntauka. Eryo ka babona kuli byá byá byá byá byá byá . . . " Ono nko kulya nko kuli batá nkwece. A te kwamba ayi nko kukukuma ? "

Ayi " Mbo mbatá mbêce abo."

Bâsensera, ayi :

" 'Naya, 'naya, kakwasu," etc.
Eryo abone eryo wasensera a kusensera mwanakaxi. Eryo a bâro bêbabo pêsure a bâro bâfwa ntabara. Ayi :

"¡Bwera, bwera," etc.
Kuñumfwa ayi :
" 'Naya, 'naya, kakwasu," etc.
A kâro kâsensera a kusensera eryo. Eryo ka akukuma a kukukuma, a kâro kakafwa ntabara pêsule. Ayi :

" Bwera, bwera," etc.
" 'Naya, 'naya, kakwasu," etc.

[66] Note that the child of the Rain-Lord thinks only of her father, while the child of vulgar origin remembers only his mother.

Neither of the two gives up trotting. The child of the Rain-Lord then sees the city itself beginning to stand in front of her. She is just going to reach it. So she sings again, while going up the rise :
" I go, I go, my little brother,
" Sins have sucked me dry,"
etc. (as above).

And the man takes up the song as before :
" Come back, come back,
" Finder of cowries and beads,
" Finder of brass coils."

At last the wife jumps into the city.

Seeing her come in this fashion, her people greet her :
" So you have put in an appearance ? "
" I have put in an appearance. . . . Ha ! Enough ! "
She just sits down.

Good gracious ! The man comes too. . . . " Now," he says, " I shall not go back to my mother's." He settles there for good.[67]

And now the little story is finished . . . altogether finished.

I am MWANA MBIRIKA, the child of I-glorify.[68]

Eryo kabasensera bôbire a kusensera. Eryo ka abona mwana wa Rêsa a muxi waboneka. Eryo, bacu ! kuya mu kuxika. Mpâ kwamba ayi atuntuke, ayi :

" 'Naya, 'naya, kakwasu,
" Mirandu yankunamina," etc.

A rakwe ayi :

" Bwera, bwera,
" Rubona-mpande na marungu
" Rubona-nsambo."

Eryo bâxikira mu muxi kunkulu.

Mpâ kwamba ayi baxike boobo. . . . " Mwaboneka ? "

" Ndaboneka . . . U !   Mbobulya."

Bacu ! Bâxikira bulyo, nkwĭkara bulyo.

Bacu ! Eryo bâxikira bulyo a musankwa. " Ono te nkayeko kuli bamá." Mpêce a kwĭkara wêkarira a rimwi.

A kwera ono kêera.

Ndime MWANA MBIRIKA.

---

[67] The Sena version ends as follows : " Now, when God rains (*sic*), if we hear thunder, we say that it is Zunguza clapping hands to his father-in-law, and when soon afterwards we hear again Rh,Rh,Rh,Rh, that is God acknowledging his son-in-law's clapping of hands."

[68] (*a*) *Mbirika*, lit. " I glorify " is said by the Bêne-Mukuni to be one of the names of God, and so are many words formed in the same manner, such as *Nkomexa* " I bring to perfection," *Nkôcexa* " I give thee rest," *Njereka* " I measure," etc. Such names describing God under one of his attributes are changed into proper names of persons by prefixing to them *Mwana* " child," as *Mwana-Mbirika, Mwana-Nkôcexa*, etc.

BANTU FOLK-LORE 145

(b) In this country there is a bird called "the son-in-law of God," *mukwe wa Rêsa*, or *mukwe Rêza*. I do not see that it has anything in common with the hero of this story. It is said to announce the coming of the rainy season. See about it Jacottet's *Textes Soubiya*, pp. 128 and 151. Only note that there *sonda imvula* does not mean properly, as Jacottet thinks "jeter les osselets pour la pluie," but " guess the rain." In Subiya, as in Tonga, Bwine-Mukuni, etc., *sonda* is the proper word for " guess." In Bwine-Mukuni " a prophet " is *mu-sonda*.

(c) In this tale, as in others, the narrators take, of course, all the liberties of fiction, but, even so, there are in it too many details reminding one of the authentic story of Moses to allow us to reject as entirely absurd the notion that some parts of it sound like an echo, however faint, of Mosaic traditions.

We have, in suggestive combination, a chief ordering the murder of new-born boys, a boy taken to the river and deposited there in some sort of cradle, a woman taking care of him, and the very mother of the boy knowing all about it, while a near relation, called Drum or Drums, is also in the secret. There is also a wonderful feather with some of the magic power of Moses' wand. Then the filth which blocks the way of out hero makes one think of the plagues of Egypt. The river Putu, which he has to cross, is said to be some-where in the direction of Egypt. Here, as in Exodus, we have a high mountain and a plague of snakes. By our hero, as by Moses, the Lord is found on a high mountain. In both narratives lightning and thunder play an important part. In both narratives the hero, to secure the treasure upon which he has set his heart, has to go twice to the mountain of God.

And after all, what did the author of the original tale mean by speaking of " a daughter " or " the daughter " of God " coming with water from the clouds ? " It is quite possible that he may have meant " the law of God " given to the hero amidst thunder and lightning. A number of passages of the tale are evidently meant to teach certain Mukuni laws supposed to come from God. And one of its notable features is that the sight of wrongdoings is enough to make the daughter of God run away.

What is beyond doubt is that the present narrators have not sought their inspiration in the Bible. They are perfectly illiterate, and the principal narrator, Mwana Mbirika, has probably never entered a church.

Just as this is going to press I note in *Anthropos* (1909, p. 946), the following observation of Father Trilles : " In our Northern Fan˞ tribes, far from all European infiltration, in villages which had never seen a white face, I found a legend in which the principal actor, *Bingo*, saviour of his people whom he frees from the persecutions of an enemy nation and whom he leads through a thousand dangers to the land they are going to occupy, reminds one strongly of the Moses of the Bible. . . ."

SECOND PART.

TALES IN RHODESIAN TONGA.

I.—DRUM, YOU HAVE HURT ME.

N.B.—This is yet another version of the tale BRANCH OFF, BLAZE OF FIRE. It is given here to provide the reader with the opportunity of observing how easily animals in folk-lore are substituted for persons, since we find here an allegorical crocodile taking the place of the little old woman of the preceding versions.

By the way, a considerable difference may be noted between the different deposits of folk-lore among the different tribes of the Zambesi region. The Bêne-Mukuni, being settled on the highlands, far from the great waterways, have scarcely any tales of animals, except two or three evidently imported. Their own tales are practically all about human beings. The Ba-Tonga and Ba-Sukulumbwe, living partly on the highlands, partly on the great rivers Zambesi and Kafúe, have mostly tales of human beings, but also a fair number of animal stories. Among the tribes settled on the great Zambesi waterway, the Ba-Luyi, Ba-Subiya, Ba-Ñayi, A-Ñungwe, A-Sena, A-Podzo, etc., the tales of animals seem to predominate. For the Subiya and the Luyi tales see Jacottet's *Textes Soubiya* and *Textes Louyi*. My own collection of Lower Zambesi folk-lore is still awaiting publication.

This is what the people of old [1] did. When they had done what has been said,[2] the following prohibition was made by the king : " Do not give birth to any more girls. If ever a girl be born, let her be strangled."

Then first a boy was born. He was called Drum

It also happened that the sister-in-law of Drum's mother gave birth to a girl. She was told to do away with her.

This she refused to do. She went and deposited the child near the river, a few steps from a crocodile, to whom she said : " Here is this child, rear her up for me."

The child grew at the crocodile's abode. When she was grown, boys herding goats, and Drum among them, appeared there. The crocodile said : " Go and tell your aunt that her child is grown up. Let her bring meal for her."

So Drum went and told his aunt. She then began to grind meal. She ground and ground before the dawn of day. She then took

---

[1] No such mention of people of old is generally made at the beginning of Tonga tales. Why this novelty here ?

[2] Nearly every tale is supposed to be the continuation of another. It reminds one of *In illo tempore* of the Sunday gospels.

the meal, went, and found the child full grown and beautiful. The daughter received the meal from the hands of her mother. Then they cooked the porridge and ate it together.

After that the mother said : " Crocodile, lend me this maid of yours to show me the way out. She will leave me on the shore there, and come back."

The daughter showed her mother the way. When they came to the shore, the mother said : " Now go back, otherwise the herd-boys will see you."

The daughter retraced her steps, transformed herself into a *ntengwa* bird,[3] and went towards a hole, into which she entered. The boys at once approached stealthily. . . . " Look, look, there is a little *ntengwa* bird which has gone into a hole."

They went and tried to drive the little bird out with sticks by poking and poking. While they were at it, there it started singing :
" Drum, you have hurt me with a stick."
       Chorus.—*Nzañini ?   Nzañini ?*[4]
" What is that ?   Drum, you have hurt me.
" There in your city the lord said
" That no girls should be born,
" Only such children should be born as can herd cattle.
" What is that ?   Drum, you have hurt me."
The child Drum was crying.[5] The other boys asked : " What did the bird say ? "
" It says it is I."
" Say, mates, what is the matter with the little bird ? "
" It says it is I. It says : Drum, you have hurt me. In your city, lord, no girls are born, only such children are born as can herd cattle."

Drum's companions then said : " Cousin, you are mistaken. Do not cry for such a trifle. . . . Go, Drum."

They went on poking, poking, the little bird singing meanwhile :
" Drum, you have hurt me with a stick," etc. (as above).

Having sung thus, it came out . . . " Cousins," they said, " let us leave the little bird alone, since it has come out at our bidding."

They turned away, the bird doing the same through the air. As it flew thus away, it went to the crocodile's home.

[3] Apparently a sort of parrot.
[4] I understood the narrator to say that *Nzañini* means something like " Dance in a ring," but more probably it is a metathesis for *nza niñi ?*   " What is that ? ", *niñi ?*   " what ? " being the word borrowed from Nungwe which occurs in another version of the same tale (*sanda, sanda, rwando*).
[5] Tonga children are comparatively sensitive and natural. A Mukuni boy would not be described as shedding tears in a case like this.

Then Drum said : " Look here, fellows, I am going to tell my uncle about this thing."

So he went to his uncle : " Father," he said, " a little bird has frightened me. It was saying it is I."

" Indeed ! How is that ? "

" It said : Drum, you have hurt me with a stick. In your city, the lord said that no girls should be born, only such children as are good to herd cattle."

The uncle said : " We will go there to-morrow morning, and you will show us."

Next morning they went at sunrise. The mother, for her part, had gone already, and there, at the crocodile's abode, had gone under the rock. . . . " My child, come ; by mother ! let us go. Show me the way." Just at that moment the father was on the bank.

There he appears already. He then hears : " Go back, child. Drum and his companions will see you. Turn away."

While going back thus, she had already become a *ntengwa* bird. The father, from the bank, was looking fixedly. . . .

" There is the *ntengwa*, mates," say the children, " there is the *ntengwa*, there is the *ntengwa*. It has gone into the hole."

They poke into it. When Drum does it too, there comes forth the song :
" Drum, you have hurt me," etc. (as above).

Then the father said : " Let us leave it alone now, to-morrow we will bring cattle. . . ."

At daybreak the herd-boys took the goats out. They also, the father and the mother, left early together with a boy leading cattle with which to redeem the girl from the crocodile.

As they came near the shore, the servants remained in the bush, but the mother went on to take meal to the child.

When they had finished eating, she said : " Now show me the way."

The child showed her the way. Then, as they came to the bank, there they found people, who surrounded her, and together got hold of her. She screamed and screamed. She then changed herself into a young eagle. . . . Again she changed herself into a grown-up eagle. . . . " Let me go, let me go."

She then pushes on towards the crocodile. He, on his side, says : " Let me have a look at my wife."

So the crocodile too comes forth : " You there in the west," he
says, " there is light in the sky." [6]
(Then confused sounds are heard) :   " No ! No ! No ! . . .
My child ! . . .   O mother there ! . . .   My child ! . . .
Crocodile, hold off. . . ."
To the crocodile they gave a cow and a bull, and an ox besides.[7]
That is the end of the story.[8]

(IN TONGA.)

WANCISA . . . NGOMA.

Nzi bâkacita bâ karekare.
Bacite boobo, kwategwa ku mwami " Mutani kuzyari basimbi,
ka muzyara basankwa.   Uti azyarwe musimbi bakamusine."
Eryo umwi mwanakazi wazyara musankwa.   Kwategwa " Nduwe
Ngoma izina ryako."
Eryo umwi mwanakazi, mulamuñina, wazyara musimbi.   Eryo
kwategwa " Ukamusine."
Ngo wakaka kumujaya.   Waya kumutula ku mulonga kuli
ciwena.   Uti " Ngo oyu mwana, kôndisaninina."
Sitare wati " Reta nkusaninine."

---

[6] *i.e.,* " Don't you fear God ?

[7] Here we have a good example of how the personification of animals in tales,
or rather, the animalising of persons, leads to fantastic absurdities.   In the
Mukuni tale " Branch off, blaze of fire," the saviour of the child is a woman,
and in her case a reward in cattle is natural enough.   Here the saviour is a
crocodile, and no doubt the tale means a true crocodile, not a person whose
proper name is Crocodile.   Now, a crocodile would always, no doubt, appre-
ciate the gift of an ox, but it may well be asked whether the donors of the
bull and the cow expected them to be used for breeding purposes.
In tales somewhat similar to this, but current among other tribes than the
Bêne-Mukuni, the absurdity is pushed still further under the influence of
superstition.   A cow and a bull are sacrificed to the spirit of the water from
which the girl is rescued.   See in my Compar. Gr. of Bantu the Xosa tale,
Tanga-lo-mlibo, p. 320.

[8] This tale was phonographed at the Chikuni Mission, Northern Rhodesia, first
in 1906 from the mouth of a little girl called Karinda, then again in 1908 from
the mouth of the little girl Miyanda.   Both texts are practically identical.
The story, as told in these versions, seems to be localised at Sesheke, which
a few years ago had a bad name among the Tonga people, when the Barotse
rulers had not yet imbibed those Christian principles on which Yeta III. now
prides himself.   This appears from the Sekololo word *basezana* " girls " instead of Tonga *basimbi* in the verse " No girls are born."
I have heard, but not recorded with the phonograph, a version of this story
in which the crocodile is described as adorning the little girl with all sorts of
cowries, pearls, and other ornaments found in the water, in the hope of winning
her as his wife.

Mwana wakomena kuli cıwena. Akomene boobo, bâsika basim-
pongo beembera a Ngoma. Sitare wati " Ka muya mukaambire
bañoko kuti " Mwana wanu wakomena," baze kumuletera busu."
Waya kubaambira Ngoma bañina. Nko kuziya bañina. Bâziya
bâziya kuciri busiku. Bâtora busu, bâya kujana mwana wakomena
kare. Watambula bañina busu. Abatambule boobo, bâjika bâlya.
Kabera bañina bâti " Sitare ndâbire muntu wako andisindikire.
Uya kujoka arya atara."
Musimbi wabasindikira bañina. Asike atara, bañina bâti " Lino
kôjoka, mwana angu, barakubona beembera."
Wajoka waba ntengwa, waya kunjira mu bwina. Eryo bâmuberera
basankwa . . . " Nka karya, nka karya kanga ntengwa, kânjira
mu bwina."
Bâya kukasoma, bâkati coko coko. Eryo, bakasome boobo,
karaimba :
" Wancisa a kasamo, Ngoma.—Nzañini ? Nzañini ?
" Nzañini, Ngoma, ncisa ?
" Mu munzi mwanu munene :
" Ta muzyarwa basezana,[9]
" Muzyarwa beembera mombe.
" Nzañini, Ngoma, ncisa ? "
Warira mwana Ngoma. Kwategwa " Waamba kutyani ? "
" Waamba ndime."
" Kâba a nzi kayuni, no barombwana-ma ? "
" Waamba ndime. Waamba kuti : Ngoma, ncisa. Mu munzi
mwanu munene : ta muzyarwa basezana, muzyarwa beembera
mombe."
Barombwana-ñina bâamba kuti " Musa, wabeja . . . Reka
kulira. . . . A kanini buyo ! Kôya, Ngoma."
Bâkasomasoma, bâkasomasoma. Kari kwimba :
" Wancisa a kasamo, Ngoma," etc. (as above).
Kaimbe boobo, kâzwa. Kwategwa " Basa, ka tusiya kayuni
kâtuzwida."
Bâunka, kâuluka kayuni. Kauluke boobo, kâunka kuli ciwena.
Eryo Ngoma waamba kuti " Ndâ kwamba kuli tata, no barom-
bwana-ma."
Waunka kuli uxi . . . " Tata, kândiyosya kayuni. Kâri
kwamba ndime."
" A ! Kâri kutyani ? "

[9] *Basezana*, Sekololo = Tonga *basimbi*.

" Kâti : Wancisa a kasamo, Ngoma. Mu munzi mwanu munene :
ta muzyarwa basezana, muzyarwa beembera rrombe."
Kwategwa " Tuzoo kuunka junza, ukatutondezye."
Junza bâunka bwaca . . . Bâkaunka kare a bâro bañina.
Baunke boobo kuli sitare oko, bênjira mu 'bwe . . . " Mwana
angu, kôbora, bama, twende, utusindikire. . . ."
A uxi a mbari . . . Ngo wasika kare uxi . . . " Joka, mwana
angu, barakubona ba-Ngoma. Kôpiruka."
Ajoke boobo, waba kare ntengwa.   Uxi ularangisya a mbari. . .
" Ngo oyo ntengwa, no barombwana-ma, ngo oyo ntengwa, ngo oyo
ntengwa, wanjira mu bwina."
Bari kucokosa . . . Akacokose Ngoma :
" Wancisa a kasamo, Ngoma," etc. (as above).
Kwategwa " Tumuleke rino, junza tukarete rrombe. . . ."
Bwaca, bâzitora mpongo beembera, a rabo bañina bâfuma a uxi,
a umwi musankwa ujisi rrombe zya kuzi kulungira sitare.
Bâsika ku mulonga.   Eryo bantu bâsyara mu xokwe.   Basyare
boobo, bañina bâtora busu ku mwana abo.
Bamane kulya, kwategwa " Ndisindikire."
Abasindikire boobo, bâjana bantu atara.   Bâmujata vú.   Bamu-
jate boobo, wabanduka musika . . . wabanduka musika. . . .
" A mundireke . . . a mundireke."
Kutora kuli sitare.   Sitare a rakwe " Ndikabone ku muka angu."
Sitare a rakwe wazwa " No muli kumbó', kujulu ngwarungwaru."
" Akaka ! . . . Akaka ! . . . Akaka ! "—Mwana angu, mayo !
Mwana angu ! "—Sitare, kaka ! "
Bama !   Bâmutora ! . . .
Sitare bâmupa rrombe zyobiro, mucende a mpwizi, a musune.
Bamutore boobo, bâamba kumunjizya mu rranda mwabo.   Nka
kâno kâsimpa.
KARINDA + MIYANDA.

II.—I DON'T WANT TO.

This is what people used to narrate.
She went to the water and there found a child of the temple,[1]
which she took home.   On her arrival there she said :   " My luck !
I have picked up a child for myself."

----

[1] " Child of the temple," *mwana wa marende.*   The *marende* are to the Ba-
Tonga what the church is to us, that is, the place where they assemble for
divine worship, particularly after the first rains.   Children sent by God to be
His messengers are supposed to be found occasionally in such spots, brought
down by the rain from the sky.   They are by that very fact *bâme* " kings."

As for the husband, he said : " All right, we are thankful."

The woman ground meal and cooked porridge, then said to the child : " Come, mother,[2] let us eat. The child answered with this song :

" I don't want to,
" Because I don't like it
" That you should speak respectfully of ugly luck,
" L-l-l-luck, yes, ugly l-l-l-luck.[3]
" Luck has puffed cheeks."

" Pray, mother, come, let us eat. . . "

" I don't want to," etc. (as above).

When they had finished eating, they went to bed . . . " Pray, come, mother, let us sleep. . . ."

" I don't want to," etc. (as above).

The woman said : " What can be, tell me, the most engaging way of addressing this child ? It refuses to sleep. To-morrow, friends, I shall take it away. It has come to the point of scratching me."

" You don't say so ! "

" It is a fact. It has scratched me."

At this moment the nails buried themselves in the flesh. . . .

" Not that," said the woman, " come, mother, let us sleep."

" I don't want to," etc. (as above).

" Pray, mother, go and call somebody from the town."

So people from the town were called. Then a different woman began to say : " I pray you, mother, let us sleep. . . ."

"" I don't want to," etc. (as above).

" Come, I pray, otherwise you will be left alone, come."

" I don't want to," etc. (as above).

At dawn those people took the child to the lake, and wanted to hide it in the sand where they had found it. When they reached the place, the woman said : I pray you, mother, come, this is the place where I found you. . . ."

" I don't want to," etc. (as above).

The people then went into the lake, at a place where the water was not yet deep, and began to say : " Pray, mother, come to this place in the lake belonging to such as you "[4] . . .

[2] This child may in the narrator s idea have been a girl. But the fact of calling it " mother " does not prove it, as this title is sometimes given also to boys. Here the context shows that it was the tenderest appellation which the woman could find. In not a few tales a boy of one version becomes a girl in another version.

[3] The narrator uses here the word *corwe* " luck," and rolls the *r* strongly, apparently to show the child's horror for the very notion of luck. In English a similar effect may be produced by trilling the *l*.

[4] " The lake belonging to such as you." Throughout the whole of the Tonga

"I don't want to," etc. (as above).

Going on and stopping where the water reached their waists, they said : "Pray, mother, come as far as this. . . ."

"I don't want to," etc. (as above).

On she went, stopping only when the water reached their chests. . . .

"I don't want to," etc. (as above).

Further, letting only the top of the child's hair appear above the water, they said : "Pray, mother, this is the place, come. . . ."

"I don't want," etc.

At this juncture all of a sudden the child got out of their hands, dived, and went away into the depths.

Here stops the little story. The people went away with the current.[5]

I am MIYANDA.[6]

(IN TONGA.)

NSEYANDI.[7]

Mbu câninga.[8]

Waya ku mênda. Waya kubweza mwana wa mu marende.

Watora ku munzi, waamba kuti "Côrwe cângu ! Ndaribwezera mwana."

A rakwe murumi uti "Mbubo, twakabomba."

Waziya, wajika nsima . . . "Kôbôra, bamá, tulye. . . ."

          "Nseyandi.
          "Nseyandi

---

lore, all royal, including white, children are supposed not only to be born of, but also to be at home in, the water. For this reason, when, a little further on, this royal child plunges into the depths, it is not supposed to come to harm, but simply to go home.

The very goods of the kings and "other" white people (the kings being all considered to be white, no matter how black they are) are all supposed to come up from the deep, or to come down from the sky with the rain. My attention was called to this detail by Mr. Sykes, late of Livingstone, who saw in it a confirmation of my theory regarding the Sabaean origin of part of the Lower Zambezi folk-lore. See "The Sabaeans on the Zambesi' in the Proceedings of the Bulawayo Scientific Assoc., June, 1905.

[5] "With the current." Distinguish in Tonga between the too verbs *bâunka* and *bâunkira*. The first means simply "they went away " ; but the second, being what may be called compositive, means "they went away with the current."

[6] This was phonographed in January, 1906. The little girl, Miyanda, was then about 12 years of age. The Tonga dialect she speaks is Bue.

[7] *Nseyandi*, Sekololoized from Tonga *Nsiyandi*.

[8] *Câninga.* Here *ci*, as often happens in Bwine-Mukuni, means "some indefinite people " (French *on*).

" Azootête côrrwe-ña,[9]
" Côrrwe, e !
" E !   Côrrwe-ña.
" Câborromana côrrwe."
" Akaka !   Kôbôra, bamá, tulye."
Bâya a bulo bâmana kulya . . . " Akaka !   Kôbôra, bama, toone. . . ."
" Nseyandi," etc. (as above).
Kwategwa " Oyu mwana atêtegwe ani, no bênzuma ?   Wakaka koona . . . Nzoo ku mutora junza mwana oyu, no bênzuma. Wakoma kunamatula."
" Akaka ! "
" Wakoma kunamatula."
Imwi mâra âbira mu ñama . . . " Akaka !   Kôbôra, bamá, toone. . . ."
" Nseyandi," etc. (as above).
" Akaka !   Bamá, mukaite bari mu munzi."
Bâya kwita bari mu munzi. A umwi wakoma kuti " Aka ! kôbôra, bamá, toone. . . ."
" Nseyandi," etc. (as above).
" Bôra, akusiye.   Kaka, bamá, bôra. . . ."
" Nseyandi," etc. (as above).
Imwi bwaca.   Bâmutora ku ziba.   Bâya ku musisa a museye nko bâkamujana.   Bâkoma kusika . . . " Aka !   Bamá, kôbôra, mpo ndâkujana. . . ."
" Nseyandi," etc.
Imwi bânjira mu ziba, mênda nku aciri mafwifwi.   Bâkoma kuti " Akaka !   Bamá, kôbôra mpa awa mu ziba rya kwanu. . . "
" Nseyandi," etc.
Imwi bâtana mu cibuno . . . " Akaka !   Bamá, kôbôra, mpa ano."
" Nseyandi," etc.
Imwi bâtana mu câmba. . . .
" Nseyandi," etc.
Imwi bâsiya kasusu . . . " Akaka !   Bamá, mpa ano, kôbôra."
" Nseyandi," etc.
Imwi bâsika akati . . . " Akaka !   Bamá, kôbôra, mpa ano ino."
" Nseyandi," etc.
" Akaka !   Ino mpa ano, bamá, kôbôra."
Byú !   Kâbira kâunka mu nkumbwi.
Nka kâno kâsimpa.   Bantu bâunkira.
Ndime MIYANDA.

[9] *Côrrwe* for *côrwe.*   See above, note 3.

Kukwe !   Kukwe rero ! [3]
Siende mu nzira.[4]
Kukwe !   Kukwe rero !
Siende mu nzira.
Mwana, ndiyowa
Câtara kare.[5]
Siende mu nzira.
Mámvwa !
Siendeende siende mu nzira.
Nkambo !
Siendeende siende mu nzira."

Erimwi bêenda bêenda bêenda . . . " Ta mwanjanina mwana wangu, no bênzuma ?   Ta baindi bajisi mwana ? "
Bâti " Bâinda."
Ma !   Ma !   Ma !   Erimwi bêenda bace angu.   Bâimba kare :
" Kukwe ?   Kukwe rero ? " etc.
Baya bubuzyabuzya.
Ma !   Ma !   Ma !   Bâya kubajana.   Bâti " Mutora kuli mwana wangu, má ? "

---

[3] *Rero*, borrowed from Sori = Tonga *suno* " to-day."   *Kukwe* " dense bush " = Mukuni *ru-kwe*.
[4] *Siende*, Sikololo for Tonga *twende* " let us go."
[5] *Tara*, word formed from Sori *tari* " far " = Tonga *rampa*.

" Twamujata buyo."
Erimwi " No bênzuma, a mundipe mwana wangu, má."
Bâti " Ngo oyu." Bâmupa.
Bêenda, bêenda, bêenda, bâswangana basimbi ku mulonga . . .
" No basimbi, ngo mwenziñokwe, ka mutêrera."
Bâti " Tulatêrera.'
Bâya kusika bañina ku munzi, basimbi bâjana cisisi câ muliro,
bâamba kuteba nkuni, bâti " A tuyoke tulye."
Ma ! Ma ! Ma ! Ngo mwana bâamba kumuyoka. . . .
    " Câtunda cana."
    " Cimanse a muliro.—*Chorus.*
    " Câbota câna.   ,,
    " Eci câna !   ,,
Bârya, bârya, bârya. Bamane kulya, bâamba kubara bufwafwa.
Babare boobo, bêenda, bêenda, bêenda. Baraimba :
    " Buyowere bwa Simamvwa,
    " Bularira buyowere, buyowere bularira.
    " Buyowere bwa Simbeza,
    " Bularira buyowere, buyowere bularira."
Bêenda erimwi . . . " No bênzuma, basimbi baimba boobo
baimba-nzi ? Baimba inga mwenziñina bâmulya buyo. Bude !
A muswirire ! Te mbabo baamba kuti buyowere bwa Simbeza
bularira ? Ino mbubo, kabaya, tuzoo kubaswirira. . . ."
    " Buyowere bwa Simamvwa," etc.
Ma ! Ma ! Ma ! Bêenda, bêenda, bêenda, bâsika kumbo . . .
" No bâna, mutora kuli mwenziñoko ? "
Bakare boobo kumbo barauzya . . . , baraimba :
    " Buyowere bwa Simamvwa," etc.
" Ino pe, mwana angu mulabara yi ? A mumpe mwana angu
ngu mwarya. Muya kufwa."
Kwaamba kusiya, bâona, bwaamba kubarya buyuni.
Nko kâno kâsimpa.
Ndime NAÑUKA.

IV.—CÂMUNDARI.

As some girls were going to fish, a little boy followed them,
thinking that he would go and keep his eyes open there while they
fished.[1]

---

[1] In Tongaland fishing is done by men with spears, by women mostly with
baskets called *myono.*

The girls drove him away again and again, saying : " Boy, where are you going to ? "

He said : " I mean to follow you."

Once more they went on driving, driving him away.   But he again followed them.

When they came to the river they caught plenty of fish.   But, meanwhile, rain came.   So they crossed the river.   Then they saw a house in the forest.   The boy at once said : " Do you not see that the path is broad ?   It is not made by men, but by a beast."

The girls said : " Boy, go back the way you came."   He refused to go.

As they came nearer to the house, the little boy said : " Do you not see how broad the doorway is ? "

They then saw horns and skulls of big game . . . " And these horns ! "   he said, " Look well, no man kills game like that.   It must be a beast that catches them, a Sizimwe." [2]

The comment was : " Never mind, let us go in."   And in they went.

Once inside they cooked and cooked fish.   One of them then said : " Give some to Câmundari.[3]   That was the name of the little boy. He would not accept any.

When they had finished eating, night came.   So they lay down to sleep, but the boy Câmundari sat down behind the entrance.

At midnight there came the owner of the house, who found the entrance closed : " There is a smell of human beings," he said. " Open to me, open to me."

The boy from inside sang :

> " Open !   No,
> " Father of a beast,
> " Father of short skins,
> " Father of Mwiza,[4]
> " I, I am Now-where-do-I-strike ? "

Once more :   " Open to me, open to me. . . ."
             " Open !   No," etc. (as above).

There was a jump, the door opened, and in came the Sizimwe, who said : " Give me, sir, this girl who is in the middle."

Then Câmundari sang :

---

[2] The Sizimwe is a fabulous beast of prey which does harm only in darkness and is notorious for its gluttony.   Jacottet has several tales about it (Textes Louyi, pp. 49, 50 ; and Textes Soubiya, pp. 51–69).

[3] *Câmundari* is a proper name which seems to mean " a trap," from *mundari*, kind of wood used mostly for traps.

[4] " Father of Mwiza."   This expression means " a heartless man."

" They, no more than I, are to be eaten.
" They have just come from the court.[5]
" They are a bitter food.[6]
" I, I am Now-where-do-I-strike ? "
Once more : " Give me, sir, give me this plump little one."
" They, no more than I, are to be eaten," etc. (as above).
The beast went out when it was still dark.   At daybreak, as they opened the door, the boy said :   Tell me now, did you hear the beast that was here, the owner of the house ? "
They said :   " Little boy, you are unbearable.   That is a lie, since we did not hear him.   When was he here ? "
The girls went to fish, while the little boy went to carve a drum. He carved and carved.   When night came, he came back and sat in the house.   He said :   " Listen well to-night, do not sleep."
They said :   " All right, we will listen."
Once more the Sizimwe came at midnight . . . " Open to me, sir, open to me. . . ."
" Open !   No," etc. (as above).
The Sizimwe then opened himself. . . .   " Give me, sir, give me this plump one. . . ."
" They no more than I, are to be eaten," etc.
This time again when the Sizimwe went out of the house, the boy said :   " Well, now, did you hear ? "
They replied :   " Yes, we heard."
At daybreak, the boy went to carve his drum.   He carved and carved and chiselled until it was finished.   He then came and put the girls into it, saying :   " Get into the drum."
They all went in, except one, who refused.   This one he got in by force.
Having them all in now, he took his drum, and went away with it, leaving rotten fish behind.
The Sizimwe, meanwhile, had gone to call all his mates, all the snakes, all the crafty leopards, all the lions, all the wild dogs, without forgetting the hyaenas.   The beasts came and went into the house, but found nobody inside.
They said :   " Where are the people you told us about ? "
The hyaenas picked up the rotten fish and ate it.
Some one said :   " Let us follow their footprints."

[5] " From the court, *mirumbe*," lit. " from law-cases."   *Mirumbe* is a Sori word = Mukuni *mirandu*.
[6] " They are a bitter food," *i.e.*, they would fight for their life.   Compare the chorus *kandiwandiwa* in the tale " *Kapepe*."

The Sizimwe then ran after them, the other beasts making a tail behind him. At last they came up to Câmundari carrying his drum, and stopped him.

They asked him : " Who art thou ? Who art thou ? "

" I am Câmundari."

" What art thou carrying on they shoulders, master ? "

" A wretched heavy drum, that is all."

" Go along and beat it on the way."

                    " Boom ! Boom ! Boom ! "

        " Sound loud ! "—*Chorus*—" Câmundari-mundari.[7]

        " I am a little child of Mônga.[8]

        " At our abode there are trees with big trunks."

Hearing this, the leopards went out of their ranks, and danced, and danced. While they were dancing, the boy left them there and disappeared.

When they had had enough of the dance, they said : " Cousins, where is he gone to, the man who was singing here ? "

They followed his footprints and came up to him. Once more he sounded his drum, once more they danced, once more he left them there, once more they went after him. But at last they lost all trace of him.

Then, not finding him any more, they devoured their mate the Sizimwe, saying : " You have deceived us."

The boy reached his parents' abode, but found nobody at home, every soul having gone to the fields. He then went into a hut with his drum, and shutting himself inside, climbed up on to a pile of firewood.

While he was there, his mother came, driven in by the rain, and said : " Let me open, quick." Having opened, she said : " Who are you ? ' '

Voices answered : " We know you : you are Mwiza's mother, and our own mother."

She ran out in haste like a rat, and said : " Have you heard the thing that has been speaking in the hut ? "

---

[7] Here the girls, who are in the drum, are supposed to join in the chorus. When the Tonga folk heard my phonograph, the first stories that came to their memories were naturally those of children singing in drums. Every one wanted to see the child concealed in the box of the instrument. These tales seem to be common to most of the black tribes. I see one in Ellis's " The Yoruba speaking peoples." There it is Mr. Tortoise who puts inside his drum a boy whose life he has saved. While Tortoise is drunk, the mothers of the boy take him out and put a crow in his place.

[8] In Jacottet's " Textes Soubiya," Mônga is the hero of a tale somewhat similar to our own Mukuni tale, " Let the Big Drum Sound," No. VI., but the song given by Jacottet, pp. 172–174, is quite different from ours.

Then came the husband saying : " Child ! Child ! There has been nothing speaking." So he added : " Let me open, let me open." And opening, he said : " Who are you ?"

" We know you. You are our father, the one who has begotten us."

Then they went to consult a seer, who said : " Perhaps that is where your children, whom you had lost sight of, are hidden. Go and kill a bullock on the doorway,[9] and roast him for them."

Father and mother then came and killed an ox, and Câmundari came out of the hut, while the girls came out of the drum.[10]

There stopped the little story at that event.[11]

(IN TONGA.)

CAMUNDARI.

Basimbi bâya ku kuzera.[12] Eryo mulombwana wacirira . . . " Ndikêbere mu bazera."

Bâmutanda basimbi, bâmutanda. Bâti " Mwana, uya yi ? " Ulaamba " Ndacirira ñwe."

Bâmutanda, bâmutanda. Mwana erimwi wabacirira.

Bâsika ku mulonga, bâzera nswi zinji-zinji. Bazere boobo, kwasika mvula. Bâzabuka bâya kubona manda iri mu saka. Mwana wati " Ta muboni, ena ?, nzira yakomena ? Ti iri ya bantu, nje ya muñama."

Eryo basimbi bâti " Mwana, kôjoka, kôjoka buyo." A rakwe nko kukaka.

Basike eryo ku manda, mwana ulaamba "Ta mulangi mulyango kukomena ? "

Bâbona zyanza zya bañama. Uti " A zyanza ezi zyonse, ena ?, têsi muntu uzijaya pe, muñama ngo uziruma, Sizimwe."

Kwategwa " Ka tunjira buyo." Baranjira.

Banjire boobo, bâjika, bâjika, bâjika ñama. Kwategwa " 'Mupe Câmundari." Ndizina rya mwana. Wakaka.

---

[9] The doorway is the Tonga altar. Some notes on this subject were published in 1906 in the *Illustrated Catholic Missions*. I find a Chinese " Spirit staircase " described in the *Century Magazine*, December, 1905. I wonder whether the idea of this and that of the Tonga Spirit-doorway have not a common origin.

[10] This killing of an ox in order to bring the children out of the drum does not look very natural. The narrator may have here mixed up his story with a different one, in which children come out of the belly of the Sizimwe.

[11] This story was told before the phonograph on March 9th, 1906, by Syabusu, a man of Sukulumbwe origin, now living on the Chikuni Stream.

[12] *Zera*, Ila for Tonga *zuba* " fish."

Bamane kulya, kwasya, bâona.	Mwana Câmundari wakara ku mulyango okuya.

Eryo akati â busiku wabôra ula a manda, Sizimwe, wajana kuli-jedwe ku mulyango. Uti " Kwanunka runtu runtu. Ndijarude,[13] ndijarude, bwene."

Uli mukati ulaimba :

   " Ka mujarula ! Kaka !
   " Syaa ciñama,
   " Syaa mapaya arerera,
   " Sya Mwiza.
   " Me ndime Romba-nguma-yiii ? "

Erimwi " Ndijarude, ndijarude. . . . "
   " Ka mujarula ! Kaka !
   " Syaa ciñama," etc.

I tu ! Wajarula, wanjira Sizimwe, wati " Ndâbire, bwene, muntu oyu uli akati."

Eryo Câmundari ulaimba :

   " A bâro ta barigwa
   " Bâzwa kwa Mirumbe
   " Bararula.
   " Me ndime Romba-nguma-yiii ? "

Erimwi " Ndâbire eci, bwene, ndâbire."
   "'A bâro ta barigwa," etc. (as above).

Wazwa muñama kuciri busiku. Bwaca bâjarula, ulaamba mwana : " Ena ? Ta mumvwide muñama wari-ko, ula a manda ? "

Bâti " Ulatusabira, mwana, wabeja, no twatamumvwa. Wari-ko riri ? "

Bâya kuzera basimbi, mulombwana waya kubeza ngoma. Wabeza wabeza. Kwasiya, wabôra wazoo kukara mu manda. Uti " Ka muswirira busiku mutaoni."

Bâti " Mbubo, tulaswirira."

Erimwi wasika Sizimwe akati â busiku . . . " Ndijarude, ndi-jarude, bwene. . . ."
   " Ka mujarula ! Kaka," etc. (as above).

Wajarula . . . " Ndâbire eci, bwene, ndâbire. . . ."
   " A bâro ta barigwa," etc. (as above).

Erimwi wazwa mu manda Sizimwe. Kwategwa " Mwamvwa, ena ? "

---

[13] Ndijarude = ndijarwide.
[14] This form zoo, much used in Tonga, is for za ku. Thus wazoo kubarongera is for waza ku kubarongera, lit. " he came to put them into . . . " A con-struction of the same sort at the beginning of this tale is bâya ku kuzera, lit. " they went to fish."

Mbo bati " Irrha, twamvwa."

Bwaca, mwana waya kubeza ngoma yakwe, wabeza, wabeza, wabeza, wabeza, yamana. Imane boobo ngoma, wazoo [14] kubarongera, wazoo kubarongera, uti " Ka munjira mu ngoma." Bânjira bamwi,umw i wati kake. A rakwe wamunjizya. Abanjizye boobo, wabweza ngoma yakwe, waunka, usiyide nswi zyabora.

Sizimwe wakaya kutamba bênziñina, zyonse nzoka, tônse turuwe zyonse nkaramu, bônse baumpe, a basuntwe. Bâbôra bañama bânjira mu manda. Banjire boobo, bâjana taba mo.

Kwategwa " Mbari bantu mba wari kwamba ? "

Basuntwe bâbweza nswi zyabora, bârya.

Kwategwa " A tubatobere mu mukondo."

Wabatobera Sizimwe, a bâro bâmucirira bâmucirira. Bâya kumwenzya Câmundari ujisi ngoma yakwe.

Bamwenzye boobo, barabuzya " Nduwe ni ? Nduwe ni ? "

" Ndime Câmundari."

" Uyumwide-nzi, bwene ? "

" Nco môma buya."

" Kôya uciumeume."

Eryo wati :
> " Ndum ! Ndum ! Ndum ! "
> " Vuruma.—Câ-mundari-mundari.
> " Ne [15] kâna kâ Mônga
> " Kwêsu kuli masamo."

Eryo bâmwayika basiruwe, bâzyana, bâzyana. Bazyane boobo, wabasiya mwana, waunka.

Bamane kuzyana, kwategwa " Basa, waya yi wari kwimba awa ? " Bâmutobera, bâya kumwenzya. Erimwi warizya ngoma, erimwi bâzyana, erimwi wabasiya, erimwi bâmutobera. Bamutobere boobo, bâmuzimina.

Bamuzimine boobo, bâmulya mwenziñina Sizimwe, bati " Watucenjezya."

Mwana wasika ku munzi kwabo. Bantu taakwe kubajana, bari ku mûnda. Waya kunjira mu manda a ngoma yakwe. Warijarira, watanta a xaka.

Atante boobo, bâbôra bañina, yabawa mvula. Bâti " Njarule,[16] njarule awa."

Bâjarula, bâti " Nduwe ni ?"

Kwategwa " Tulikuzi kutegwa ndiñwe bîna-Mwiza,[17] ndiñwe mwatuzyara."

---

[15] *Ne* = Tonga *me*.

[16] *Njarule*=Tonga *ndijarule*. *Njarule* is the Mukuni and Ila form.

[17] *Bîna-Mwiza*, Ila for Tonga *bana-Mwiza*=Mukuni *bêna-Mwinsa*.

Uti cu cu cu . . . " Mulimvwide câambaula mu manda ? "
Wabôra mwanarume, uti " Mwana ! Mwana ! Tawo câambaula
pe."
Erimwi mwanarume "Njarule, njarule."
Wajarula . . . " Nduwe ni? "
" Tulikuzi kutegwa ndiñwe tata, ndiñwe mwatuzyara."
Eryo nko kuya ku kusonda. Kwategwa " Ndono nko kwari
bâna bânu bâkazimide. Mukajaye musune a mulyango, muzoo
kubaumpaude."
Eryo bâbôra bazoo kujaya mombe. Eryo Câmundari wazwa mu
manda, a basimbi bâzwa mu ngoma.
Nka kâno eryo kâsimpa.

V.—I SHALL REVEAL THEE.

This is what was done by Sya-Mwiza with his child. . . .

At that time they went to hunt, but got no game whatever.

Finding himself thus in a sore plight, the man bethought himself
of killing his child. He pulled out some fibrous bark to tie him up
with, and bound him by the neck to a tree. He then went further
with the intention of coming back.

On his return he found his child dead, strangled by the string.

He then skinned him and cut him into pieces, that they should
mistake him for meat at home.

To make doubly sure, he got a small hairy beast, then rubbed and
rubbed it against the flesh which he had cut up, making the hair
stick on it. After that, he strung the pieces together on a stick, put
the load on his shoulder and carried it on the way home.

As he carried it, a little bird came and sang :

" The father of Mwiza ! [1]
" He had left his child alone.
Chorus.—" In the forest."
" He afterwards tied him up along with a dirty hairy beast
Chorus.—" In the forest."
" Wiriryo ! [2] I shall reveal thee.
" Wiriryo ! I shall reveal thee."

[1] " The father of Mwiza." This expression (in Tonga Sya-Mwiza, in Mukuni
Ixi-Mwinsa) seems to come naturally to the lips of storytellers every time
they speak of a heartless man. See the note 4 of the preceding tale.

[2] Wiriryo may be Sukulumbwe (Ila) for Tonga We, rirye-o " Thou, eat
thyself." By my informants it is supposed to be an onomatopeia imitating
the whistling of the bird. In the Tonga folk-lore poetic freedom goes further
than borrowing words from any human language one may please. It has

Hearing the little bird sing thus, the man put down his load and chased and chased the importunate creature. Finally, giving up the chase, he came back to carry his load. But once more the little bird came and sang as before :

" The father of Mwiza ! " etc.

Once more he put down the load. Once more he drove the bird away. Once more he took up the load. Once more the little bird came back. When he had driven it away enough, and carried his load enough, at last he reached the village.

The wife said : " Father of Mwiza, where have you taken my child to ? "

He said : " He has gone over to his cousin's."

" Indeed ? To his cousin's ! What has he gone to do there ? "

" He has gone to herd with him."

Then he added : " Wife, just take this meat."

She said : " Let my child come first."

" He won't return for some time. He has gone to his mate."

Then the woman said : " Let my child come, let him come, my child of this hut."

He said : " He will come, sure enough."

She waited and waited for him. Again : " Where exactly have you left my child ? "

" He stayed behind with his cousin."

Just then the little bird came and was heard singing :

" The father of Mwiza ! ", etc. (as above).

The woman then said: " What does the little bird mean by crying in that way ? "

The husband said: " No, this little bird is telling lies."

The woman then went to call some people at her mother's home, and brought them together. They asked : " What is the matter ? "

She said : " He has killed my child."

Her husband had, meanwhile, gone to lie down in the hut, and shut the door.

The people came at night and set fire to the hut on the top of him. Now the little story is preserved.

KALINDA.

---

at its disposal even the language of birds and other animals, nay, the whole vocabulary of nature. Hence to interpret with a sure pen even the fragments of poetry contained in these tales is not so easy a task as one might imagine.

168 BANTU FOLK-LORE

(IN TONGA.)

WIRIRYO ! NDARÛLA.

Nzyakacita Sya-Mwiza a mwana wakwe.
Eryo bâya kuweza, bâbula bañama.
Babule boobo, wayeya kujaya mwana wakwe. Wamufundira
rôzi, waamba kumwanga mu nsingo. Eryo waamba kwenda azoo
kubwedere.
Abwedere boobo, wajana mwana wakwe wafwa, rumutingide
rôzi mu nsingo.
Eryo wamufunda, wamubendabenda, bakacite ñama ku munzi.
Eryo wamuyandira ciñama cira a bôya. Nko kumupukapuka
oko ñama nji ari kubenda, wamubika wamubika bôya. Eryo nko
kutunga watunga, wagulika, wayumuna.
Abweze boobo, kwabôra kayuni :
" Sya-Mwiza !
" Ngwakasiya mwana wakwe
" Mu saka.
" Wamusingirira ciñama ciri bôya
" Mu saka.
" Wiriryo ! Ndarûla.
" Wiriryo ! Ndarûla."
Kaimbe boobo kayuni, watula, wakatanda, wakatanda kayuni.
Wareka wabôra, wazoo kubweza muguli wakwe.
Erimwi kâbôra kayuni :
" Sya-Mwiza," etc.
Erimwi watula, erimwi wakatanda, erimwi wabweza, erimwi
kâbôra kayuni. Amane kukatanda, amane kubweza,
waya kusika ku munzi.
Kwategwa " Sya-Mwiza, mwana angu wamutora yi ? "
Uti " Wainda ku musa a ñina."
" Ena ? Ku musa a ñina waya ku kucita-nzi ? "
" Waya ku kwembera."
Nko kuti " Muntu, kôtambula buyo ñama eyi."
Nko kuti " Mwanângu abôre."
" Tawo ulabôra, wainda ku bênziñina."
Nko kuti mwanakazi " Abôre, abôre mwanângu wa manda."
Uti " Ulabôra."
Wari kulangira, wari kulangira. Erimwi " Mwana wangu wamu-
siya yi ? "
" Wasyara ku musa a ñina."

Eryo nko kubôra kayuni.

"Sya-Mwiza," etc.

Eryo nko kuti mukayintu "Katyani kayuni nko karira?"
Mulume [3] wati "Pe, kâamba mânga kayuni aka."
Nko kutamba oyu mwanakazi, waya kutamba ku bañina.
Eryo atambe boobo, kwategwa "Wabona-nzi?"
Uti "Wamujaya mwana wangu."
Mulume nko kôna mu manda. Wajara a mulyango. Bâbôra
bantu masiku, bâmuumpirira.
Nka kâno kâsimpa.
KALINDA.

VI.—MY BERRIES !

N.B.—The following is one of the most widespread of S. African stories,
and has been more than once published in one form or another. But it is,
generally, divided into two, one part being that of the animals guarding their
well against the rabbit, the other being the litany of the successive acquisitions
of the deceitful rabbit. *Cf.* Jacottet's *Textes Soubiya*, pp. 35, 36.

This is what Master Rabbit did.

The beasts were dying of thirst. They then dug a well, but Master
Rabbit refused to dig, saying : "I have enough juicy food."

He went and met the crane. They resolved to gather certain
berries called *mfulimuninga* or *nkoroondo*, and found them. Then
they ate some and put the others aside. This done, they went and
walked each his own way in the forest.

While they were on their walk, Master Rabbit bethought himself
of coming back, and he came and ate the berries all up.

He then called the crane and asked : "Who has eaten my berries?
It must be you, crane, since you were here."

"Friend," said the crane, "I have not seen them."

"Now," said the rabbit, "what will you pay me for the berries,
my berries which you have eaten?" And he went on singing :

"My berries !
"I am dead, I am eaten up."

Mother ! There is the crane shaking off and shaking off some of
his feathers . . . "Which is the biggest?" he said. He threw
a big one to Master Rabbit, who picked it up, and went on his way
home.

There he goes. . . . He happened to meet on the road some
people who were dancing the war-dance, throwing assegais at one
another. "Here is a feather," he said, " for one of you to put on."

---

[3] *Mulume*, commonly *mwanarume*.

So one of them stuck the feather on his head, but a gush of wind came and blew it off. . . .

" Helloa ! *munsanje*," [2] said the man, " there is thy feather going away."

" Let it go," said the rabbit, " let it go. What is it worth ? "

" Well, Rabbit," asked some of the people, " does it not look as if we were men ? "

The sun was going down. Some one said : " Have they given thee back thy feather ? "

" They have not."

So he sang :

> " Alas ! My big feather,
> " That I got from my brother the crane,
> " The crane that ate my berries,
> " My berries that I found on a dry tree.
> " My berries ! I am dead, I am eaten up."

They gave him a fish-spear. He picked it up and went and met some people who were fishing : " Here is a spear," he said, " for one of you to spear the fishes."

One man took it and went on killing fish after fish, until he hit a big one. There was the spear disappearing in the water, and, dear ! dear ! going to stop only at the bottom.

" O *munsanje*, thy spear is gone."

" Let it go. What is it worth ? "

When the rabbit saw the sun go down, he said : " It looks as if the sun were going, while we rabbits are still here."

" Let them give thee thy spear first."

" Yes," he sang, " my spear that I got from people playing at war
> " The people playing at war that lost my big feather,
> " The big feather that I got from my brother the crane,
> " The crane that ate my berries," etc. (as above.)

They made for him a parcel of fish, and he picked it up.

He went on and met some people who were eating porridge without relish. He asked them : " Do you really eat without relish ? Here is some fish."

They put the pot on the fire, then ate and finished the fishes. He then awoke : " Have you," he asked, " finished them ? "

> " Alas ! My fishes which you have eaten,
> " The fishes that I got from people fishing with Kafir corn stalks,
> " The fishermen that lost my fish-spears,
> " The fish-spear that I got from people playing at war," etc. (as
> above).

---

[2] *Munsanje* is the totemic name for " rabbit," more or less what the family name is for us.

They gave him Kafir corn.   He took it and went and met some people who were eating sour milk :   " Here is some grain," he said, " grind it and cook some light porridge."

They cooked and ate it all up. . . . Then he remembered : " Have they given thee back thy Kafir corn, rabbit ? "

The sun was going down.   So he said :   " Give me back my Kafir corn."

" What ? " they replied, " did you not give it to us ? "

" And I, did I tell you to eat it ?   O mother ! "

" Alas !   My Kafir corn, that you have eaten,

" The Kafir corn that I got from people who were eating porridge without relish,

" The people eating without relish that ate my fishes,

" The fishes that I got," etc. (as above).

They gave him sour milk.—So he went on and on, walking carefully. He then saw clouds :   " Now," he says, " it looks as if this little cloud were going to drench me.   Somebody will have to pay for it."

So he went to the top of an anthill.   And there the little cloud burst upon him.   He began to slip and fell over there.   There was the sour milk spilt on the ground . . . " To think," he said, " that my sour milk should be spoilt like that ! "

" My sour milk that I got from people eating thick milk,

" The people eating thick milk, that ate my Kafir corn !

" Anthill !

' Give me my sour milk.

" Anthill !

" Give me my sour milk."

O mother !   Did not the anthill actually send out winged ants for him ! "

He picked them up and went to meet the lion, who was guarding the animals' well :   " Give me some water," he said, " I am thirsty."

" This is no water for the rabbit," said the lion.   " Didst thou not refuse to dig ? "

The rabbit said :   " Do you know what I have here ? "

" What is it that thou hast ? " asked the lion.

" They are winged ants," answered the rabbit.

" Well ! " said the lion, " tie me up while I eat, but let me have the winged ants."[3]

The rabbit tied him up properly, then gave him the winged ants. After that he went and drank his fill, and, when he had had enough,

---

[3] Winged white ants are by some natives considered a great delicacy.   In similar tales it is honey that the rabbit gives to the lion and other watch-guards of the well.

he took a bath in the well, then said : " Your water is all dirtied, as
we are rabbits."
He went away.
Soon after that the beasts came to drink from their well.   They
found the water all dirty and asked :   " Who is it that has made our
water so dirty ? "
The lion said :   " It is the rabbit.   Do you not see how he has
tied me up ? "
" What !   The little rabbit tie such a big person !   How did
that happen ? "
" He deceived me by giving me winged ants."
The beasts hearing that got up and, coming up to the rabbit, fired
a cannon at him, boom !   and he came to an end.[4]
So does my little story.
I am ÑANGA.

(IN TONGA.)
ME NKOROONDO.

Nzyacita Syana-Sulwe.
Bañama bâri kufwa ñotwa.   Bâkaba cikara, Syana-sulwe ngo
wakaka kukaba.   Uti me ndira a ziryo zyangu zitontora."
Waunka waswankanya a nakara.   Kwategwa " Tuye tukacere
mfulimuninga."   Bâya kucera, zimwi bâzirya, zimwi bâzibika
ansi.   Bamane kuzibika, baamba kuvundika ku saka.
Bavundika boobo, kanga Syana-sulwe kâamba kubôra, kâamba
kuzirya-rya-rya.
Eryo waya kwita nakara.   Aite nakara, kwategwa " Basa, nguni
wandida mfulimuninga zyangu ?   Ndiwe, nakara, wakari-wo."
" No bênzuma, nsizibwene."
" Ino mfulimuninga undirungire-nzi, mfulimuninga zyangu nzi
warya ?
       " Me nkoroondo
       " Ndafwa ndarigwa."
Ma !   Ngo nakara buku buku buku . . .   " Uri mupepe ! "
Waamba kumupa, kâbweza, kêenda ku munzi.
Karaya.   Kâya kujana basimuzyana mugwata, basikuyasana
rumamba.   Kabera " Ngo oyu mupepe, asame."   Asame ku mutwe,
kâbôra kapepere, ngo mupepe waamba kuunka.

----

[4] The story can go on indefinitely with further tricks on the part of Master
Rabbit.

" O munsanje, ryaunka pepe ryako."
" Ka riya, ka riya. A ! Nde-nxi ? "
" Ya ! Swe inga to bâmuna,[5] Syana-sulwe."
Ryaamba kubira zuba. Kwategwa " Bâkupa pepe ryako ? "
" Ta bakwe.
" Me mupepe wangu,
" Mupepe ngu ndajana kuli nakara mukwesu,
" Nakara waamba kundida mfulimuninga,
" Mfulimuninga nzi ndajana ku musamo muyumu,
" Nkoroondo, ndafwa ndarigwa."
Bâmupa mûmba. Wabweza, waya kujana basimuzuba inswi.
Abajane boobo, uti " Ngo oyu mûmba, ayase nswi." Bâamba
kutambula. Uciya kuyasa buya, wayasa muswi mupati. Nde
sumo ryaamba kuunkira m̂u mênda. Ya ! Ya ! Ka rikede.
" Omunsanj e, ryaunka sumo ryako.
" Ka riya bu yo. A ! Nde-nzi ? "
Kabone kuti zuba ryabira " Inga ryabira, to bâna-sulwe."
" Bakupe a risumo ryako."
" E, isumo ryangu ndi ndâjana kuli basimuyasana-rumamba,
" Basimuyasana-rumamba bândisowera mupepe wangu,
" Mupepe ngu ndâjana kuli nakara mukwesu," etc. (as above).
Bâamba ku mwangira cikungo câ nswi, wabweza.
Abweze boobo, waya kujana basimubuya-nsima. Wa buzya kuti
" Mubuya nsima buya ? Nzeezi nswi."
Bâamba kujika dongo, bârya, bâzimana. Bazimane boobo.
Syana-sulwe wabuka. Uti " Mwazimana ? "
" Me nswi zyangu, nzi mwarya,
" Nswi nzi ndâjana kuli basimuzuba-makuba,
" Basimuzuba-makuba bândisowera mûmba wangu,
" Mûmba wangu ngu ndâjana kuli basimuyasana-ru mamba," etc.
(as above).
Bâmupa maira. Wabweza waya kujana basimulya-mabisi. Wati
" Nga awa maira, muziye mujike cêre." Bâamba kujika, bârya.
Bamane kurya . . . " A ! Inga bâkupa ari maira âko, to Syana-
sulwe ? "
Ryabira zuba, wati " Mundipe maira ângu."
Kwategwa " Macu ! O mwenzuma, erimwi watupa."
" Me ndaamba kuti mulye ? Mama !
" Me maira angu, nga mwarya,
" Maira nga ndajana kuli basimubuya-nsima
" Basimubuya-nsima bândida nswi zyangu," etc. (as above).
Bâmupa mabisi. Bamupe mabisi boobo, weenda a kwenda

---

[5] *Amuna* " men (*viri*)," Nungwe for Tonga *bânarume*.

mantu mantu mantu. Eryo wabona mayoba. Uti " Kayoba kano inga karandiwa ime." Uti " Ta kayi kundiwa buya." Watanta a cûlu. Atante a cûlu boobo, nká kayoba mpú kumuwa. Waamba kutezerera, nkuwa a kuwa oko. Ngá mabisi âtika . . . " Ino obo mabisi ângu me ! "
 " Mabisi nga ndâjana kuli basimulya-mabisi,
 " Basimulya-mabisi bândida maira ângu.
 " Cûlu ! "
 " Ndipe mabisi ângu.
 " Cûlu !
 " Ndipe mabisi ângu."
Ma ! Ma ! Te cûlu câamba kuzwa tûkauka. Wabweza wa- swankanya syanza ulinda mênda â bañama. Uti " Ndipe mênda ndiñwe."
 " Têsi mênda â Syana-sulwe. Têsi nduwe wakaka kukaba ? " Syana-sulwe uti " Ulizi nci ndijisi awa ? "
 " Ujisi-nzi ? "
 " Me ndijisi tûkauka."
Kabera uti " Ndiange ndipake, undipe tûkauka."
Syana-sulwe wamutebega, wamupa bûkauka, waya kuñwa mênda a bañama. Amane kuñwa wasamba-mo. Eryo " Ngá mênda. âfumuntuka, to yoyo." Waunka.
Kabera bâsika bañama bazoo kuñwa ku cikara câbo. Bâbuzya kwategwa " Watufumuntwida mênda êsu nguni ? "
Nko kuti " Ngu sulwe. Ta mubwene mbwakandianga ? "
 " Kasulwe kwanga mupati wonse ! Câba buti ? "
 " Wandicenjezya wandipa bûkauka."
Eryo bâbuka bañama bâya kumujana Syana-sulwe, bâmuti muzinga bú, wafwa.
Kâfwa kâno.
Ndime ÑANGA.

VII.—THE LITTLE IRON HOUSE.[1]

Master Rabbit did this.

He found a pretty rabbit girl,[2] and put up for her a little house of galvanised iron.

When the house was ready, and the rabbit girl had taken posses- sion of it, Master Rabbit went to call his friends.

These came together, from the lions to the duikers.

[1] Already published in the Zambesi Mission Record, No. 34, pp. 138–141.
[2] Some say " a duiker girl," musimbi wa nsya.

Then first of all the elephant came to knock at the little iron house. She who was inside said : " Thou who knockest at my iron house, who art thou ?" (Then the song started) :

" I am the elephant.
    Chorus.—" We are a hundred." [3]
" I chase you,[4]
" Learn to go away ;—*Chorus.*
" I want the rabbit—*Chorus.*
" He fits nicely on the palms of my hands.—*Chorus.*
" Have you, perhaps, pledged yourself to him ?—*Chorus.*
" Yes, I have pledged myself to him—*Chorus.*
" At the mouth of the hole of Father-deceive-me.—*Chorus.*
" Learn to go away."—*Chorus.*

The elephant went away. Father Soft-Paws [5] came towards him : " Say, friend, what has happened to thee ? "

" She has refused me," said the elephant. " She wants you, Father Soft-Paws. Go, friend, go. You are so good-looking with that mane and those whiskers of yours."

So Father Soft-Paws went to knock at the door of the little house, *gú !*

The person who was inside said : " Thou who knockest at the little iron house, who art thou ? "

Then the same song as above :

    " I am Lord Roarer . . .
    " I chase you . . .
    " Learn to go away," etc.

The lion went away and said : " Go, friend, go thou, gnu ; go, as thou hast a lovely tail."

Well ! Well ! Well ! He went, did the gnu. He went and knocked at the little house, *gú !*

Same story : " Who art thou," etc.

    " I am the gnu . . .
    " I chase you . . .
    " Learn to go away, etc."

Away went the gnu. The eland too went, but came back. The zebra too with all his fine stripes went and came back. Then came the leopard : " Now you, cousin, go, go, go, go. With such pretty

---

[3] Var. " Thou art as good as a hundred, *oli mwanda* (Subiya for Tonga *uli mwanda*)."

[4] In the Tonga text *ndákutanda.* This, if it is Tonga, means " I chase you." If it were Zulu, it would mean " I love you." As the suitors are supposed to be foreign, the rabbit girl seems to use on purpose an expression with a double meaning, just to laugh at them.

[5] " Father Soft Paws," *i.e.*, the lion.

spots as yours, the girl cannot refuse you. By Jove ! You are the man she is crying for, the man she is crying for."

The leopard went. Mother ! Mother ! There he is knocking at the door. But the story was repeated once more : " Who art thou ? " etc.

> " I am the leopard . . .
> " I chase you . . .
> " Learn to go away," etc.

Well ! Well ! He went away, did the leopard. " Did you see her ? "—" Fancy that ! She has refused him ! She wants Master Rabbit."

So Master Rabbit went at last, trotting in his own way, then walking on tiptoes, *krú, krú, krú*. Mother ! Just one knock at the house. From inside comes the answer : " *Wo !* Thou who art knocking at my little iron house, who art thou ? "

> " I am the rabbit.
> *Chorus.*—" Thou art a hundred.
> " I accept thee.—*Chorus.*
> " Yes, come in.—*Chorus.*
> " Yes, I pledged myself to thee—*Chorus.*
> " At the mouth of the antbear's hole.—*Chorus.*
> " Thou fittest so nicely on the palms of my hands.—*Chorus.*
> " I accept thee"—*Chorus.*

Master Rabbit made no delay in going. The young lady made him sit " here."

After a time the comrades said : " Where has he gone to ? Cousins, go and say good morning to Master Rabbit. Ask him how he is getting on."

The fellows were afraid to go : " Go you, Lord Soft-Paws, go and bring out Little Rabbit. Little Rabbit is too small altogether for the young lady."

"Well, cousins, no, we do not care to go."

The beasts then began to disperse.

And that was the end of the story.[6]

Ñanga.

---

[6] This tale was phonographed on February 11th, 1906, when the railway construction in Northern Rhodesia was in full swing, as much as 6 miles being sometimes laid in one day. What reminded the narrator of the existence of this tale was, perhaps, the fact that Tonga women were then being approached by white people and well-paid foreign boys on the construction work. I was told that the true Tonga women generally preferred to remain faithful to their legitimate, though poor, lovers or husbands.

(IN TONGA.)

KANDA KA RUBULO.

Wacita Syana-sulwe.

Wajana musimbi mubotu wa sulwe, wamuyakira kânda kâ rubulo.
Amuyakire kânda, anjire mu kânda musimbi, waya ku kuyo-
borora bênzinina. Bâsika bênzinina, a baravu a nsya.
Basike boobo, wasanguna muzovu, waya kuuma kânda kâ rubulo.
Uli mukati uti " Ongumina [7] kânda kâ rubulo nduwe ni ? "
    " Ndime muzovu.
       " Seli mwanda.[8]
   "Ndâkutanda   ,,
   " Kôzi kuya.   ,,
   " Me ñanda sulwe.   ,,
   " Werera mu taxi.   ,,
   " Inga wamukumbata ?   ,,
   " Irrha, ndâmukumbata ,,
   " A bwina bwa siñenge ,,
   " Kôzi kuya."   ,,
Waunka muzovu. Wabôra Syanza. Kwategwa " Wakuba-
nzi ? "
  " Waya kundikaka. Uyanda nduwe, Syanza. Kôya, basa,
kôya ; uli mubotu nduwe, mbo ula a ngara."
Syanza waya kuti kânda gú.
Wati uli mukati " Ongumina kânda kâ rubulo nduwe ni ? "
    " Ndime Syumbwa. . . .
    " Ndâkutanda. . . .
    " Kôzi kuya," etc.
Waunka Syanza, uti " Kôya, basa, kôya nduwe muñumbwe,
kôya, mbo ula a mucira mubotu."
Má ! Má ! Má ! Waunka muñumbwe, waya kuuma kânda
gú . . . " Ongumina kânda kâ rubulo nduwe ni ? "
    " Ndime muñumbwe, . . .
    " Ndâkutanda . . .
    " Kôzi kuya," etc.
Waunka muñumbwe. Waya musefu, wabôra ; waya cibise a
mabara âkwe, wabôra. Wasika siruwe " Basa, kôya, kôya, kôya,
mbo ulâ mabara mabotu. Musimbi uya kukuzumina. No barombwana-ma, ulira nduwe buyo, ulira nduwe."
Waunka Siruwe, má ! má ! azoo kuuma kânda. Aume kânda,
wati uli mukati " Ongumina kânda," etc.

[7] *Ongumina = O undiumina.*
[8] *Seli mwanda,* Sekololo = Tonga *tuli mwanda.*

" Ndime Siruwe . . .
" Ndakutanda . . .
" Kôzi kuya," etc.
A !   Má !   Waunka   Siruwe . . . " Wamubona ? "—" Má !
Wamukaka !   Uyanda Syana-sulwe."
Waunka Syana-sulwe kakata . . . krú, krú, krú . . . Ma ! igú
kânda.   Wavuwa uli mukati " Wo ! Ongumina kânda kâ rubulo
nduwe ni ? "
                        " Ndime sulwe.
                                    " Oli mwanda.
          " Ndâkuzumina.   ·   ,,
          " A ! Kôzi kunjira.   ,,
          " Imha ! Ndâkukumbata ,,
          " A bwina bwa Siñenge.   ,,
          " Werera mu taxi.   ,,
          " Ndâkuzumina.   ,,
Syana-sulwe waamba kunjira.
Anjire boobo, wamuzumina mukayintu awa.
Bênziñina bâti " Waya yi ?   Basa, a mukamujuzye Syana-sulwe,
wabuka buyani ? "
Bênziñina bâamba kuyowa " Kôya, basa ; unka nduwe, Syanza,
ukabuzye kânga-sulwe.   Kanga-sulwe nkanini buyo."
" Má !   Ta tukwe, basa."
Mba bañama bâamba kumwayika.
Nka kâno kâjinka.
ÑANGA.

========

VIII.—DANCE LIKE THAT !

Miss Rabbit, going one day to the river, found there some little
girls drawing water.   They shook hands together, then began to
play.

Soon the little girls gave some of their strings of beads to Miss
Rabbit, telling her to put them on.   They further dressed her head
with other beads, so that she looked just like a civilised little girl.
Then she started dancing and dancing, the other little girls clapping
their hands.   The song was as follows :

" *Ozibane !   Zibane !   Zibane !*
          Chorus.—" *Ozibane !* "
" Dance like that !   Like that !   Like that !   Dance like that !
" Miss Rabbit, they have strung beads on her near the river.

" Miss Rabbit, the little girls have strung beads on her.
" She is as pretty as Na-Mandu.
" How well dressed she is !
" Uwî-i ! [1] *Ozibane !* "

They danced, and danced, and danced.   The day went on . . .
" Mates, mates, the sun is down, let us go."

Miss Rabbit gave them back their beads, and they moved away.
She then said to them :   " You little girls, to-morrow come here
early ;   we will play near the river, you will dress me with beads,
and I will dance."

The girls went, reached their kraal, and slept

At daybreak they left their huts, came back to the river, and
found Miss Rabbit already there, dressed her, and said :   " Now let
us dance."

" Ozibane !   Zibane !   Zibane ! ", etc. (as above).

Miss Rabbit danced and danced, and danced, the little girls
clapping their hands.   Mother !   This time too the sun went down
So she gave them back their beads, saying :   " To-morrow again
come early, little girls, that we may play near the river.   Also bring
me a nice apron, that I may put it on."

The little girls went home, and soon turned to bed.

Early in the morning they picked up an apron for Miss Rabbit,
then went to the river, and there found her waiting for them. . . .
" Here is a pretty apron," they said, " which we have brought to-day.
Put it on."

" No," said Little Rabbit, " to-day I have no wish to dance."

They said :   " No, no, you have to dance, put it on."

She dressed, dressed, dressed, and they strung beads in her hair.
Then she started dancing, the song being the same as before :

" Ozibane !   Zibane !   Zibane ! . . .
" How nicely dressed she is !
" She is as pretty as Na-Mandu.
" Uwî-i !   Ozibane ! "

They went on dancing and dancing, until Miss Rabbit noted
that the sun was going down.   But they went on, though from a
distance was heard the cry *Uwi-i !*

O mother !   Then she begins to go away, but continues dancing
and singing on her way. . . .   " Friend Rabbit, give us our aprons.
. . . When will you give them back to us ? " . . . "

[1] *Uwî-i* !   represents a cry at a distance from a hyaena joining in the
chorus.

They go on following her as far as the middle of the forest.   There
Miss Rabbit stops, and starts this new song :
>   " You children !   You who have come !
>   *Chorus.*—" Come !   Come !
>   " It will be far where a beast gave me birth.
>   " Lovers of high meat ! [2]   You who have come !
>   " What is it ?
>   " You who are lost for good, lost, lost for good !
>   " What is it ?
>   " You who are lost for good, lost, lost for good! "

Little Rabbit started running.   And the girls after her crying for
their aprons.

Mother !   Mother !   Mother !   They found themselves this time
right in the thickest of the forest, and the song started again :
>   " You children ! " etc. (as above).

Mother !   Mother !   Mother !   There she is gone once more.
They go, they go.   One of the girls dies of thirst on the way . . .
" Alas !   Let us go back," say the others.

" Mother !   Mother !   Mother ! " say some, " let us simply go
on."

" Is Miss Rabbit going to give us back at all our things ? "

" Let us simply go on, let us go on."

Mother !   She sings again :
>   " You children ! " etc. (as above).

By going on and on they arrive as far as Munenga's.[3]   There the
hyaenas ate them all.

That is where the story dies.[4]

ÑANGA and NAÑUKA.

(IN TONGA.)

OZIBANE !   ZIBANE !   ZIBANE !

Kanga-sulwe musimbi kâya ku mulonga, kâjana basimbi bateka
mênda. Bâanzyana. Bamane kwanzyana, barasobana, baraso-

---

[2] *i.e.*, hyaenas.
[3] *Munenga*, a kraal on the Lower Magoye.   The narrators are on the Upper
Magoye.
[4] Quite likely this tale is an allegory describing the tricks by which kidnappers used to deceive the Tonga girls whom they wished to carry into slavery.
The Tonga children, as a rule, are exceptionally playful and confident, hence
easily deceived.

bana. Bâkapa bulungu bwabo " Tusame." Bumwi bulungu bâkatunga ku mutwe. Kâba anga musimbi wa mu munzi.

Kamane kusama boobo, kâtarika kuzyana, karai mba, basimbi
barakamba :

" Ozibane ! Zibane ! Zibane !—Ozibane ! [5]
" Kanga-sulwe bâmutunga ubulungu [6] ku mulonga . . .
" Kanga-sulwe bâmutunga ubulungu abasimbi [6] . . .
" Ngu Na-Mandu [7]
" Ngu Nâmbete [8] . . .
" Uwî-i ! Ozibane !
(This song is repeated several times.)

Bâzyana, bazyana, bâzyana. Bazyane boobo. . . . " Basa,
basa, ryabira, a twende."

Kanga-sulwe kâbapa bulungu bwabo. Bâamba kuunka eryo.
Kati " Kamufuma junza, no basimbi, tuzoo kusobane ku mulonga,
muzoo kunditunge bulungu, nzoo kusame.

Eryo bâunka basimbi, bâya kusika ku maribo, bâona.

Kabera bwaca, bâamba kufuma basimbi, bâya ku mulonga, bâka-

---

[5] *Ozibane.* From some unknown dialect of Barotseland for Tonga *uzizyane.*
[6] *U bulungu, a basimbi,* These articles *u, a* are foreign to Tonga and are
here employed only by poetic licence.
[7] The prefix *Na* means " mother of "=Mukuni *Ina.*
[8] *Nâmbete,* lit. " Mother of well-dressed," from Zulu *ambata* " dress " for
Tonga *zwata* (used by some tribes, the others saying *sama*).

jana kanga-sulwe kâsika kare karixire. Bâkatunga bulungu, bâka-
samika bati " A tuzyane rino. . . ."

            " Ozibane ! Zibane ! Zibane ! ", etc.

Kâzyana, kâzyana, kâzyana, barakamba basimbi. Ma ! Ryabira erimwi. Kâbapa bulungu bwabo kati " Ka mufuma junza,
no basimbi, tuzoo kusobane ku mulonga. A manda mundetere,
muzoo kundisamike."

Bâunka ku maribo basimbi, bâya kularira.

Bwaca, bâbweza manda bazoo kusamike kanga sulwe, bâunka
ku mulonga bâkajana karikede, bâti " Ngaya mabotu manda, nga
twareta suno, kôsama."

Kâti " Pe, suno nsiyandi kuzyana."

Bâti " Pe, pe, ulazyana, kôsama."

Kâsama, kâsama, kâsama, a bulungu bâkatunga ku mutwe
Bamane kukasamika, kâtarika kuzyana. . . .

            " Ozibane ! Zibane ! Zibane ! . . .

            " Ngu Nâmbete . . .

            " Ngu Na-Mandu . . .

            " Uwî-i ! Ozibane ! "

Kazyana, kâzyana, kâbera zuba riya kumbo . . .

            "Ozibane ! Zibane ! Zibane !

            " Uwî-i ! Ozibena ! "

Ma ! Kâamba kuunka, kaya bwimba, kaya bwimba. . . " No
bênzuma, sulwe, tupe manda êsu . . . Uya kutupa riri ? "

Bâya kusika a kati â saka. Nko kwima kanga sulwe. Kâreta
rwimbo rumbi . . .

    " No bânike, no mwabwera !—Bwerani ! Bwerani !

    " Kwaya kurampa nkwanzyarira muñama.—Bwerani! Bwerani !

    " Bakabwenga, no mwabwera !—Bwerani ! Bwerani !

    " Ningi ?—Bwerani ! Bwerani !

    " No mwaninganinga, no mwaninga, no mwaninganinga !—
        Bwerani ! Bwerani !

    " No mwaninganinga, no mwaninga, no mwaninganinga !—
        Bwerani ! Bwerani ! " [1]

Kâunka kanga-sulwe kâcijana. Bâtobera basimbi, baya bulira
manda.

---

[9] This song is evidently meant by the narrators to give an idea of the
language of the kidnappers hidden in the forest. It is a kitchen Kafir of its
kind, half Tonga, half Ñungwe. *Bwera*, pl. *bwerani* is Ñungwe and means
" come, you come "=Tonga *bôra, a mubôre*. It is practically the sort of
kitchen Kafir that used to be heard in Tongaland on the railway construction
work at the time this story was told (February, 1906). *Ningi ?* is for Ñungwe
niñi ?=Tonga *ncinzi ?* What is it ?

Má ! Má ! Má ! Erimwi barasika a kati â saka . . .
  " No bânike, no mwabwera," etc.
Má ! Má ! Má ! Kâunka. Baraya bwenda, baraya bwenda.
Eryo umwi waamba kufwa mu nzira, wamana kufwa ñotwa . . .
" No bênzuma, tubwede."
" Má ! Má ! Má ! Ka tuya buyo."
" Zyuma zyêsu zya bulungu akatupe riri kanga-sulwe ? "
" Ka tuya buyo, ka tuya."
Má ! Karaimba :
  " No bânike, no mwabwera," etc.
Erimwi beende boobo, bâya kusika a Munenga, bâya kubarya
basuntwe.
Nko kâfwida ka kâno.
Ñanga and Nañuka.

IX.—GIVE ME A LITTLE TOBACCO.

This is what an old woman did.

She was very hungry. So she went to steal meat from people's
granaries.[1] When she was caught, she said : " Let me go, I will
give you at home a child round whose neck you will see a collar."

Having thus sold her child, the little woman came back home, and
said : " Child, child, go into the hut."

Meanwhile the owners of the meat were coming, singing on the
way :

" There at the fig-trees,[2]
  Chorus.—Give me a little tobacco (bis)."
" There is a little old woman.
" She said : Give me meat,
" I will give birth for you to Mucinda,[3]

---

[1] The granaries of the Ba-Tonga, Bêne-Mukuni, etc., are little constructions
made of wickerwork, raised on posts in order that any attempt by the white
ants to get into them may be discovered in time. They are, generally, some
50 or 100 yards from the sleeping huts for fear of accidental fire. Occasionally
dried meat, or biltong, is kept in them.

[2] The little old woman is represented as living among the fig-trees, because
where these grow their fruit is the food of the poor for several months of
the year.

[3] This verse shows that in the true story the child is sold before being born.
But the narrator began it without, it seems, remembering this detail. In
fact, in a number of stories current on the same theme, the child is thus sold
for some meat before it is born. The owner of the meat is, generally, a
hyaena. *Cf.* Jacottet's *Textes Louyi*, p, 49, also my story of *Kaskapaleza* in
the *Zeitschrift für Afr. und oc. Sprachen*, 1st, year, p. 243. By the way, I may
here observe, what I did not notice then, that *Kaskapaleza* in the Quelimane
story is a noun borrowed from Rhodesian Tonga. It should be properly
Kasika-pa-Leza, lit. " He who reached God's place." In the Ñungwe tales
the hero of this story is *Pimbirimano*.

"Mucinda will have a prominent navel,[4]
"And a collar round his neck."
Hearing that, the child ran away into the forest.
The people came and said : "Where is thy child ? "
The mother said : "Look at it running away there."
She added : "Come back to-morrow, you will find it in the garden."
They went away. When it was dark, the child came back home to his mother.
Next morning she said : "Go and bring me pumpkins from the garden."
The child went, but, instead of going to the garden, he went and sat down on an antheap. Then seeing a duiker pass, he said to him : "Go and bring me some pumpkins from the garden." He sang :
Solo : "Duiker ! Duiker ! "
Chorus : "Go and bring me pumpkins from the garden,
        "Go and bring me pumpkins."
Solo : "Duiker good boy ! "
Chorus : "Go and bring me," etc. (as above).
The duiker went to fetch the pumpkins.
Now there are those people reaching the little old woman's abode .. . "I have sent him," she said, "I have sent my child ; you will find him in the garden. Just go there."
They go singing as before :
        "There at the fig-trees," etc.
Mother ! They came to the garden, but found there only a duiker. So they came back to the kraal and said : "Old woman, where is thy child, whom thou didst sell us for meat ? We have not found him."
"All right," she said, "to-morrow you will find him at the surface well."
They went away.
The following day the same story. In the early morning, the mother said to the child : "Go and bring me clay from the well."
This time the child sent a black hornet.[5]
The hornet went to fetch clay.
Now here are those people coming and singing as before :
        "There at the fig-trees," etc.

[4] "A prominent navel," because the mother is too poor to pay some one to cut the umbilical cord properly.
[5] The black hornet builds nests in the huts.

They came to the surface well, but, instead of the child, found there only a hornet.

As they came back to the old woman's abode, they caught the child in a hut and got hold of him.

They took him away.

On the road they saw some *nego* berries.[6] Then the child said : " Let me go up and pluck some fruit for you."

Up he went and said : " Now open your mouths."

Those people opened their mouths. He then dropped berries, one into one mouth, another into another. The men were simply choked.

There is the story ; that is where it dies.[7]

NAÑUKA and ÑANGA

(IN TONGA.)
NGWAYIRE. [8]

Nzyakacita kacembere.

Yakakora nzara. Kâya kuba ñama ku matara â bantu. Bâkajana bantu, kâti " Mundireke, nzoo kumupa mwana ku munzi wa ciyingu mu nsingo.

Kamuule boobo mwana wakwe, kâbôra ku munzi kacembere, kâti " Mwana, mwana, njira mu manda."

Bábôra bantu bara a ñama, baya bwimba :

" Okuya ku makuyu.
                Ngwayire, ngwayire !
" Nko kuli kacembere.   ,,
" Kâti ' A mumpe ñama,'   ,,
" Nkamuzyarire Mucinda.   ,,
" Mucinda ula a kombo,   ,,
" Wa ciyingu mu nsingo.   ,,

---

[6] The *nego* is a grey fruit of the size of a big cherry with very little substance, except stones ; a sort of " monkey apple." To show, by the way, how significant native names of localities become corrupted, we may mention that the railway through Tongaland happened to pass at a place called *Na-ka-nego*, lit. " The mother of a little monkey apple," and that the railway authorities transformed the name into the well-sounding, but meaningless, *Neganega*. It hardly looks like progress. Nay, who knows whether the name *Na-ka-nego* had not been given to that place precisely to localise there the present story ? For is not the exact meaning of *Na-ka-nego* " the mother of the proverbial *nego*."

[7] This tale, no doubt, is meant to teach that anyone who is in slavery by no other than the supposed right of birth may with a clear conscience vindicate his freedom if he can, and that every sensible creature will help him in the attempt.

[8] *Gwayira* " give a little tobacco." Verb coined from *gway* " tobacco." kitchen Kafir for Tonga *tombwe*.

Eryo nko kutija mwana, waya ku saka.

Kwategwa " Nguli mwana wako ? "

Ñina waamba kuti " Ngo oyu watija."

Uti " Kamubôra junza, muzoo kumujane ku mûnda."

Bâunka.　Kwasiya, mwana wabôra kuli bañina.

Bwaca, kwategwa " Kôya kancerere myungu ku mûnda."

Waunka mwana, waya kukara a cûlu.　Wabona nsya iinda, **wati**
" Nsya, kancerere myungu ku mûnda."

Ulaimba ·

> ¨Nakasya !　Nakasya ! [9]
> " Kancerere myungu ku mûnda,
> " Kancerere myungu
> " Nakasya mulombe !
> " Kancerere myungu ku mûnda,
> " Kancerere myungu."

Yaunka nsya, yaya kuleta myungu.

Eryo mbá bantu bâsika kuli kacembere . . . " **Ndâmutuma**
mwana wangu . Muzoo kumujana ku mûnda.　Kamuya buyo."

Baya bwimba :

> " Okuya ku makuyu," etc. (as above).

Bâsika ku mûnda.　Má !　Bâjana nsya, bêenda bâya **ku munzi,**
bâti " Mucembere, mwanâko nguli, ngu wakaula ñama vêsu ? **Ta**
twakumujana."

Nko kuti " Mbubo, junza mulamujana ku cikara.

Bâunka.

A rimwi mbomuña buyo.　Bwaca, bâamba kuti bañina " Kan-
detere bulongo ku mukara."

A rimwi mwana waya kutuma rôma . . .

> " Rôma, rôma !
> " Kamfumbire bulongo ku mukara,
> " Kamfumbire bulongo.
> " Rôma, rôma !
> " Kamfumbire bulongo ku mukara,
> " Kamfumbire bulongo."

Waya kubuleta rôma.

Eryo mbá bantu bâbora .

> " Okuya ku makuyu," etc.

Bâsika bantu ku cikara, bâjana mwana tawo, bâjana rôma,
bâbôra ku munzi.

Babôre buyo, bâmujana mu manda mwana, bâya kumujata.

---

[9] *Nakasya* for *insya* " duiker " =Mukuni *nakaxa*.

Bâmujata bâmutora.

Bamutore boobo, bâya kubona manego, wati " Ntante mujulɩ ndimucerere manego."

Watanta uti " Murakame."

Bârakama bantu. Barakame boobo, wabarokesya manego munkanwa, a umwi ndinego, a umwi ndinego. Manego âbatinga bantu a môyo.

Nkaκ kâno mpo kâfwida awo.

Naᷠuκa and Nanga.

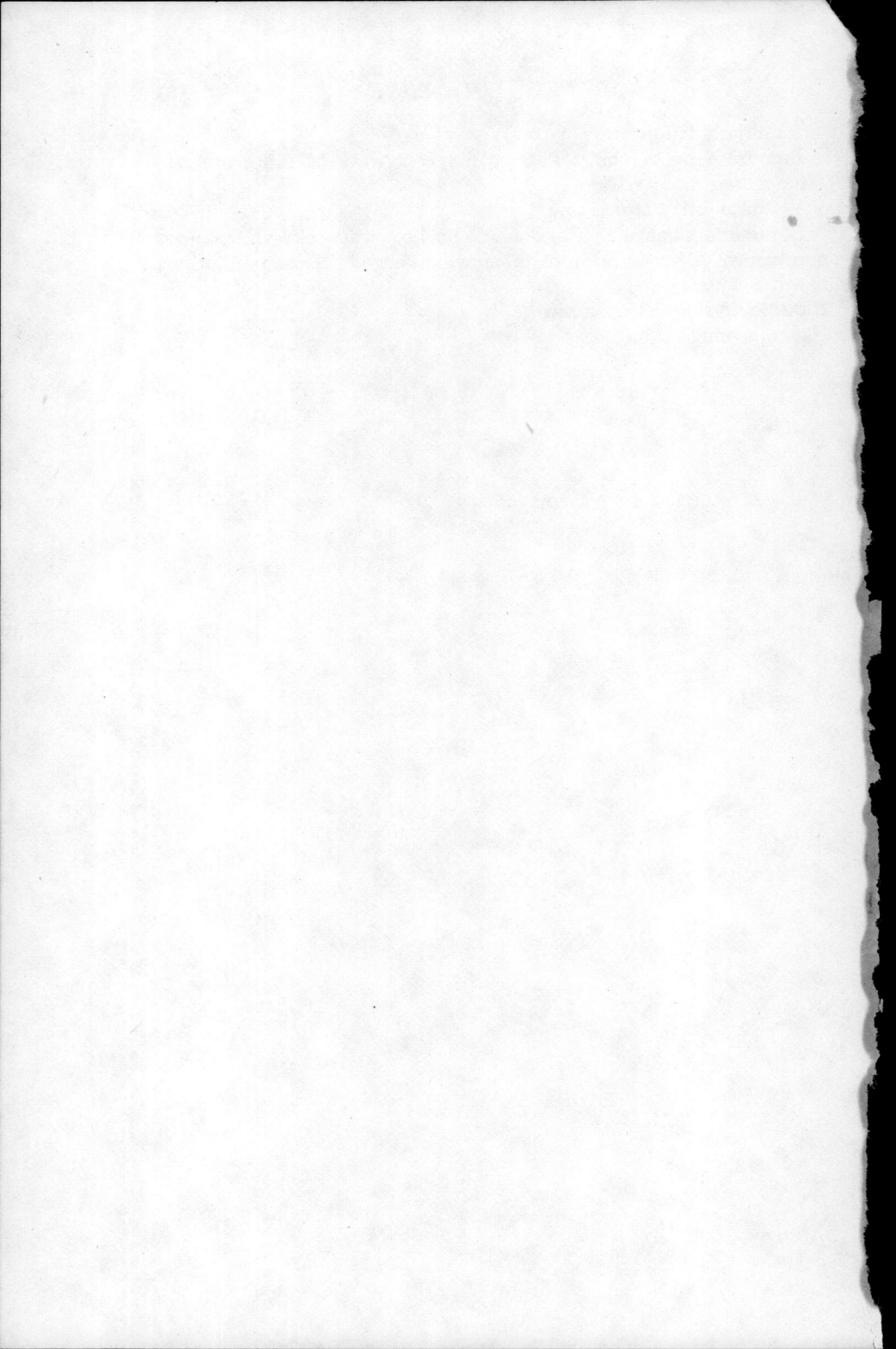